CBSE Term II
2022

Computer Science
Class XII

- Complete Theory Covering NCERT
- Case Based Questions
- Short/Long Answer Type Questions
- 3 Practice Papers with Explanations

Authors
Sanjib Pal
Neetu Gaikwad

arihant
ARIHANT PRAKASHAN (School Division Series)

ARIHANT PRAKASHAN (School Division Series)

ॐ **Administrative & Production Offices**

Regd. Office

'Ramchhaya' 4577/15, Agarwal Road, Darya Ganj, New Delhi -110002
Tele: 011- 47630600, 43518550

ॐ **Head Office**

Kalindi, TP Nagar, Meerut (UP) - 250002, Tel: 0121-7156203, 7156204

ॐ **Sales & Support Offices**

Agra, Ahmedabad, Bengaluru, Bareilly, Chennai, Delhi, Guwahati, Hyderabad, Jaipur, Jhansi, Kolkata, Lucknow, Nagpur & Pune.

ॐ **ISBN :** 978-93-25797-05-5

ॐ **PRICE :** ₹125.00

PO No : TXT-XX-XXXXXXX-X-XX

Published by Arihant Publications (India) Ltd.

For further information about the books published by Arihant, log on to www.arihantbooks.com or e-mail at info@arihantbooks.com

Follow us on   

Contents

CHAPTER 01
Data Structures   *1-17*

CHAPTER 02
Computer Networks and Web Services   *18-50*

CHAPTER 03
Database Concepts   *51-63*

CHAPTER 04
Structured Query Language   *64-93*

CHAPTER 05
Interface Python with SQL   *94-107*

Practice Papers (1-3)   *108-120*

Watch Free Learning Videos

Subscribe **arihant** You Tube Channel

- ☑ Video Solutions of CBSE Sample Papers
- ☑ Chapterwise Important MCQs
- ☑ CBSE Updates

Syllabus

CBSE Term II Class XII

Distribution of Theory Marks

Unit No.	Unit Name	Marks
I	Computational Thinking and Programming - 2	05
II	Computer Networks	10
III	Database Management	20
	Total	**35**

Unit I   Computational Thinking and Programming – 2

- Data Structure: Stack, operations on stack (push & pop), implementation of stack using list.

Unit II   Computer Networks

- Evolution of networking: introduction to computer networks, evolution of networking (ARPANET, NSFNET, INTERNET)

- Data communication terminologies: concept of communication, components of data communication (sender, receiver, message, communication media, protocols), measuring capacity of communication media (bandwidth, data transfer rate), IP address, switching techniques (Circuit switching, Packet switching)

- Transmission media: Wired communication media (Twisted pair cable, Co-axial cable, Fiber-optic cable), Wireless media (Radio waves, Micro waves, Infrared waves)

- Network devices (Modem, Ethernet card, RJ45, Repeater, Hub, Switch, Router, Gateway, WIFI card)

- Network topologies and Network types: types of networks (PAN, LAN, MAN, WAN), networking topologies (Bus, Star, Tree)

- Network protocol: HTTP, FTP, PPP, SMTP, TCP/IP, POP3, HTTPS, TELNET, VoIP

- Introduction to web services: WWW, HyperText Markup Language (HTML), Extensible Markup Language (XML), domain names, URL, website, web browser, web servers, web hosting

Unit III Database Management

- Database concepts: introduction to database concepts and its need

- Relational data model: relation, attribute, tuple, domain, degree, cardinality, keys (candidate key, primary key, alternate key, foreign key)

- Structured Query Language: introduction, Data Definition Language and Data Manipulation Language, data type (char(n), varchar(n), int, float, date), constraints (not null, unique, primary key), create database, use database, show databases, drop database, show tables, create table, describe table, alter table (add and remove an attribute, add and remove primary key), drop table, insert, delete, select, operators (mathematical, relational and logical), aliasing, distinct clause, where clause, in, between, order by, meaning of null, is null, is not null, like, update command, delete command

- Aggregate functions (max, min, avg, sum, count), group by, having clause, joins : Cartesian product on two tables, equi-join and natural join

- Interface of python with an SQL database: connecting SQL with Python, performing insert, update, delete queries using cursor, display data by using fetchone(), fetchall(), rowcount, creating database connectivity applications

CBSE Circular

Acad - 51/2021, 05 July 2021

Exam Scheme Term I & II

केन्द्रीय माध्यमिक शिक्षा बोर्ड

(शिक्षा मंत्रालय, भारत सरकार के अधीन एक स्वायत संगठन)

CENTRAL BOARD OF SECONDARY EDUCATION

(An Autonomous Organisation under the Ministryof Education, Govt. of India)

CBSE/DIR (ACAD)/2021

Date: July 05, 2021
Circular No: Acad-51/2021

All the Heads of Schools affiliated to CBSE

Subject: Special Scheme of Assessment for Board Examination Classes X and XII for the Session 2021-22

COVID 19 pandemic caused almost all CBSE schools to function in a virtual mode for most part of the academic session of 2020-21. Due to the extreme risk associated with the conduct of Board examinations during the second wave in April 2021, CBSE had to cancel both its class X and XII Board examinations of the year 2021 and results are to be declared on the basis of a credible, reliable, flexible and valid alternative assessment policy. This, in turn, also necessitated deliberations over alternative ways to look at the learning objectives as well as the conduct of the Board Examinations for the academic session 2021-22 in case the situation remains unfeasible.

CBSE has also held stake holder consultations with Government schools as well as private independent schools from across the country especially schools from the remote rural areas and a majority of them have requested for the rationalization of the syllabus, similar to last year in view of reduced time permitted for organizing online classes. The Board has also considered the concerns regarding differential availability of electronic gadgets, connectivity and effectiveness of online teaching and other socio-economic issues specially with respect to students from economically weaker section and those residing in far flung areas of the country. In a survey conducted by CBSE, it was revealed that the rationalized syllabus notified for the session 2020-21 was effective for schools in covering the syllabus and helped learners in achieving learning objectives in a less stressful manner.

In the above backdrop and in line with the Board's continued focus on assessing stipulated learning outcomes by making the examinations competencies and core concepts based, student-centric, transparent, technology-driven, and having advance provision of alternatives for different future scenarios, the following schemes are introduced for the Academic Session for Class X and Class XII 2021-22.

Special Scheme for 2021-22

A. Academic session to be divided into 2 Terms with approximately 50% syllabus in each term:

The syllabus for the Academic session 2021-22 will be divided into 2 terms by following a systematic approach by looking into the interconnectivity of concepts and topics by the Subject Experts and the Board will conduct examinations at the end of each term on the basis of the bifurcated syllabus. This is done to increase the probability of having a Board conducted classes X and XII examinations at the end of the academic session.

B. The syllabus for the Board examination 2021-22 will be rationalized similar to that of the last academic session to be notified in July 2021. For academic transactions, however, schools will follow the curriculum and syllabus released by the Board vide Circular no. F.1001/CBSE-Acad/Curriculum/2021 dated 31 March 2021. Schools will also use alternative academic calendar and inputs from the NCERT on transacting the curriculum.

C. Efforts will be made to make Internal Assessment/ Practical/ Project work more credible and valid as per the guidelines and Moderation Policy to be announced by the Board to ensure fair distribution of marks.

Details of Curriculum Transaction

- Schools will continue teaching in distance mode till the authorities permit in-person mode of teaching in schools.

- **Classes IX-X: Internal Assessment** (throughout the year-irrespective of Term I and II) would include the *3 periodic tests, student enrichment, portfolio and practical work/ speaking listening activities/ project.*

- **Classes XI-XII: Internal Assessment** (throughout the year-irrespective of Term I and II) would include end of topic or unit tests/ exploratory activities/ practicals/ projects.

- Schools would create a student profile for all assessment undertaken over the year and retain the evidences in digital format.

- CBSE will facilitate schools to upload marks of Internal Assessment on the CBSE IT platform.

- Guidelines for Internal Assessment for all subjects will also be released along with the rationalized term wise divided syllabus for the session 2021-22.The Board would also provide additional resources like sample assessments, question banks, teacher training etc. for more reliable and valid internal assessments.

केन्द्रीय माध्यमिक शिक्षा बोर्ड

(शिक्षा मंत्रालय, भारत सरकार के अधीन एक स्वायत संगठन)

CENTRAL BOARD OF SECONDARY EDUCATION

(An Autonomous Organisation under the Ministryof Education, Govt. of India)

Term I Examinations:

- At the end of the first term, the Board will organize **Term I Examination** in a flexible schedule to be conducted between November-December 2021 with a window period of 4-8 weeks for schools situated in different parts of country and abroad. Dates for conduct of examinations will be notified subsequently.

- The Question Paper will have Multiple Choice Questions (MCQ) including case-based MCQs and MCQs on assertion-reasoning type. Duration of test will be **90 minutes** and it will cover only the rationalized syllabus of **Term I only** (i.e. approx. 50% of the entire syllabus).

- Question Papers will be sent by the CBSE to schools along with marking scheme.

- The exams will be conducted under the supervision of the External Center Superintendents and Observers appointed by CBSE.

- The responses of students will be captured on OMR sheets which, after scanning may be directly uploaded at CBSE portal or alternatively may be evaluated and marks obtained will be uploaded by the school on the very same day. The final direction in this regard will be conveyed to schools by the Examination Unit of the Board.

- Marks of the **Term I** Examination will contribute to the final overall score of students.

Term II Examination/ Year-end Examination:

- At the end of the second term, the Board would organize **Term II or Year-end Examination** based on the rationalized syllabus of Term II only (i.e. approximately 50% of the entire syllabus).

- This examination would be held around **March-April 2022** at the examination centres fixed by the Board.

- The paper will be of **2 hours duration** and have questions of different formats (case-based/ situation based, open ended- short answer/ long answer type).

- In case the situation is not conducive for normal descriptive examination a **90 minute MCQ based exam** will be conducted at the end of the Term II also.

- Marks of the Term II Examination would contribute to the final overall score.

Data Structures

In this Chapter...

- Needs of Data Structure
- Types of Data Structure
- Common Data Structures
- Operations on Data Structure
- Stack
- Item Node in Stack
- Evaluation of Postfix Expression

Data structure is a way of storing and organising information in the computer. A data structure is a group of data that have different data types which can be accessed as a unit. It has well defined operations, properties and behaviours. General data structure types include array, file, record, table, tree and so on.

Needs of Data Structure

Different kinds of data structures are meant for different kinds of applications and some are highly specialised to specific tasks.

Data structures are important for the following reasons

(i) Data structures are used in almost every program or software.

(ii) Specific data structures are essential ingredients of many efficient algorithms and make possible the management of huge amounts of data, such as a large integrated collection of databases.

(iii) Some programming languages emphasize on data structures rather than algorithms as the key organising factor in software design.

Types of Data Structure

There are two types of data structure as follows

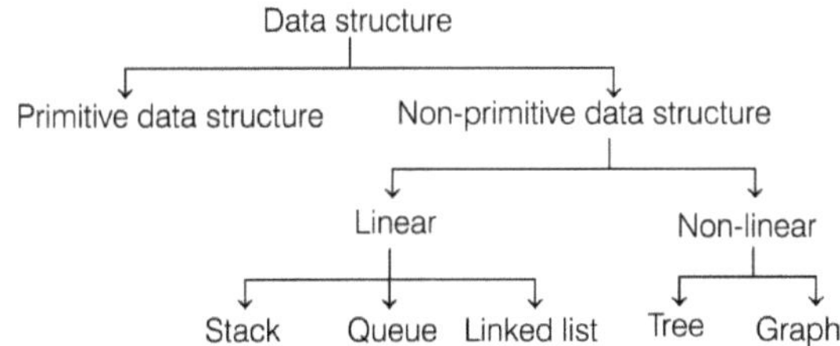

(i) **Primitive data structures** Data structures that are directly operated by machine level instructions are known as primitive data structures. Integer, real, character, pointer and reference are primitive data structures.

(ii) **Non-primitive data structures** These are more complex data structures. These data structures are derived from the primitive data structures. They include formation of sets of homogeneous and heterogeneous data elements.

The non-primitive data structure is divided into two types

- **Linear data structures** These are single level data structures, having their elements in a sequence. e.g. array, stack, queue and linked list.
- **Non-linear data structures** These are multilevel data structures. e.g. tree and graph.

Data structures can also be classified as

(i) **Static data structures** These data structures are those whose size, structure and associated memory locations are fixed at compile time. e.g. array.

(ii) **Dynamic data structures** These data structures are those, which can shrink or expand as required during the program execution and their associated memory locations that will be changed. e.g. linked list.

Common Data Structures

Common data structures are as follows

(i) **Array** It refers to the name of list of elements in a specific order, typically all elements are of the same type. Elements are accessed using index number. Arrays may be fixed length or resizable.

(ii) **Stack** It is limited form of array based on LIFO (Last In First Out), where insertion and deletion of elements take place at one end called the top of the stack. It serves as a collection of elements with two principle operations : Push, which adds an element to the collection and Pop, which removes the last element that was added.

(iii) **Queue** It is also a limited form of array based on FIFO (First In First Out), where insertion of elements take place at one end called the Front and deletion of elements take place at the other end called the Rear.

(iv) **Linked list** It is a data structure which consists of a set of data records (nodes) linked together and organised by references (links or pointers). Every node has a data field and an address field. The link between data can also be called a connector.

It is a collection of structures ordered not by their physical placement in memory but by logical links that are stored as part of the data in the structure itself. It is not necessary that it should be stored in the adjacent memory locations.

Operations on Data Structure

The basic operations that are performed on data structure are as follows

(i) **Insertion** It means addition of a new data element in a data structure.

(ii) **Deletion** It means removal of a data element from a data structure. The data element is searched before its removal.

(iii) **Searching** It involves searching for the specific data element in a data structure.

(iv) **Traversal** Traversal of a data structure means processing all the data elements of it.

(v) **Sorting** Arranging data elements of a data structure in a specific order (ascending or descending) is called sorting.

(vi) **Merging** Combining elements of two similar data structures to form a new data structure of same type is called merging.

Stack

In computer science, a stack is an abstract data type and a linear or user-defined data structure based on the principle of Last In First Out (LIFO).

A stack is a list where insertion and deletion can take place only at one end called Top.

A stack can be implemented using array and using linked list structure, depending upon the requirement.

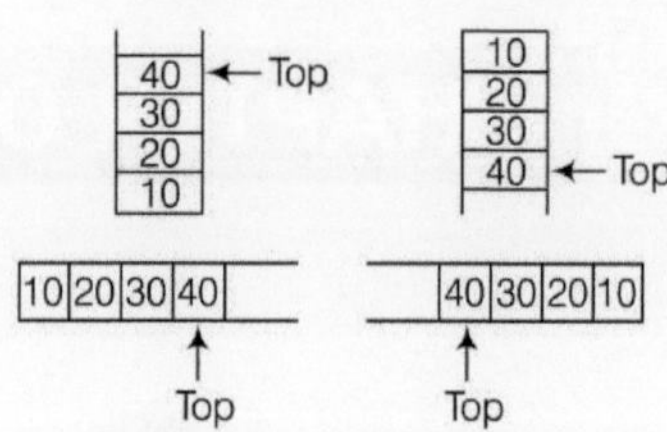

Different forms of stack

Stacks are used extensively at every level of a modern computer system.

e.g. a modern PC use stack at the architecture level, which are used in the basic design of an operating system for interrupt handling and operating system method calls.

Some of the examples of stack in real life are

- Stack of coins.
- Plates placed one above another.
- Pile of books.
- Pile of clothes in an almirah.
- Multiple chairs in a vertical pile.

Basic Operations and Implementation of Stack

Stack is open at one end, so operations can be performed on single end. We have two primitive operations that can be performed on stack data structure:

(i) Push

(ii) Pop

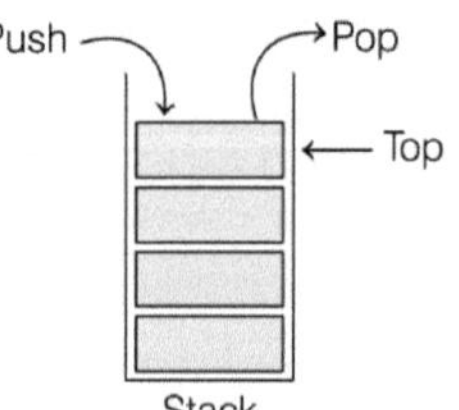

Push Operation

Whenever we add any element "data" in the list then it will be called as Push operation on stack.

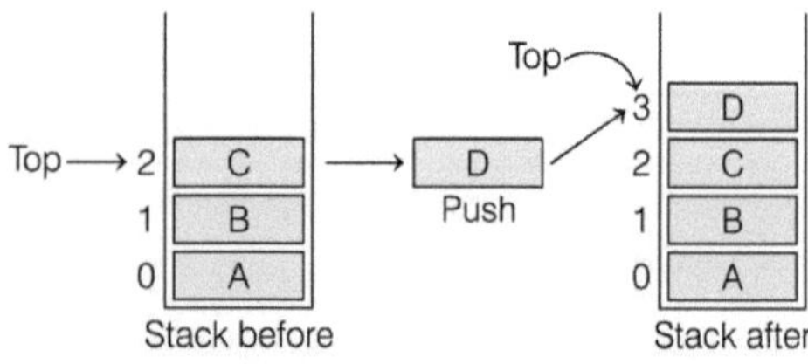

Before every Push operation, the value of "Top" is incremented by one and then value is inserted at the Top of the stack.

Pop Operation

Whenever we try to remove elements from the stack then the operation is called as Pop operation on stack.

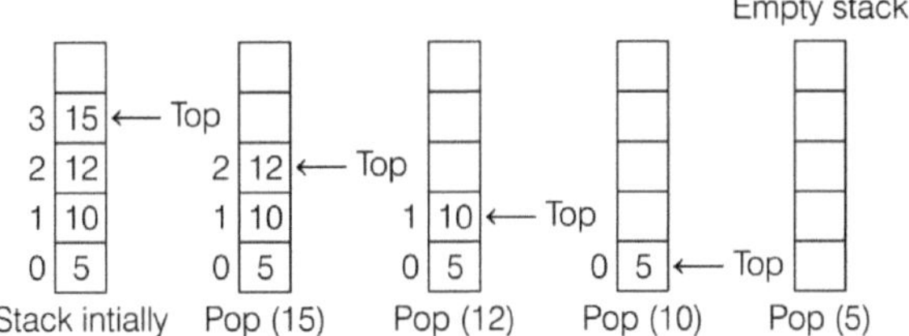

After every Pop operation, the value of "Top" is decremented by one and then value is deleted from the Top of the stack.

Some basic terms are given below

Terms	Definition
Peek	Refer to the inspecting the value at the stack's top without moving it. It is also sometimes referred as inspection.
Stack Top	Points at the top most position or point to the last item in stack.
Stack Push	The procedure of inserting a new element to the top of the stack is known as Push operation.
Stack Overflow	Any attempt to insert a new element in already full stack results shows overflow.
Stack Pop	The procedure of removing element from the top of the stack is called Pop operation.
Stack Underflow	Any attempt to delete an element from already empty stack results as underflow.

Insertion in a Stack as a List (Pushing)

Before inserting a new data into the stack, it is necessary to check that the stack is full (overflow) or not.

If it is not full then the Push operation can be performed otherwise not. This test is performed by comparing the value of Top with value MAX-1, the largest index.

Algorithm for Push Operation

In this algorithm, we insert an element called ITEM on the Top of the linear stack called data [MAX], which can hold maximum of MAX elements.

The variable Top is the counter pointing to the topmost element of stack.

Algorithm Steps

```
1. if (Top == (MAX-1))
   write "Stack is full" and go
   to step 4
2. Top   = Top + 1
3. data [Top] = ITEM
4. Stop
```

Deletion in a Stack as a List (Poping)

Before removing a data from the stack, it is necessary to check that the stack is empty (underflow) or not. If it is not empty then the Pop operation can be performed otherwise not.

Algorithm for Pop Operation

In this algorithm, we remove an element from the stack and copy the contents of topmost element into a variable called ITEM.

Algorithm Steps

```
1. if (Top == - 1)
   write "Stack is empty" and go to step 4
2. ITEM = data [Top]
3. Top = Top - 1
4. Stop
```

Traversal in a Stack as an Array

Moving through the elements of the stack is known as traversal. Traversing is the basic operation to display elements in a stack.

Algorithm Steps to Display all the Elements of the Stack

```
1. Start
2. if (Top == - 1)go to step 3
   else go to step 4
3. Print "Stack is empty" and go to step 7
4. Print the Top element of the stack
5. Decrement Top by 1
6. if (Top == - 1) go to step 7
   else go to step 4
7. Stop
```

Program To illustrate the basic operation of stack, i.e. Push, Pop and Show elements of stack.

```
def Empty(s):
    if s==[]:
        return True
    else:
        return False
def Push(s,x):
    s.append(x)
    Top=len(s) - 1
def Pop(s):
    if Empty(s):
        return "Underflow"
    else:
        x=s.Pop()
        if len(s)==0:
            Top=None
        else:
            Top=len(s) - 1
        return x
def Show(s):
    if Empty(s):
        print("Stack is Empty")
    else:
        Top=len(s)
        for i in range(Top-1,-1,-1):
            print(s[i])
#------ Main -------
```

```
stk=[]
Top=None
a="y"
while a=="y":
    print("1. Push")
    print("2. Pop")
    print("3. Show")
    print("4. Exit")
    choice=int(input("Enter your choice :"))
    if choice==1:
        x=int(input("Enter the number :"))
        Push(stk,x)
    elif choice==2:
        x=Pop(stk)
        if x=="Underflow":
            print("Stack is Empty")
        else:
            print("Popped element is :",x)
    elif choice==3:
        print("---Stack---",)
        Show(stk)
    elif choice==4:
        break
    else:
        print("Wrong input")
```

Output

1. Push
2. Pop
3. Show
4. Exit
   Enter your choice :1
   Enter the number :23
1. Push
2. Pop
3. Show
4. Exit
   Enter your choice :1
   Enter the number :56
1. Push
2. Pop
3. Show
4. Exit
   Enter your choice :1
   Enter the number :45
1. Push
2. Pop
3. Show
4. Exit
   Enter your choice :3
   ---Stack---
   45
   56
   23
1. Push
2. Pop
3. Show
4. Exit
   Enter your choice :2
   Popped element is : 45
1. Push
2. Pop
3. Show
4. Exit
   Enter your choice :3
   ---Stack---
   56
   23
1. Push
2. Pop
3. Show
4. Exit
   Enter your choice :1
   Enter the number :78
1. Push
2. Pop
3. Show
4. Exit
   Enter your choice :3
   ---Stack---
   78
   56
   23
1. Push
2. Pop
3. Show
4. Exit
   Enter your choice :6
   Wrong input
1. Push
2. Pop
3. Show
4. Exit
   Enter your choice :4

Item Node in Stack

Stored element or item in the stack is called item node. Item node can be of different types as

- When item nodes are integer types, stack will be mentioned as stack of integers.

- When item nodes are string types, stack will be mentioned as stack of string.
- When item nodes are list types, stack will be mentioned as stack of lists.

Applications of Stack

A stack is a LIFO structure, so it is a useful data structure for applications in which information must be stored and later retrieved in reverse order. Stacks are used by operating systems, application softwares as well as compilers.

Some applications of the stack in computer data processing are as follows

1. Processing of Method (Subprogram) Calls

Stacks are frequently used to keep track of the order of execution of the methods called by a main program. It is used to store information about the active subroutines of a computer program.

2. Matching Parentheses

The compilation process is very complex as the compiler checks the syntax minutely. The compiler has to ascertain if the number of left parentheses is equal in number with that of right parentheses and for every left bracket, there is a right bracket. This matching is performed by using a stack.

3. Polish String for Arithmetic Expression

An arithmetic expression is an expression having variables, constants and operators. Assume that an expression has only constants (numeric and logical) and operators (arithmetic-exponentiation, multiplication, division, addition and subtraction or logical-NOT, AND and OR).

Hierarchy of these operations is given below

Arithmetic Operators	Precedence
Exponentiation ($\wedge$ or $\uparrow$)	Highest
Multiplication and Division (* , /)	Middle
Addition and Subtraction (+, −)	Lowest
Logical Operators	**Precedence**
NOT	Highest
AND	Middle
OR	Lowest

Operations at the same level are executed in a left to right order. Operators may be enclosed within parentheses to override the above rules of hierarchy. There are three different but equivalent ways of writing expressions: Infix, Postfix and Prefix.

Infix Notation

Operators are written in between their operands. This is an usual way we write expressions

$$A * (B + C)/D$$

Prefix Notation

Operators are written before their operands. It is also known as "Polish Notation".

The infix expression given is equivalent to

$$/*A + BCD$$

Postfix Notation

Operators are written after their operands. It is also known as "Reverse Polish Notation".

The infix expression given is equivalent to $ABC + *D/$

Advantage of Postfix or Prefix Expression Over Infix Expression

The main advantage of using postfix or prefix expression is that parentheses is not required to enclose the operations. So, the problem of nesting of expressions is removed. Every operator in a postfix or prefix expression is placed according to its precedence. Therefore, no ambiguity exists in interpreting arithmetic expressions.

Algorithm to Convert Infix Expression to Postfix Expression

Assume that, STACK is the name of stack that is used to store operators, EXP represents the given infix expression, PE is the string array containing resultant postfix expression and TOP is the pointer pointing at the topmost element of the stack.

Algorithm Steps

```
1. First of all enclose the EXP in
   parentheses, i.e. ( ).
2. Read next symbol of EXP and repeat
   steps 3 to 6 until the STACK is empty.
3. if the symbol read is operand then add it
   to PE.
4. if the symbol read is '( ' then Push it
   into STACK.
5. if the symbol read is operator then
   (i) Repeat while (Priority of TOP (STACK)
       ≥ Priority of operator)
       Pop operator from STACK and add
       operator to PE
   (ii) Push operator into STACK
6. if the symbol read is ')' then
   (i) Repeat while (TOP (STACK)! = ' ( ' )
       Pop operator from STACK
       Add operator to PE
   (ii) Remove the '('. [It must not be
        added to PE].
7. PE is the desired equivalent postfix
   expression.
8. Stop
```

e.g. Evaluate the postfix expression from the following infix expression using a stack and show the contents of stack after execution of each operation :

$$((True \&\& False)|| \; ! \; (False \; || \; True))$$

Scan (EXP)	Stack	Output (PE)
(	(	
(	((	
True	((	True
&&	((&&	True
False	((&&	True False
)	(	True False &&
||	(||	True False &&
!	(||!	True False &&
(	(||!(	True False &&
False	(||!(	True False && False
||	(||!(||	True False && False
True	(||!(||	True False && False True
)	(||!	True False && False True||
)	Stack empty	True False && False True||!||

Output True False && False True\|\|!\|\|

Evaluation of Postfix Expression

A postfix expression has no parentheses. So, it can be evaluated as two operands and an operator at a time (except NOT operator) or a NOT operator, which is applied on a single operand. As mentioned earlier, it is easy to handle a postfix expression by the compiler and the computer than an infix expression.

Algorithm Stepsr

```
1. Create an empty stack STACK
```

```
2. Read next symbol of the postfix
   expression PE and repeat steps 3 and 4
   until end of expression is reached.
3. if (symbol read = = operand) then
   Push (STACK, symbol read)
4. if (symbol read = = operator) then
   if (operator = = NOT) then
   Pop (STACK, symbol)
   Evaluate the expression so formed
   Push the result onto STACK
   else
   Pop (STACK, symbol1)
   Pop (STACK, Symbol2)
   Evaluate
   result = symbol2
   operator symbol1
   Push (STACK, result)
5. Pop (STACK, result)
6. Stop
```

e.g. Evaluate the following postfix expression using a stack and show the contents of stack after execution of each operation :

$$50, \; 40, \; +, \; 18, 14, \; -, \; 4, \; *, \; +$$

Scan	Stack	Output
50	50	
40	50, 40	
+	90	50 + 40 = 90
18	90, 18	
14	90, 18, 14	
−	90, 4	18 − 14 = 4
4	90, 4, 4	
*	90, 16	4 * 4 = 16
+	106	90 + 16 = 106

Output 106

Chapter Practice

Objective Questions

• Multiple Choice Questions

1. Data structures are
(a) network structures
(b) group of data
(c) different types of data
(d) different operations on data

Ans. (*b*) Data structures are group of data that have different data types, which can be accessed as a unit.

2. Which of the following is/are linear data structure(s)?
(a) Array   (b) Stack   (c) Queue   (d) All of these

Ans. (*d*) Stack, queue and array all are linear data structures.

3. .... of data structure means processing all the data elements of it.
(a) Traversal   (b) Searching
(c) Insertion   (d) Merging

Ans. (*a*) Traversal of data structure means processing all the data elements of it.

4. Which data structure is needed to convert infix notation to postfix notation?
(a) Branch   (b) Tree
(c) Queue   (d) Stack

Ans. (*d*) Stack is needed to convert infix notation to postfix notation.

5. Process of inserting an element in stack is called
(a) Create   (b) Push
(c) Evaluation   (d) Pop

Ans. (*b*) When we add or insert any element 'data' in the list, then it will be called as 'Push' operation on stack.

6. Process of removing an element from stack is called
(a) Create   (b) Push
(c) Evaluation   (d) Pop

Ans. (*d*) When we try to remove elements from the stack, then the operation is called as 'pop' operation on stack.

7. Pushing an element into stack already having five elements and stack size of 5, then stack becomes
(a) Overflow   (b) Uses flow   (c) Crash   (d) Underflow

Ans. (*a*) Any attempt to insert a new element in already full stack results shows 'Overflow'.

8. In a stack, if a user tries to remove an element from empty stack is called
(a) Underflow   (b) Overflow
(c) Empty   (d) Garbage collection

Ans. (*a*) In a stack, if a user tries to remove an element from empty stack is called 'Underflow'.

9. Integer, real, character, pointer and reference are .... data structures.
(a) primitive   (b) non-primitive
(c) linear   (d) non-linear

Ans. (*a*) Integer, real, character, pointer and reference are primitive data structures. Primitive data structures are directly operated by machine level instructions.

10. Pile of books is an example of ....
(a) stack   (b) queue   (c) array   (d) linked list

Ans. (*a*) Pile of books is an example of stack.

• Case Based MCQs

11. Direction *Read the case and answer the following questions.*

Mr. Rajeshwar has created a stack whose size is fixed for 10 elements and wants to perform some operations on it. He wants to push certain elements and pop some elements from it. He is confused about the operations and how the elements will behave on pushing and popping?

Chevrolet
Suzuki
Honda
Mercedes
RolsRoyce

Help him to find the answers of the following questions.

(i) How many elements can he push more to the stack?

(a) 3   (b) 5
(c) 4   (d) 1

(ii) How many elements he needs to take out before "RolsRoyce" will come out?

(a) 2   (b) 3
(c) 4   (d) 1

(iii) If 3 elements are popped out and 2 pushed in , what will be the strength of the stack?

(a) 2   (b) 4
(c) 0   (d) 1

(iv) If "Tata" and "Datsun" are pushed to the initial stack respectively , which element will be popped out as a result of a pop operation now?

(a) Chevrolet
(b) Datsun
(c) Tata
(d) RolsRoyce

(v) If 2 elements are popped out and 4 pushed into the initial stack, how many times a loop needs to iterate to traverse the stack?

(a) 6   (b) 3
(c) 7   (d) 4

Ans. (i) (*b*) Though the capacity of the stack is 10 , so he can push a maximum of 5 elements.

(ii) (*c*) Though there are 4 elements above "RolsRoyce", so 4 elements need to be taken out.

(iii) (*b*) Popping 3 elements means 2 remain. Now, pushing 2 elements means strength becomes 4.

(iv) (*b*) Since 'Datsun' is pushed at the end, it will be popped out first.

(v) (*c*) Since, there are 5 elements in stack and we popped out 2 elements from it, then 3 elements remain. Now, we push 4 elements into stack, then total elements are 7. Hence, a loop needs to iterate to traverse the stack is 7 times.

PART 2
Subjective Questions

• Short Answer Type Questions

1. What is data structure ? Name any two non-primitive data structures.

Ans. Data structure is a way of storing and organising information in the computer, so that it can be retrieved and used most productively. Two non-primitive data structures are array and linked list.

2. What is the value of the postfix expression?

$$6 \ 3 \ 2 \ 4 \ + \ - \ *$$

Ans. Postfix expression is : $(6 * (3 - (2 + 4)))$
$$= (6 * (3 - 6))$$
$$= (6 * (-3)) = -18$$

3. Define any two operations on data structure.

Ans. Two operations on data structure are as follows

(i) **Insertion** It means addition of a new data element in a data structure.

(ii) **Searching** It involves searching for the specific data element in a data structure.

4. Write the applications of stack.

Ans. There are some applications of stack are as follows

(i) Infix to postfix conversion using stack.
(ii) Evaluation of postfix expression.
(iii) Reverse a string using stack.
(iv) Implement two stacks in an array.

5. Evaluate the following postfix expression. Show the status of stack after execution of each operation separately.

$$T, \ F, \ NOT, \ AND, \ T, \ OR, \ F, \ AND$$

Ans. Given postfix expression is

$$T, \ F, \ NOT, \ AND, \ T, \ OR, \ F, \ AND$$

Scanned Elements	Operation	Stack Status
T	Push	T
F	Push	T, F
NOT	Pop one operand from stack NOT F = T Push	T, T
AND	Pop two operands from stack T AND T = T Push	T
T	Push	T, T
OR	Pop two operands from stack T OR T = T Push	T
F	Push	T, F
AND	Pop two operands from stack T AND F = F Push	F

Output F

6. Evaluate the following postfix expression. Show the status of stack after execution of each operation.

$$60, \ 6, \ /, \ 5, \ 2, \ *, \ 5, \ -, \ +$$

Ans. Given postfix expression is

    60, 6, /, 5,2, *, 5, −, +

Scanned Elements	Operation	Stack Status
60	Push	60
6	Push	60, 6
/	Pop two operands from stack 60/6 = 10 Push	10
5	Push	10, 5
2	Push	10, 5, 2
*	Pop two operands from stack 5 * 2 = 10 Push	10, 10
5	Push	10, 10, 5
−	Pop two operands from stack 10 − 5 = 5 Push	10, 5
+	Pop two operands from stack 10 + 5 = 15 Push	15

Output 15

7. Evaluate the following postfix notation. Show status of stack after every step of evaluation (i.e. after each operator).

    True, False, NOT, AND, False, True, OR, AND

Ans. Given postfix expression is

    True, False, NOT, AND, False, True, OR, AND

Scanned Elements	Operation	Stack Status
True	Push	True
False	Push	True, False
NOT	Pop one element from the stack. Apply NOT on False and Push the result.	True, True
AND	Pop two elements from the stack. Apply AND between them and Push the result.	True
False	Push	True, False
True	Push	True, False, True
OR	Pop two elements from the stack. Apply OR between them and Push the result.	True, True
AND	Pop two elements from the stack. Apply AND between them and Push the result.	True

Output True

8. Convert the following infix expression to its equivalent postfix expression. Showing stack contents for the conversion

    (A + B * (C − D)/E)

Ans. Given infix expression is

    (A + B * (C − D)/E)

Scanned Elements	Operation	Stack Status
(	(	
A	(	A
+	(+	A
B	(+	AB
*	(+ *	AB
(	(+ * (	AB
C	(+ * (	ABC
−	(+ * (−	ABC
D	(+ * (−	ABCD
)	(+ *	ABCD −
/	(+ /	ABCD − *
E	(+ /	ABCD − * E
)		ABCD − *E/+

Output ABCD −*E/+

9. Evaluate the following postfix expression. Show the status of stack after execution of each operation :

    25, 8, 3, −, /, 6, *, 10, +

Ans. Given postfix expression is

    25, 8, 3, −, /, 6, *, 10, +

Scanned Elements	Operation	Stack Status
25	Push	25
8	Push	25, 8
3	Push	25, 8, 3
−	Pop twice 8 − 3 = 5 Push	25, 5

Scanned Elements	Operation	Stack Status
/	Pop twice $25/5 = 5$ Push	5
6	Push	5, 6
*	Pop twice $5*6 = 30$ Push	30
10	Push	30, 10
+	Pop twice $30 + 10 = 40$ Push	40

Output 40

10. Evaluate the following postfix expression. Show the status of stack after execution of each operation :

    10, 20, +, 25, 15, −, *, 30, /

Ans. Given postfix expression is

    10, 20, +, 25, 15, −, *, 30, /

Scanned Elements	Operation	Stack Status
10	Push	10
20	Push	10, 20
+	Pop twice $10 + 20 = 30$ Push	30
25	Push	30, 25
15	Push	30, 25, 15
−	Pop twice $25 - 15 = 10$ Push	30, 10
*	Pop twice $30 * 10 = 300$ Push	300
30	Push	300, 30
/	Pop twice $300 / 30 = 10$ Push	10

Output 10

11. Evaluate the following postfix expression. Show the status of stack after execution of each operation :

    20, 10, +, 5, 2, *, −, 10, /

Ans. Given postfix expression is

    20, 10, +, 5, 2, *, −, 10, /

Scanned Elements	Operation	Stack Status
20	Push	20
10	Push	20, 10
+	Pop twice $10 + 20 = 30$ Push	30

Scanned Elements	Operation	Stack Status
5	Push	30, 5
2	Push	30, 5, 2
*	Pop twice $5 * 2 = 10$ Push	30, 10
−	Pop twice $30 - 10 = 20$ Push	20
10	Push	20, 10
/	Pop twice $20 / 10 = 2$ Push	2

Output 2

12. Obtain the postfix notation for the following infix notation of expression showing the contents of the stack and postfix expression formed after each step of conversion:

    (A * B + (C − D/F))

Ans. Given infix expression is

    (A * B + (C − D/F))

Scanned Elements	Operation	Stack Status
(	(	
A	(	A
*	(*	A
B	(*	AB
+	(+	AB*
(	(+(	AB*
C	(+(	AB*C
−	(+(−	AB*C
D	(+(−	AB*CD
/	(+(−/	AB*CD
F	(+(−/	AB*CDF
)	(+	AB*CDF/−
)		AB*CDF/−+

Output AB*CDF/−+

13. Evaluate the following postfix expression using stack and show the contents of stack after execution of each expression.

    120, 45, 20, +, 25, 15, −, +, *

Ans. Given postfix expression is

    120, 45, 20, +, 25, 15, −, +, *

Scanned Elements	Operation	Stack Status
120	Push	120
45	Push	120, 45
20	Push	120, 45, 20
+	Pop twice 45 + 20 = 65 Push	120, 65
25	Push	120, 65, 25
15	Push	120, 65, 25, 15
−	Pop twice 25 − 15 = 10 Push	120, 65, 10
+	Pop twice 65 + 10 = 75 Push	120, 75
*	Pop twice 120 * 75 = 9000 Push	9000

Output 9000

14. Use a stack to evaluate the following postfix expression and show the content of the stack after execution of each operation. Do not write any code. Assume as if you are using Push and Pop member methods of the stack.

$$AB - CD + E * +$$

(where A = 5, B = 3, C = 5, D = 4 and E = 2)

Ans. Putting the values of the operands, we get the postfix expression as

$$5, 3, -, 5, 4, +, 2, *, +$$

Scanned Elements	Operation	Stack Status
5	Push	5
3	Push	5, 3
−	Pop twice 5 − 3 = 2 Push	2
5	Push	2, 5
4	Push	2, 5, 4
+	Pop twice 5 + 4 = 9 Push	2, 9
2	Push	2, 9, 2
*	Pop twice 9 * 2 = 18 Push	2, 18
+	Pop twice 2 + 18 = 20 Push	20

Output 20

15. Change the following infix expression into postfix expression : $((A + B)*C + D/E - F)$

Ans. Given infix expression is

$$((A + B) * C + D/E - F)$$

Scanned Elements	Operations	Stack Status
(	(	
(	((	
A	((	A
+	((+	A
B	((+	AB
)	(	AB +
*	(*	AB +
C	(*	AB + C
+	(+	AB + C *
D	(+	AB + C * D
/	(+ /	AB + C * D
E	(+ /	AB + C* DE
−	(−	AB + C * DE/+
F	(−	AB + C* DE/ + F
)		AB + C * DE/ + F −

Output AB+C*DE/+F−

16. Evaluate the following postfix expression using a stack and show the contents of stack after execution of each operation :

$$100, 40, 8, +, 20, 10, -, +, *$$

Ans. Given postfix expression is

$$100, 40, 8, +, 20, 10, -, +, *$$

Scanned Elements	Operation	Stack Status
100	Push	100
40	Push	100, 40
8	Push	100, 40, 8
+	Pop twice 40 + 8 = 48 Push	100, 48
20	Push	100, 48, 20
10	Push	100, 48, 20, 10
−	Pop twice 20 − 10 = 10 Push	100, 48, 10
+	Pop twice 48 + 10 = 58 Push	100, 58
*	Pop twice 58 * 100 = 5800 Push	5800

Output 5800

17. Evaluate the following postfix expression using a stack and show the contents of the stack after execution of each operation :

$$5, 6, 9, +, 80, 5, *, -, /$$

Ans. Given postfix expression is

$$5, 6, 9, +, 80, 5, *, -, /$$

Scanned Elements	Operation	Stack Status
5	Push	5
6	Push	5, 6
9	Push	5, 6, 9
+	Pop twice $6 + 9 = 15$ Push	5, 15
80	Push	5, 15, 80
5	Push	5, 15, 80, 5
*	Pop twice $80 * 5 = 400$ Push	5, 15, 400
−	Pop twice $15 - 400 = -385$ Push	5, −385
/	Pop twice $5/-385 = -1/77$ Push	−1/77

Output $-1/77$

18. Evaluate the following postfix expression using a stack. Show the contents of stack after execution of each operation.

```
True, False, True, False, NOT, OR, True, OR,
OR, AND
```

Ans. In the given expression True and False are operands and AND, NOT and OR are operators.

Scanned Elements	Operation	Stack Status
True	Push	True
False	Push	True, False
True	Push	True, False, True
False	Push	True, False, True, False
NOT	Pop one operand NOT False = True Push	True, False, True, True
OR	Pop two operands Evaluate : True OR True = True Push	True, False, True
True	Push	True, False, True, True
OR	Pop two operands Evaluate : True OR True = True Push	True, False, True
OR	Pop two operands Evaluate : False OR True = True Push	True, True
AND	Pop two operands Evaluate : True AND True = True Push	True

Output True

19. Consider the following sequence of numbers:

$$1, 2, 3, 4$$

These are supposed to be operated through a stack to produce the following sequence of numbers:

$$2, 1, 4, 3$$

List the Push and Pop operations to get the required output.

Ans. (i) Push (1) (ii) Push (2)
(iii) Pop (2) (iv) Pop (1)
(v) Push (3) (vi) Push (4)
(vii) Pop (4) (viii) Pop (3)

20. Consider the following stack of characters, where STACK is allocated N = 8 memory cells.

STACK : A, C, D, F, K, ..., ..., ...

Describe the STACK at the end of the following operations. Here, Pop and Push are algorithms for deleting and adding an element to the stack.

(i) Pop (STACK, ITEM) (ii) Pop (STACK, ITEM)
(iii) Push (STACK, L) (iv) Push (STACK, P)
(v) Pop (STACK, ITEM) (vi) Push (STACK, R)
(vii) Push (STACK, S) (viii) Pop (STACK, ITEM)

Ans. The stack contents will be as follows after the operations of stack

(i) STACK : A, C, D, F (ii) STACK : A, C, D
(K is deleted) (F is deleted)
(iii) STACK : A, C, D, L (iv) STACK: A, C, D, L, P
(L is inserted) (P is inserted)
(v) STACK : A, C, D, L (vi) STACK : A, C, D, L, R
(P is deleted) (R is inserted)
(vii) STACK : A, C, D, L, R, S
(S is inserted)
(viii) STACK : A, C, D, L, R
(S is deleted)

21. Suppose STACK is allocated 6 memory locations and initially STACK is empty (Top = 0). Given the output of the program segment.

```
AAA = 4
BBB = 6
Push (STACK, AAA)
Push (STACK, 4)
Push (STACK, BBB +2)
Push (STACK, AAA + BBB)
Push (STACK, 10)
while (Top>0) :
     Element = STACK. Pop ( )
     print(Element)
```

Ans. Output

10

10

8

4

4

22. Evaluate the following postfix notation of expression

```
True, False, NOT, AND, True, True, AND, OR
```

Ans. Given postfix expression is

```
True, False, NOT, AND, True, True, AND, OR
```

Scanned Elements	Operation	Stack Status
True	Push	True
False	Push	True, False
NOT	Pop one element from the stack NOT False = True Push	True, True
AND	Pop two elements from the stack True AND True = True Push	True
True	Push	True, True
True	Push	True, True, True
AND	Pop two elements from the stack True AND True = True Push	True, True
OR	Pop two elements from the stack True OR True = True Push	True

Output True

23. Evaluate the following postfix expression:

```
20, 10, −, 15, 3, /, +, 5, *
```

Ans. Given postfix expression is

```
20, 10, −, 15, 3, /, +, 5, *
```

Scanned Elements	Operation	Stack Status
20	Push	20
10	Push	20, 10
−	Pop twice 20 − 10 = 10 Push	10
15	Push	10, 15
3	Push	10, 15, 3
/	Pop twice 15/3 = 5 Push	10, 5
+	Pop twice 10 + 5 = 15 Push	15
5	Push	15, 5
*	Pop twice 15 * 5 = 75 Push	75

Output 75

24. Evaluate the following postfix using stack and show the content of the stack after the execution of each.

```
20, 4, +, 3, −, 7, /
```

Ans. Given postfix expression is 20, 4, +, 3, −, 7, /

Scanned Elements	Operation	Stack Status
20	Push	20
4	Push	20, 4
+	Pop (4) Pop (20) Push (20 + 4) = 24	24
3	Push	24, 3
−	Pop (3) Pop (24) Push (24 − 3) = 21	21
7	Push	21, 7
/	Pop (7) Pop (21) Push (21/7) = 3	3

Output 3

25. Evaluate the following postfix expression using a stack. Show the contents of stack after execution of each operation:

$$10, 40, 25, -, *, 15, 4, *, +$$

Ans. Given postfix expression is

$$10, 40, 25, -, *, 15, 4, *, +$$

Scanned Elements	Operation	Stack Status
10	Push	10
40	Push	10, 40
25	Push	10, 40, 25
−	Pop (25) Pop (40) Push (40 − 25) = 15	10, 15
*	Pop (15) Pop (10) Push (10 * 15) = 150	150
15	Push	150, 15
4	Push	150, 15, 4
*	Pop (4) Pop (15) Push (15 * 4) = 60	150, 60
+	Pop (60) Pop (150) Push (150 + 60) = 210	210

Output 210

• Long Answer Type Questions

26. Explain the different operations possible in a stack.

Ans. The stack provides three major operaions, which are as follows

(i) Push   (ii) Pop

(iii) Traversal

(i) **Push Operation** Whenever we add any element "data" in the list, then it will be called as 'Push operation' on stack.

Before every Push operation, the value of "Top" is incremented by one and then value is inserted at the top of the stack.

(ii) **Pop Operation** Whenever we try to remove elements from the stack, then the operation is called as 'Pop operation' on stack.

After every Pop operation, the value of "Top" is decremented by one and then value is deleted from the top of the stack.

(iii) **Traversal Operation** The traversal operation means traversing through the elements of the stack starting from the 1st element to the last. It does not involve any modifications to the contents of the stack.

27. Write Push (contents) and Pop (contents) methods in Python to add numbers and remove numbers considering them to act as Push and Pop operations of stack.

Ans.
```python
def Push (contents) :
    if(len(stack) >= limit) :
        print("Stack Overflow!")
    else :
        stack . append (contents)
    print ("Stack after Push", stack)
def Pop ( ) :
    if (len (stack) <= 0 ) :
        print("Stack Underflow!")
        return 0
    else :
        return stack. Pop( )
```

28. Write the Push operation of stack containing person names. Notice that the name should only accept characters, spaces and period (.) except digits. Assume that Pname is a class instance attribute.

Ans.
```python
def insert():
    name_pattern = re.compile
                      (r "[A-Za-zs.]")
    while True :
        n = input ("Enter name:")
        while name_pattern. search (n) :
            print ("Invalid name")
            print ("Enter name correctly")
            n = input( )
        Sname. append (n)
        c = input ("Enter more name
                      <y/n>").upper ( )
        if (c! = 'y'):
            break
```

29. A linear stack called status contains the following information :

(i) Phone number of Employee

(ii) Name of Employee

Write the following methods to perform given operations on the stack status :

(i) **Push_element ( )** To Push an object containing Phone number of Employee and Name of Employee into the stack.

(ii) **Pop_element ( )** To Pop an object from the stack and to release the memory.

Ans. (i)
```
def Push_element (Status, Top) :
    phone_no = int (input ("Enter phone
    number :"))
    emp_name = input ("Enter employee
                              name :")
    St = (phone_no, emp_name)
    Status.append (St)
    Top =Top + 1
    return Top
```
(ii)
```
def Pop_element (Status, Top) :
    Slen = len (Status)
    if (Slen <= 0) :
        print ("Status is empty")
    else :
        phone_no, emp_name = Status. Pop ( )
        Top = Top - 1
        print("Phone number %s and name %s
        deleted" % (phone_no, emp_name))
    return Top
```

30. Convert the expression given below from infix to postfix using stack , showing each operation.

(A+ B/(C *D)-E)

Ans. Given infix expression is (A+B/(C*D)-E)

Scanned Elements	Operation	Stack Status
(	(	
A	(	A
+	(+	A
B	(+	AB
/	(+/	AB
(	(+/(	AB
C	(+/(	ABC
*	(+/(*	ABC
D	(+/(*	ABCD
)	(+/	ABCD*
−	(−	ABCD*/+
E	(−	ABCD*/+E
)		ABCD*/+E−

Output ABCD*/+E−

31. Evaluate the following postfix expression using stack, showing stack 7 8 2 * 4 / + status after execution of each operation.   **(NCERT)**

Ans. Given postfix expresion is
7 8 2 * 4/+

Scanned Elements	Operation	Stack Status
7	Push	7
8	Push	7, 8
2	Push	7, 8, 2
*	Pop two operands from stack 8*2 = 16 Push	7, 16
4	Push	7, 16, 4
/	Pop two operands from stack 16/4 = 4 Push	7, 4
+	Pop two operands from stack 7 + 4 = 11 Push	11

Output 11

32. Change the following infix expression into postfix expression

$$(A +(B * C) - D/ E + C \wedge H$$

Ans. Given infix expresion is

$$(A +(B * C) - D/ E + C \wedge H$$

Scanned Elements	Operations	Stack Status
(	(	−
A	(	A
+	(+	A
(	(+(	A
B	(+(	AB
*	(+(*	AB
C	(+(*	ABC
)	(+	ABC*
−	(−	ABC*+
D	(−	ABC*+D
/	(−/	ABC*+D
E	(−/	ABC*+DE
+	(+	ABC*+DE/−
C	(+	ABC*+DE/− C
^	(+ ^	ABC*+DE/− C
H	(+ ^	ABC*+DE/− CH
)		ABC*+DE/−^CH+

Output ABC*+DE/− CH ^ +

33. Find the output of the following code   (NCERT)

```
answer=[]; output=''
answer.append('T')
answer.append('A')
answer.append('M')
ch=answer.pop()
output=output+ch
ch=answer.pop()
output=output+ch
ch=answer.pop()
output=output+ch
print('Result=',output)
```

Ans. answer is a blank list and output is a blank string. The three append operatins add T →A→ M into the stack with M at the top. First Pop operation takes out 'M' and adds it to 'ch' and then 'output'. Similarly, the subsequent pop operations are popping out 'A' and 'T' and adding them to output, which is printed as 'MAT'.

Output Result = MAT

Chapter Test

Multiple Choice Questions

1. A tree is a .... data structure.
   (a) linear
   (b) non-linear
   (c) primitive
   (d) non-primitive

2. A stack is a
   (a) data structure
   (b) file system
   (c) type of network
   (d) type of file

3. A static stack cannot store
   (a) integers
   (b) strings
   (c) float
   (d) any number of elements

4. The condition of a stack full is applicable for
   (a) static stack
   (b) dynamic stack
   (c) stack with Boolean values
   (d) All of the above

5. Which of the following stack cannot be traversed ?
   (a) An empty stack
   (b) A full stack
   (c) A stack implemented by a list
   (d) None of the above

Short Answer Type Questions

6. What is the use of "Top" in a stack.

7. Evaluate the following postfix expression. Show the status of stack after execution of each operation separately.
   True,False,True,AND,OR

8. List some of the advantages of data structure.

9. Write a function popdata() with a list of student names as parameter and display only those names that are of length more than 10.

10. Write the algorithm steps for pop in a static stack.

Long Answer Type Questions

11. Write the rules that are used while converting an infix expression to postfix using stack.

12. Write the algorithm for push in a static stack.

Answers

Multiple Choice Questions

1. (b)   2. (a)   3. (d)   4. (a)   5. (a)

For Detailed Solutions

Scan the code

CHAPTER 02

Computer Networks and Web Services

In this Chapter...

- Evolution of Networking
- Data Communication
- Switching Techniques
- Data Communication Terminologies
- Transmission Media
- Types of Network
- Network Devices
- Network Topology
- Network Protocols
- Web Services

A **computer network** is a collection of computers and other hardwares interconnected by communication channels that allows sharing of resources and information.

A computer networking is the practice for exchanging information between two or more computer devices together for the purpose of data sharing.

Benefits of Networking

Computer network is very useful in modern environment. Some of the benefits of networking are discussed here:

(i) **File Sharing** Networking of computer helps the user to share data files.

(ii) **Hardware Sharing** Users can share devices such as printers, scanners, CD-ROM drives, hard drives, etc. in a computer network.

(iii) **Application Sharing** Applications can be shared over the network and this allows implementation of client/server applications.

(iv) **User Communication** This allows users to communicate using E-mail, newsgroups, video conferencing within the network.

(v) **Access to Remote Database** This allows users to access remote database, e.g. airline reservation database may be accessed for ticket booking.

Evolution of Networking

Evolution of networking is described below

ARPANET

The Advanced Research Projects Agency NETwork (ARPANET) was the world's first operational packet switching network.

The U.S department of defence sponsored a project named ARPANET, whose goal was to connect computers at different universities and U.S defence.

In 1969, the University of California at Los Angeles, the University of California and the University of Utah were connected as the beginning of the ARPANET using 50 Kbits circuits.

In mid 80's, the National Science Foundation created a new network called **NSFnet**, which was more capable than ARPANET.

WWW

The World Wide Web (WWW) is a system of interlinked hypertext documents accessed *via* Internet. With a web browser, one can view web pages that may contain text, images, videos and other multimedia and can navigate between them *via* hyperlinks.

The Internet is a global system of interconnected computer networks. In short, the web is a way of exchanging information between computers on the Internet.

Internet (INTERconnection NETwork)

The Internet is a network of the interlinked computer networking worldwide, which is accessible to the general public.

Internet is a huge network of several different interlinked networks relating to the business, government, academic and even smaller domestic networks. Therefore, Internet is known as the network of all the other networks.

These networks enable the Internet to be used for various important functions, which include the several means of communications like the file transfer, the online chat and even the sharing of the documents and websites on the WWW or the World Wide Web.

Interspace

It is a client/server program that allows multiple users to communicate online with real-time audio, video and text chat in dynamic 3D environments.

Interspace provides the most advanced form of communication available on the Internet today.

The Interspace is a future vision of what the Internet will become tomorrow, when users cross-correlate the information of multiple sources. It will be an application environment for interconnecting spaces to manipulate information like Internet.

Intranet

An intranet is a network that connects the computers and networks with in an organisation that is based on Internet technology.

It uses the TCP/IP protocols, server and browser software used for the Internet. With an intranet, the basic services of the Internet like E-mail, FTP, etc. are used.

Data Communication

Communication is an act of sending or receiving data. Thus, data communication refers to the exchange of data between two or more networked or connected devices.

These devices must be capable of sending and receiving data over a communication medium. Examples of such devices include personal computers, mobile phones, laptops etc.

Components of Data Communication

Whenever we talk about communication between two computing devices using a network, five most important aspects come to our mind.

These are sender, receiver, communication medium, the message to be communicated and certain rules called protocols to be followed during communication. The communication media is also called transmission media.

Five components in data communication are :

(i) **Sender** It is a computer or any such device which is capable of sending data over a network. It can be a computer, mobile phone, smartwatch, walkie-talkie, video recording device, etc.

(ii) **Receiver** It is a computer or any such device which is capable or receiving data from the network. It can be any computer, printer, laptop, mobile phone, television, etc. In computer communication, the sender and receiver are known as nodes in a network.

(iii) **Message** It is the data or information that needs to be exchanged between the sender and the receiver. Messages can be in the form of text, number, image, audio, video, multimedia, etc.

(iv) **Communication Media** It is the path through which the message travels between source and destination. It is also called medium or link which is either wired or wireless.

(v) **Protocols** It is a set of rules that need to be followed by the communicating parties in order to have successful and reliable data communication.

Switching Techniques

Switching techniques are used for transmitting data across networks. Different types of switching techniques are employed to provide communication between two computers. These are as follows

Circuit Switching

Circuit switching is a methodology of implementing a telecommunication network in which two network nodes establish a dedicated communication channel (circuit).

The main advantage of circuit switching is guaranteed delivery. The circuit switching guarantees the full bandwidth of the channels and remains connected for the duration of the communication session.

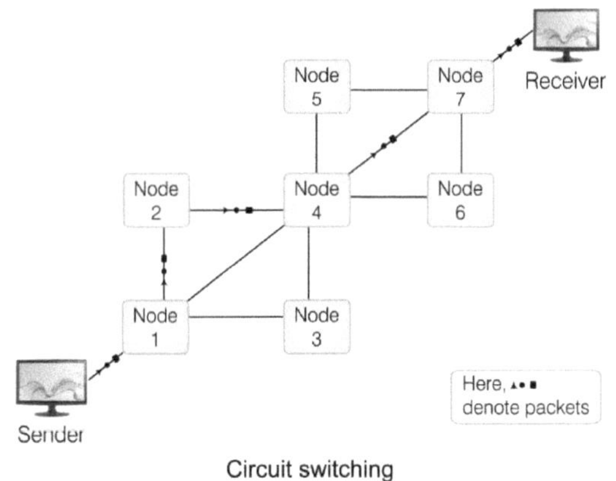

Circuit switching

The defining example of a circuit switched network is the early analog telephone network. When a call is made from one telephone to another, switches within the telephone exchanges create a continuous wire circuit between the two telephones for as long as the call last.

Message Switching

Message switching is a network switching technique, in which data is routed entirely from the source node to the destination node. In this technique, no physical path is established between source and destination.

During message routing, every intermediate switch in the network stores the whole message.

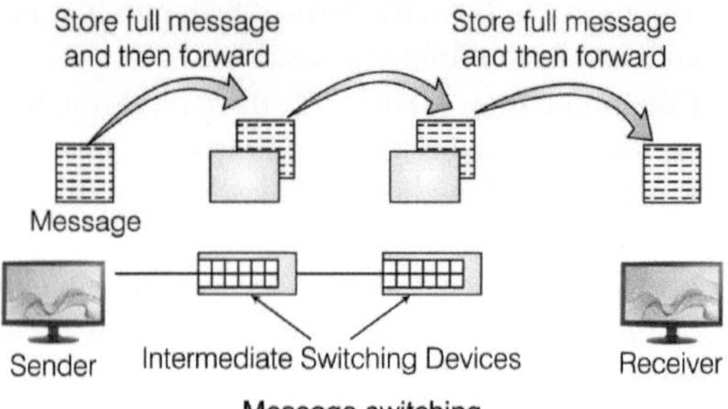

Message switching

If the entire network's resources are engaged or the network becomes blocked, the message switched network stores and delays the message until some resource become available for effective transmission of the message.

Packet Switching

In packet based networks, the message gets broken into small data packets.

These packets are sent out from the computer and they travel around the network seeking out the most efficient route to travel as circuits become available.

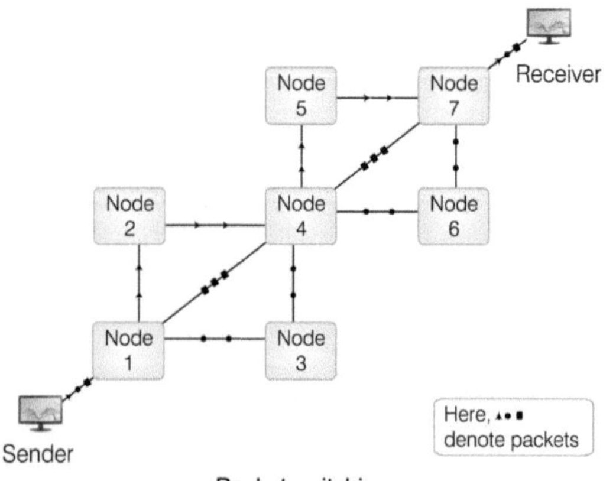

Packet switching

The main advantage of packet switching is that the packets from many different sources can share a line, allowing for very efficient use of the communication medium.

Comparison between the various switching techniques

Criteria	Circuit Switching	Message Switching	Packet Switching
Path established in advance	Yes	No	No
Store and forward technique	No	Yes	Yes
Message follows multiple routes	No	Yes	Yes

Data Communication Terminologies

The various data communication terminologies are as shown below

Channel

A communication channel is a medium that is used in the transmission of a message from one point to another. It may refer to the entire physical medium such as a tele- phone line, optical fibre, co-axial cable or twisted pair wire.

Depending on their speed, there are three broad categories of communication channels

- **Narrow band** is slow and used for telegraph lines and low speed terminals.
- **Voice band** used for ordinary telephone communication.
- **Broad band,** is fastest and used for transmitting large volumes of data at high speed.

Baud Rate

It is a measure of the number of symbols (signals) transferred or line changes every second. It may represent more than one binary bit. Each symbol can represent or convey one (binary encoded signal) or several bits of data. For a binary signal of 20 Hz, this is equivalent to 20 baud (there are 20 changes per second).

Bandwidth

It is the frequency range of a channel, measured as the difference between the highest and lowest frequencies that the channel supports. The maximum transmission speed is dependent upon the available bandwidth.

The larger the bandwidth, the higher the transmission speed. In analog systems, bandwidth is defined in terms of the difference between the highest frequency signal component and the lowest frequency signal component. Frequency is measured in cycles per second, i.e. hertz (Hz). One Hz equals one cycle per second.

A kilohertz (kHz) represents a thousand Hz per second and a megahertz (MHz) represents a thousand kHz per second.

Data Transfer Rate (DTR)

A data transfer rate (or just data rate) is the amount of digital data that is moved from one place to another in a given time, usually in a second on a network. In telecommunication, data transfer is usually measured in bits per second.

Bits Per Second (bps)

This is an expression of the number of data bits per second. Where, a binary signal is being used, this is same as the baud rate. When the signal is changed to another form, it will not be equal to the baud rate, as each line change can represent more than one bit (either two or four bits).

Measurement of Data Transfer Rate

Measurement of data transfer rate is as follows

- One **Kilobit Per Second** (Kbps) equals 1000 bits per second (bps). (Kbps is sometimes also written as 'kbps' both carry the same meaning.)
- One **Megabit Per Second** (Mbps) equals 1000 kbps or one million bps.
- One **Gigabit Per Second** (Gbps) equals 1000 mbps or one million kbps or one billion bps.
- One **Terabit Per Second** (Tbps) equals 1000 gbps or one million mbps or one billion kbps or one trillion bps.

Data rates for non-network equipment are sometimes shown in Bytes Per Second (BPS) rather than bits per second. In those cases:

- One KBPS equals one kilobyte per second.
- One MBPS equals one megabyte per second.
- One GBPS equals one gigabyte per second.
- One TBPS equals one terabyte per second.

Finally, one kilobyte per second equals 8 kilobits per second.

Transmission Media

The media through which data is transferred from one place to another is called transmission or communication media. Transmission media is grouped into two types

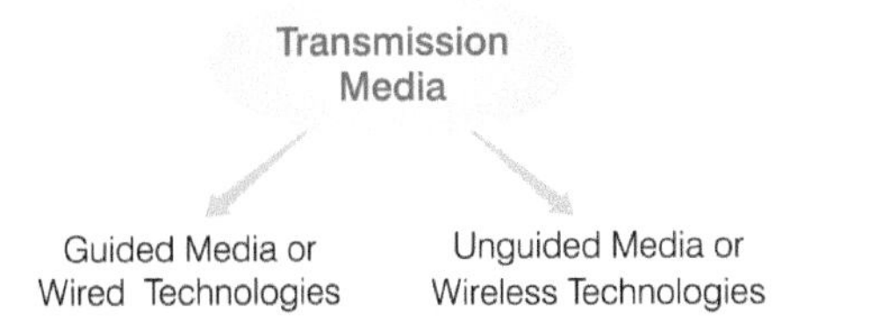

Guided Media or Wired Technologies

In guided media or wired technologies, the computers in a network are connected through wire or cable. The data signal physically gets transferred from the transmitting computer to the receiving computer through the wired transmission medium. Some of guided media are given below

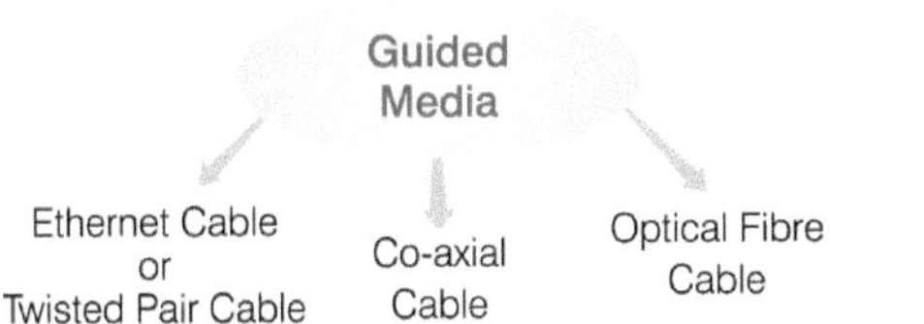

1. Ethernet Cable or Twisted Pair Cable

In this cable, wires are twisted together, which are surrounded by an insulating material and an outer layer called jacket. One of the wire is used to carry signals to the receiver and the other is used only as a ground reference. e.g. Local Area Networks (LAN's) are used twisted pair cable.

There are two types of twisted pair cables

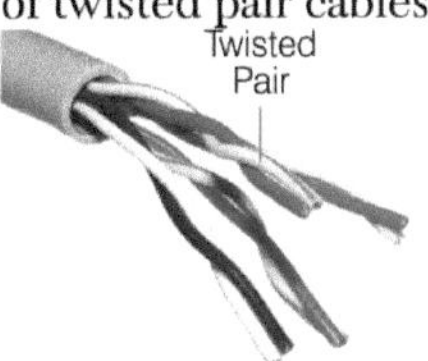

(i) **Shielded Twisted Pair** (STP) **Cable** It has shielding of the individual pair of wires, which protects it from external interference and crosstalk.

Shielded Twisted Pair (STP)

(ii) **Unshielded Twisted Pair** (UTP) **Cable** It has two unshielded wires twisted around each other. UTP cables are found in many LAN networks and telephone systems.

Unshielded Twisted Pair (UTP)

Advantages of Twisted Pair Cable

- Simple structure.
- Physically flexible.
- Easy to install.
- Low weight.
- Very inexpensive.

Disadvantages of Twisted Pair Cable

- Due to high attenuation, signals cannot be transported over a long distance without using repeaters.
- Due to low bandwidth, it is unsuitable for broadband application.
- Data rates supported are 1 Mbps to 10 Mbps.

2. Co-axial Cable

It consists of a solid wire core surrounded by foil shields or conducting braid or wire mesh, each separated by some kind of plastic insulator. The inner solid wire core carries the signal through the network and the shield is used to provide earthing or ground. Co-axial cable is commonly used in transporting multi-channel television signals in cities. The two most commonly used types of co-axial cable are:

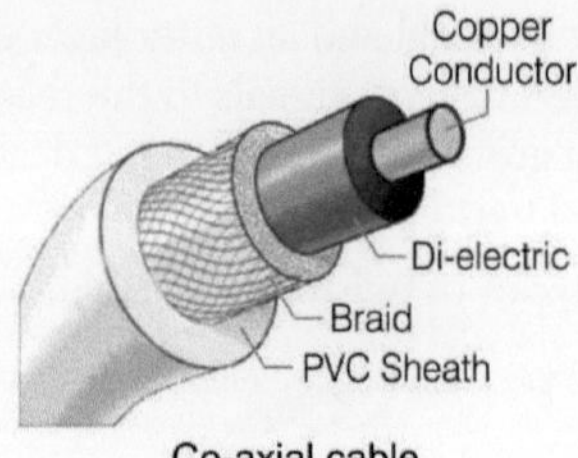

Co-axial cable

(i) **Thicknet** This form of co-axial cable is thick. The length of thicknet co-axial cable segments can be upto 500 metre long.

(ii) **Thinnet** This form of co-axial cable is thinner and using this cable, nodes having maximum distance of 185 metre can be joined.

Advantages of Co-axial Cable

- Transmission quality of co-axial cable is better than twisted pair cable.
- It can be successfully used for shared cable network.
- It can transmit several channels simultaneously, so that used for broadband transmission.
- It offers high bandwidth.

Disadvantages of Co-axial Cable

- It is expensive compared to twisted pair cable.
- These are difficult to manage and reconfigure as compared to twisted pair cable.

3. Optical Fibre

Optical fibre or fibre optic cable consists of thin threads made up of glass or glass like material, which are capable of carrying light signals from a source at one end to another end. At the source, there are either Light Emitting Diodes (LEDs) or Laser Diodes (LDs) present, which modulate the data into light beam using frequency modulation techniques. At the receiver's end, the signals are demodulated. There are three main parts in optical fibre:

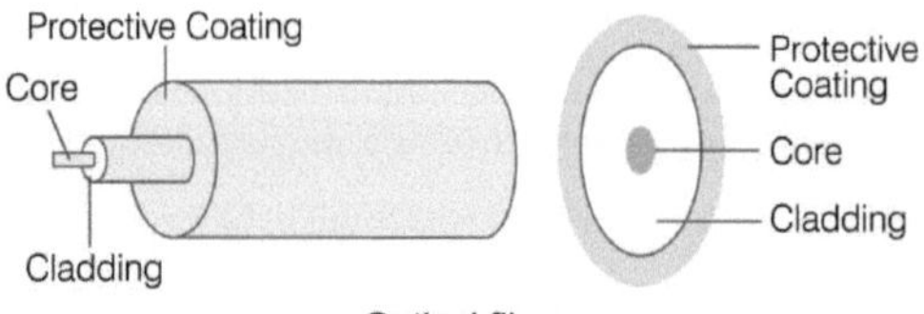

Optical fibre

(i) **Core** It is the section through which data travels in the form of light.

(ii) **Cladding** The cladding is covering of the core. Its function is to reflect back the light into the core, as it is a denser medium.

(iii) **Protective Coating** It is the outer cover of cladding for the protection of the optical fibre.

There are two types of fibre optic cables

(i) **Single Mode** It supports a segment length of upto 2 kms and bandwidth of upto 100 Mbps.

(ii) **Multi Mode** The maximum segment length of multi mode is upto 100 kms and bandwidth of upto 2 Gbps.

Advantages of Optical Fibre Cable

- It is immune to electrical and magnetic fields. So, the data does not get disturbed and pure data is retrieved on the other end.
- Highly suitable for harsh industrial environment.
- It guarantees secure transmission and has a very high transmission capacity.
- It can be used for broadband transmission, where several channels are handled in parallel.
- Bandwidth is upto 10 Gbps.

Disadvantages of Optical Fibre Cable

- Connecting two fibres together or a light source to a fibre is difficult.
- Because of noise immunity, these are virtually impossible to tap.
- Optical cables are expensive to install but last longer than copper cables.
- Optical fibres require more protection around the cable as compared to copper cables.
- Installation problem. Fibre optic cables are quite fragile and may need special care to make them sufficiently robust for an office environment.

Unguided Media or Wireless Technologies

When the computers in a network are interconnected and data is transmitted through waves, then they are said to be connected through unguided media. Some of the unguided media are given below:

1. Bluetooth

It is used for exchanging data over a short distance from fixed and mobile devices. The name bluetooth is derived from Harald Bluetooth, a king in Denmark.

Advantages of Bluetooth

- We are able to share data without any cord.
- We are able to share data without disclosing our private data.
- We can use bluetooth on many different devices, as it is available in all devices such as laptops, cell phones, music players, hand sets, printers and a lot more other products.

Disadvantages of Bluetooth

- Battery consumption
- Data transfer is very slow

2. Infrared

It is the frequency of light that is not visible to human eye. These high frequencies allow high speed data transmission.

Infrared communiucation requires a transceiver (a combination of transmitter and receiver) in both devices that communicate. Infrared communication is playing an important role in wireless data communication due to the popularity of laptop computers, personal digital assistants (PDAs), digital cameras, mobile phones, pagers and other devices but being a line-of-sight transmission, it is sensitive to fog and other atmospheric conditions.

Advantages of Infrared

- Power consumption is less.
- Circuitry cost is less.
- Circuitry is simple.
- Secure mode of transmission.

Disadvantages of Infrared

- Line of sight, need to be in a straight line for communication.
- Limited in a short range.
- Can be blocked by common materials like walls, people, plants, etc.

3. Radiowave

When two terminals communicate by using radio frequencies, then such type of communication is known as radiowave transmission.

Radiowave transmission set-up has two parts; Transmitter and Receiver.

(i) Devices which transmits signals are termed as **transmitter.**

(ii) Devices which receives signals are termed as **receiver**.

Both the transmitter and receiver use antennas to radiate and capture the radio signal.

Advantages of Radiowave

- Cheaper than wired network.
- Provides mobility.
- Easy to use over difficult terrain.

Disadvantages of Radiowave

- Insecure communication can be easily taped.
- It is affected by the weather conditions such as rain, storms, thunder, etc.

4. Microwave

It permits data transmission rates of about 16 gigabits per second. This type of transmission uses high frequency radio signals to transmit data through space. Like radio waves, microwaves can pass through obstacles viz. buildings, mountains etc. Microwaves offer a line of sight method of communication.

A transmitter and receiver of a microwave system are mounted on very high towers and both should be visible to each other (line of sight). In case of microwave transmission, curvature of the earth, mountains and other structures often block the line of sight. Hence several repeater stations are required for long distance transmission thereby increasing the cost considerably. It is generally used for long distance telephonic communications.

Advantages of Microwave

- Microwave transmission does not require the expense of laying cables.
- It can carry 25000 voice channels at the same time.
- Since no cables are to be laid down so it offers ease of communication over difficult terrains like hilly areas.

Disadvantages of Microwave

- Signals become weak after travelling a certain distance and require amplification. To overcome this problem, repeaters are used at regular intervals (25-30 kms). The data signals are received, amplified and then retransmitted. This makes it a very expensive mode of communication
- Installation and maintenance of microwave links is very expensive.
- The transmission is affected by weather conditions like rain, thunderstorms etc.

5. Satellite Communication

Satellites are an essential part of telecommunications systems worldwide. They can carry a large amount of data in addition to TV signals. When the data is transmitted using satellite then it is said to be satellite communication.

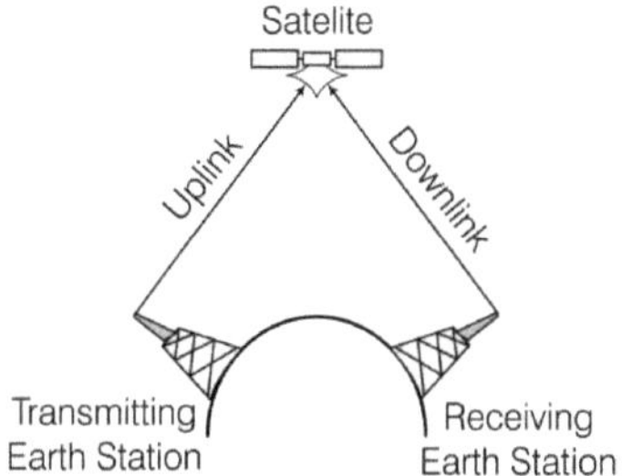

Satellite communication

Satellite communication is a special use of microwave transmission system. A satellite is placed precisely at 36000 km above the equator where its orbit speed exactly matches the earth's rotation speed. Hence it always stays over the same point with respect to the earth. This allows the ground station to aim its antenna at a fixed point in the sky.

Satellites are especially used for remote locations, which are difficult to reach with wired infrastructure. Also communication and data transfer on Internet, is only possible through satellites.

Advantages of Satellite Communication

- It covers a vast range of area.
- The wired communication is almost impossible and too costly to use across the continents, where the satellite communication proves to be the best alternative.
- It is very useful in long distance television distribution.
- Earth station, which receives the signals can be fixed position or relatively mobile.

Disadvantages of Satellite Communication

- It is very costly. So, it is not used for personal or low budget communication.
- There is atmospheric loss of transmitted signals.
- Due to low antenna signals, bandwidth are over crowded.

Types of Network

Networks can be widely divided into following types

Local Area Network (LAN)

In a LAN, a group of computers and other devices are connected over a relatively short distance. Generally, it is a privately owned networks within a single building or campus, upto a few kilometres in size. Users can share expensive devices, such as laser printers, as well as data on LAN and can also use the LAN to communicate with each other, by sending mails or engaging in chat sessions.

Mostly, cables are used to connect the computers in LANs. However, there is also a limit on the number of computers that can be attached to a single LAN.

Now-a-days, we also have WLAN(Wireless LAN) which is based on wireless network.

Metropolitan Area Network (MAN)

This is basically a bigger version of LAN and normally uses similar technology. It might cover few buildings in a city and might either be private or public. This is a network which spans a physical area (in the range of 5 to 50 km) that is larger than a LAN but smaller than a WAN.

MANs are usually characterised by very high-speed connections using optical fibres or other digital media and provides uplink services to Wide Area Networks (WANs) and the Internet. e.g. in a city, a MAN, which can support both data and voice might even be related to local cable television network.

It is also frequently used to provide a shared connection to other networks using a link to a WAN.

Wide Area Network (WAN)

WAN spans a large geographical area, often a country or a continent and uses various commercial and private communication lines to connect computers. Typically, a WAN combines multiple LANs that are geographically separated.

Like the LAN, most WANs are not owned by any one organisation, but rather exist under collective or distributed ownership and management. The world's most popular WAN is the Internet.

Personal Area Network (PAN)

PAN refers to a small network of communication. It is a computer network organised around an individual person. These networks typically involve a mobile computer, a cell phone and/or a handheld computing devices such as a PDA. Person can use these networks to transfer files including e-mail and calendar appointments, digital photos and music. These are used in a limited range, which is in the reachability of individual person. It generally covers a range of less than 10 metres and can be constructed with cables or wirelessly. Few examples of PAN are Bluetooth, Wireless USB, Z-wave and Zig Bee.

Virtual Private Network (VPN)

VPN is an encrypted connection over the Internet from a device to a network. It can be used to access region - restricted websites, shield your browsing activity from prying eyes on public Wi-Fi and more.

It prevents unauthorised people from eavesdropping on the traffic and allows the user to conduct work remotely. VPN technology is widely used in corporate environments.

Network Architecture

Network architecture is the logical and structural layout of the network, consisting of transmission equipment, software, communication protocols and infrastructure (i.e. wired or wireless), transmission of data and connectivity between components.

There are two types of network architecture

Point-to-Point (P2P) Network

In P2P or Peer-to-Peer network, each node can receive from exactly one sender and each sender sends to exactly one receiver. Sending and receiving can be done on separate wires or they can take turns over the same wire using a variety of techniques.

Client/Server Network

The model of interaction between two application programs in which a program at one end (client) requests a service from a program at the other end (server). It is a network architecture which separates the client from the server. It is scalable architecture, where one computer works at server and other as client.

In this architecture, client acts as the active device and server behaves as passively.

Network Devices

Hardware device that are used to connect computers, printers, fax machines and other electronic devices to a network are called network device.

There are many types of network devices used in networking and some of them are described below

Repeater

It is a hardware device which is used to amplify the signals when they are transported over a long distance. The basic function of a repeater is to amplify the incoming signal and retransmit it, to the other device.

Repeaters are mainly used for extending the range. If you want to connect two computers, which are more than 100 metres apart you need repeater.

Hub

A hub is a device, used with computer systems to connect several computers together. It acts as a centralised connection to several computers with the central node or server.

It is a multiport device, which provides access to computers. All incoming data packets received by the hub are sent to all hub ports and from them the data is sent to all the computers connected in a hub network.

There are two types of hub

  (i) **Active Hub** It acts as repeaters. It amplifies the signal as it moves from one device to another.
  (ii) **Passive Hub** It simply passes the signal from one connected device to another.

Switch

A switch is a hardware device, which is used to connect devices or segments of the network into smaller subsets of LAN segments.

The main purpose of segmenting is to prevent the traffic overloading in a network.

Switch forwards a data packet to a specific route by establishing a temporary connection between the source and the destination. After the transmission or once the conversation is done, the connection is terminated. There is a vast difference between switch and hub. A hub forward each incoming packet (data) to all the hub ports, while a switch forwards each incoming packet to the specified recipient.

Gateway

A gateway is a device, which is used to connect dissimilar networks. The gateway establishes an intelligent connection between a local network and external networks, which are completely different in structure.

The gateway is a node in a network, which serves as a proxy server and a firewall system and prevents the unauthorised access. It holds the information from a website temporarily, so that the repeated access to same website or web page could be directed to the proxy server instead of actual web server. Thus, it helps in reducing the traffic load.

Bridge

It serves a similar function as switches. A bridge filters data traffic at a network boundary. Bridges reduce the amount of traffic on a LAN by dividing it into two segments.

Traditional bridges support one network boundary, whereas switches usually offer four or more hardware ports. Switches are sometimes called multiport bridges.

Router

It is a hardware device, which is designed to take incoming packets, analyse the packets, moving and converting the packets to another network interface, dropping the packets, directing packets to the appropriate locations, etc.

Modem (MOdulator DEModulator)

It is a device that converts digital signal to analog signal (modulator) at the sender's site and converts back analog signal to digital signal (demodulator) at the receiver's end, in order to make communication possible *via* telephone lines.

It enables a computer to transmit data over telephone or cable lines.

Modems are of two types
 (i) **Internal Modem** Fixed within a computer.
(ii) **External Modem** Connected externally to a computer.

When a network contains largest number of system/ computer it needed modem.

RJ45 Connector

RJ45 stands for Registered Jack-45. It is an eight wire connector. RJ45 connector is used to connect computers onto a Local Area Network (LAN).

It is commonly used in telephony applications and networking. It is also used for serial connections.

RJ11 Connector

RJ11 connector is the typical connector used on two pair, four wire handset wiring.

RJ11 connector wiring comes in two standard assortments Unshielded Twisted Pair (UTP) and flat-satin cable or the untwisted. RJ11 connectors are used to terminate phone lines and are typically deployed with single line Plain Old Telephone Service (POTS) telephone jacks.

Ethernet Card

An ethernet card is a kind of network adapter. These adapters support the ethernet standard for high-speed network connections *via* cables. Ethernet cards are sometimes known as **Network Interface Cards** (NICs).

Ethernet cards are available in several different standard packages called form factors. Newer ethernet cards installed inside desktop computers use the PCI standard and are usually installed by the manufacturer.

Ethernet cards may operate at different network speeds depending on the protocol standard they support.

Wi-Fi Card

These are small and portable cards that allow to connect to the Internet through a wireless network. In these cards, transmission is done through radio waves. The antenna transmits the radio signals to those equipment, which has Wi-Fi cards.

Wi-Fi cards can be external or internal. If a Wi-Fi card is not installed in your computer, you may purchase a USB antenna attachment and have it externally connected to your device. Many newer computers, mobile devices, etc., are equipped with wireless networking capability and do not require a Wi-Fi card.

Network Topology

The arrangement of computers and other peripherals in a network is called its topology.

The main network topologies are as follows

Bus Topology (Linear Topology)

A bus topology is an arrangement in which the computers and the peripheral devices are connected to a common single data line.

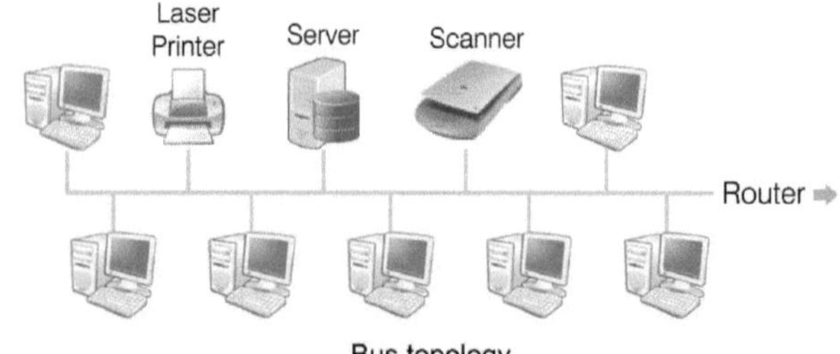

Bus topology

All the computers or devices are directly connected to the data line. The data is transmitted in small blocks known as **packets.** Each packet has a header containing the destination address. When data is transmitted on the cable, the destination node identifies the address on the packet and thereby processes the data.

Advantages of Bus Topology

- All the nodes are connected directly, so very short cable length is required.
- The architecture is very simple, reliable and linear.
- Bus topology can be extended easily on either sides.

Disadvantages of Bus Topology

- In case of any fault occurred in data transmission, fault isolation is very difficult. We have to check the entire network to find the fault.
- Becomes slow with increase in number of nodes.
- Only a single message can travel at a particular time.

Ring or Circular Topology

In this type of topology, the node is connected to two and only two neighbouring nodes. The data travels in one direction only from node to node around the ring. After passing through each node, the data returns to the sending node.

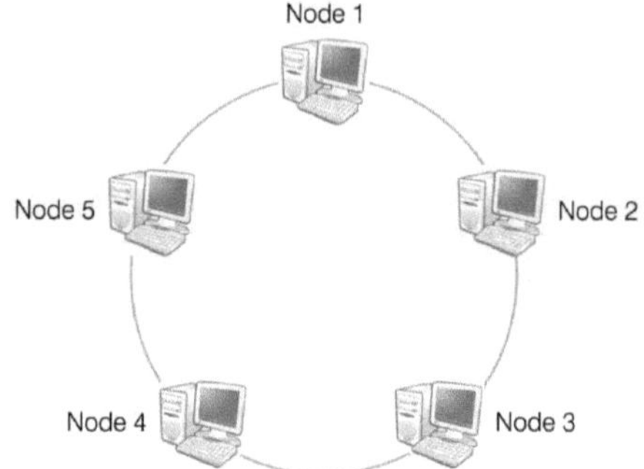

Ring or Circular topology

Advantages of Ring or Circular Topology

- Short length cable is required.
- Suitable for optical fibre as the data flow in one direction.

Disadvantages of Ring or Circular Topology

- In ring topology, each node is connected in a circular way with its two neighbouring nodes, so when there is transmission problem anywhere in the network, entire network stops functioning.
- Fault diagnosis is very difficult.

Star Topology

In star topology, each communicating device is connected to a central node which is a networking device like a hub or a switch.

The central node can be either a broadcasting device means data will be transmitted to all the nodes in the network or a unicast device means the node can identify the destination and forward data to that node only.

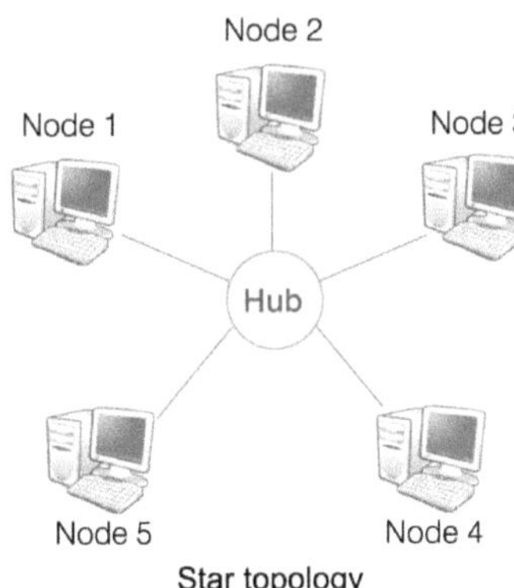

Star topology

Advantages of Star Topology

- Installation of star topology is very easy as all the nodes are directly connected to the central node or server.
- Easy to detect faults and remove it.
- Failure of single system will not bring down the entire network.
- Allows several types of cables in same network.

Disadvantages of Star Topology

- Requires more cable length than bus topology.
- If hub or server fails, the entire network will be disabled.
- Difficult to expand, as the new node has to connect all the way to central node.

Tree Topology

A tree topology is an extension and variation of bus topology. Its basic structure is like an inverted tree, where the root acts as a server. In tree topology, the nodes are interlinked in the form of tree. If one node fails, then the node following that node gets detached from the main tree topology.

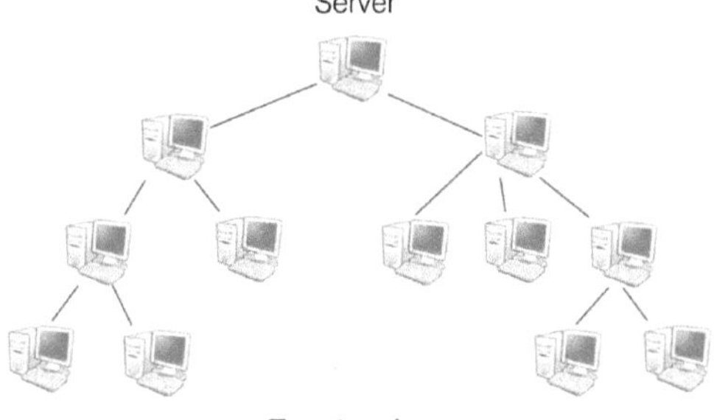

Tree topology

Advantages of Tree Topology

- The tree topology simulates hierarchical flow of data. So, it is suitable for applications, where hierarchical flow of data and control is required.
- We can easily extend the network.
- Faulty nodes can easily be isolated from the rest of the network.

Disadvantages of Tree Topology

- Long cables are required.
- There are dependencies on the root node.
- Installation and reconfiguration is very difficult.

Mesh Topology

It is also known as completely interconnected topology. In mesh topology, every node has a dedicated point-to-point link to every other node. This topology is also more secure as compared to other topologies because each cable between two nodes carries different data.

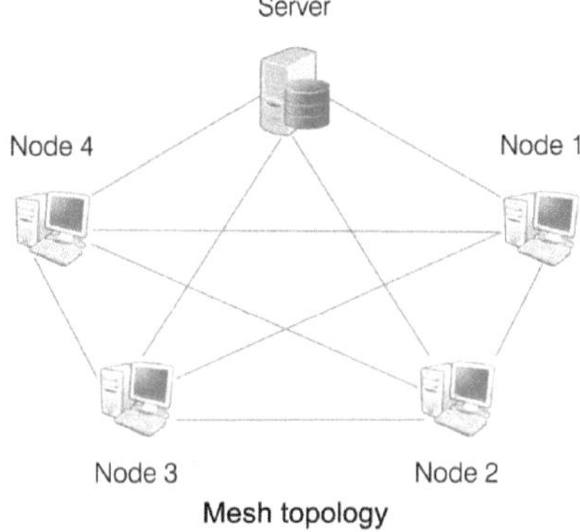

Mesh topology

Advantages of Mesh Topology

- Excellent for long distance networking.
- Communication possible through the alternate e-route, if one path is busy.
- A network can handle large amount of traffic since multiple nodes can transmit data simultaneously.

Disadvantage of Mesh Topology

- Long wire/cable length is required.
- Wiring is complex and cabling cost is high in creating such networks.

Network Protocols

Protocol refers to the set of rules applicable for a network. The protocol defines standardised format for the data packet to be transmitted through the network.

Some of the commonly used protocols are as follows

HTTP (HyperText Transfer Protocol)

HTTP is an application layer protocol. It is widely used protocol. This protocol is used by the world wide web. HTTP defines how messages are formatted and transmitted and what actions web servers and browsers should take in response to various commands. It is a request/response standard between a client (end-user) and a server (website).

e.g. when you enter a URL in your browser, this actually sends an HTTP command to the web server directly to fetch and transmit the requested web page. It is generic, stateless and object oriented protocol.

TCP/IP (Transmission Control Protocol/Internet Protocol)

TCP/IP is the communication protocol for the Internet. It defines the rules, computers must follow to communicate with each other over the Internet. The TCP/IP is a protocol used in E-mail transmission.

The TCP/IP is a protocol, which is responsible for finding path for the destination. It also splits the message into several datagrams, if it does not fit in one datagram. Therefore, these datagrams are sent through different alternate paths towards the destination. The TCP makes sure that the datagram arrives at the destination correctly. While IP is responsible for moving packet of data from source to destination. It handles the address part of each packet so that it reaches to the right destination.

PPP (Point-to-Point Protocol)

It is a data link layer protocol, which encapsulates other network layer protocols for transmission on synchronous and asynchronous communication lines.

The PPP is used with dial-up Internet connections including ISDN. It is a layered protocol, which is used for transmitting the IP data packets over usual telephone lines. It encapsulates packets into PPP frames and then forwards them to the server over the serial transmission lines. PPP defines the format of frame to be exchanged between devices on one or multiple links and also defines the authenticity of the two devices.

FTP (File Transfer Protocol)

It is a standard network protocol used to transfer files from one host to another host over a TCP-based network, such as the Internet.

FTP is based on client/server principle. It establishes two connections between the hosts. One connection is used for data transfer, which is opened and closed for each file transfer and the other for control information, which remains connected during the entire interactive FTP session.

Remote Login (Telnet)

Telnet is a protocol used for creating a connection with a remote computer. Once your telnet client establishes a connection to the remote host, telnet client becomes a virtual terminal, allowing you to communicate with the remote host from your computer. It establishes a connection either with command line client or with a programmatic interface. Telnet provides an error free connection, which is always faster than the latest conventional modems.

Post Office Protocol (POP)

POP is an application-layer Internet standard protocol, used by local E-mail clients to retrieve E-mail from a remote server over a TCP/IP connection.

POP3 (Post Office Protocol version 3) is the most recent version of a standard protocol for receiving E-mail. POP3 is a client/server protocol in which E-mail is received and held for you by your Internet server.

Each POP3 mail server has a different address, which is usually provided to an individual by their web hosting company. This address must be entered into the E-mail program so that the program can connect effectively with the protocol.

Simple Mail Transfer Protocol (SMTP)

SMTP is the protocol used for sending E-mail over the Internet. Your E-mail client uses SMTP to send a message to the mail server and the mail server uses SMTP to relay that message to the correct receiving mail server.

Basically, SMTP is a set of commands that authenticate and direct the transfer of electronic mail. When configuring the settings for your E-mail program, you usually need to set the SMTP server to your local Internet Service Provider's SMTP settings.

Voice over Internet Protocol (VoIP)

VoIP is a technology that enables voice communications over the Internet through the compression of voice into data packets that can be efficiently transmitted over data networks and then converted back into voice at the other end. It required broadband connection.

Various benefits of VoIP are as follows

(i) Using services of VoIP, subscribers can call one another at no cost to other party.

(ii) Routing phone calls over existing data networks eliminate the need for separate voice and data networks.

(iii) The ability to transmit more than one telephone call over a single broadband connection.

(iv) VoIP consists advance telephone features, e.g. call routing, screen POP and IVR.

Web Services

Web services are built on many technologies, which work in conjunction with emerging standards to ensure the manageability and standards, which extend the World Wide Web infrastructure to provide the means for software to connect to other software applications. Applications access web services *via* web protocols and data formats such as HTTP, XML and SOAP, with no need to worry about how each web service is implemented. Web services combine the best aspects of component based development.

Some of the web services are as follow

World Wide Web (WWW)

The World Wide Web (WWW) is an Internet service, which allows a particularly configured server computer to distribute documents across the Internet in a standard way. This web standard allows programs on many different computer platforms to properly format and display the information server. These programs are called web browsers. The WWW is a collection of millions of files stored on thousands of computers all over the world. The flow of information is controlled by a protocol. The protocol used in this exchange is called **HyperText Transfer Protocol** (HTTP).

HyperText Markup Language (HTML)

HyperText Markup Language (HTML) is the main markup language for creating web pages and other information that can be displayed in a web browser.

HTML is written in the form of HTML elements consisting of tags enclosed in angular brackets (like <html>), within the web page content. HTML tags most commonly come in pairs like <h1> and </h1>, which are known as container tags, although some tags known as **empty elements**, are unpaired, e.g. <img>. The <html> tag is the start tag and the </html> tag is the end tag (they are also called **opening tags** and **closing tags**). In between these tags, web designers can add text, some other tags, comments and other types of text based content. An HTML document has the extension .htm or .html. The purpose of a web browser is to read HTML documents and compose them into visible or audible web pages. The browser does not display the HTML tags, but uses the tags to interpret the content of the page.

HTML elements form the building blocks of all websites. HTML allows images and objects to be embedded and can be used to create interactive forms. It provides a means to create structured documents by denoting structural semantics for text such as headings, paragraphs, lists, links, quotes and other items. It can embed scripts written in languages such as JavaScript, which affect the behaviour of HTML web pages.

eXtensible Markup Language (XML)

XML is a markup language that defines a set of rules for encoding documents in a format, that is both human-readable and machine-readable. It is defined in the XML 1.0 specification produced by the W3C and several other related specifications. The design goals of XML emphasise simplicity, generality and usability over the Internet. e.g. in web services. Because the Internet is based on IP addresses, not domain names, every web server requires a Domain Name System (DNS) server to translate domain names into IP addresses.

Domain Name

A domain name is a unique name that identifies a particular website and represents the name of the server, where the web pages store. Domain names are formed by the rules and procedures of the Domain Name System (DNS). Domain names are used in various networking contexts and application specific naming and addressing purposes.

In general, a domain name represents an Internet Protocol (IP) resource, such as a personal computer used to access the Internet, a server computer hosting a website or the website itself or any other service communicated via the Internet.

Uniform Resource Locator (URL)

A uniform resource locator, abbreviated URL, also known as **web address**, is a specific character string that constitutes a reference to a resource. In most web browsers, the URL of a web page is displayed on top inside an address bar.

A URL is a formatted text string used by web browsers, E-mail clients and other software to identify a network resource on the Internet. Network resources are files that can be plain web pages, other text documents, graphics or programs.

URL consists of three parts
  (i) Network protocol
  (ii) Host name or address
  (iii) File or resource location.

These parts are separated by special characters as follows

```
Protocol://host/location
```

An example of a typical URL would be

```
"http://en.example.org/wiki/Main_Page".
```

IP Address (Internet Protocol Address)

The Internet Protocol (IP) is the method or protocol by which data is sent from one computer to another on the Internet. Each computer (known as a **host**) on the Internet has atleast one IP address that uniquely identifies it from all other computers on the Internet.

The format of an IP address is a 32 bits numeric address written as four numbers separated by periods (.). Each number can be in range 0 to 255. e.g. 1.160.10.240

Web Page

The backbone of the World Wide Web is made up of files or documents called pages or web pages, that contain information and links to resources both text and multimedia. It is created using HTML. The web is a collection of large number of computer documents and web pages that stored on computers around the world which are connected to one another using hyperlink.

A web page can be of two types

Static Web Page

A web page which displays same kind of information whenever a user visits, it is known as a static web page. A static web page generally has .htm or .html as extension.

Dynamic Web Page

An interactive web page is a dynamic web page. A dynamic web page uses scripting languages to display changing content on the web page. Such a page generally has .php, .asp or .jsp as extension.

Website

A group of related web pages that follow the same theme and are connected together with hyperlinks is called a website. A website displays related information on a specific topic. Each website is accessed by its own address known as URL (Uniform Resource Locator). The main or first page of a website is known as home page.

Web Browser

A web browser (commonly referred to as a **browser**) is a software application for retrieving, presenting and traversing information resources on the World Wide Web. An information resource is identified by a Uniform Resource Identifier (URI) and may be a web page, image, video or other piece of content.

Although, browsers are primarily intended to use the World Wide Web, they can also be used to access information provided by web servers in private networks or files in file systems. The major web browsers are Google Chrome, Firefox, Internet Explorer, Opera and Safari.

Web Server

The term web server can refer to either the hardware (the computer) or the software (the computer application) that helps to deliver web content, accessible through the Internet. The most common use of web server is to host websites, but there are other uses such as gaming, data storage or running enterprise applications.

Any computer can be turned into a web server by installing server software and connecting the machine to the Internet. There are many web server software applications including public domain software from NCSA and Apache and commercial packages from Microsoft, Netscape and others.

Web Hosting

A web hosting service is a type of Internet hosting service that allows individuals and organisations to make their website accessible *via* the World Wide Web.

A web host is the business of providing server space, web services and file maintenance for websites controlled by individuals or companies that do not have their own web servers. Many ISPs (Internet Service Providers), such as America Online will allow subscribers a small amount of server space to host a personal web page.

Web hosting can be of four types as follows

  (i) Free Hosting   (ii) Virtual or Shared Hosting

(iii) Dedicated Hosting   (iv) Co-location Hosting

Chapter Practice

Objective Questions

• Multiple Choice Questions

1. Which of the following is a collection of independent computers and other hardware interconnected by communication channels?
(a) Computer   (b) Networking
(c) Sharing   (d) None of these

Ans. (b) A computer networking is the practice for exchanging information between two or more computer devices together for the purpose of data sharing.

2. Which of the following is an advantage of networking?
(a) Application sharing   (b) File sharing
(c) User communication   (d) All of these

Ans. (d) Computers connected in a network are able to share applications, files, resources etc. They also can communicate with each other.

3. Network formed between computers which are spread across the continents is called
(a) LAN   (b) WAN   (c) MAN   (d) WLAN

Ans. (b) Network formed between computers which are spread across the continents is called WAN. A WAN combines multiple LANS that are geographically separated.

4. Which of the following refers to a small, single site network?
(a) DSL   (b) RAM   (c) WAN   (d) PAN

Ans. (d) PAN refers to a small network of communication. It is a computer network organised around an individual person. These networks typically involve a mobile computer, a cell phone and/or a handheld computing devices such as a PDA.

5. Modulation and demodulation is performed by
(a) microwave   (b) satellite
(c) modem   (d) gateway

Ans. (c) It is a device that converts digital signal to analog signal (modulator) at the sender's site and converts back analog signal to digital signal (demodulator) at the receiver's end.

6. A modem is connected in between a telephone line and a
(a) computer   (b) serial port
(c) network   (d) communication adapter

Ans. (a) Modems has to be connected internally or externally with a computer.

7. Geometric arrangement of devices on the network is called
(a) topology   (b) protocols
(c) media   (d) LAN

Ans. (a) Geometric arrangement of devices on the network is called topology. It is the arrangement of how computers will be connected with each other.

8. In which of the topology, network components are connected to the same cable?
(a) Star   (b) Ring
(c) Bus   (d) Mesh

Ans. (c) In bus topology, network components are connected to the same cable. The figure explains the arrangement:

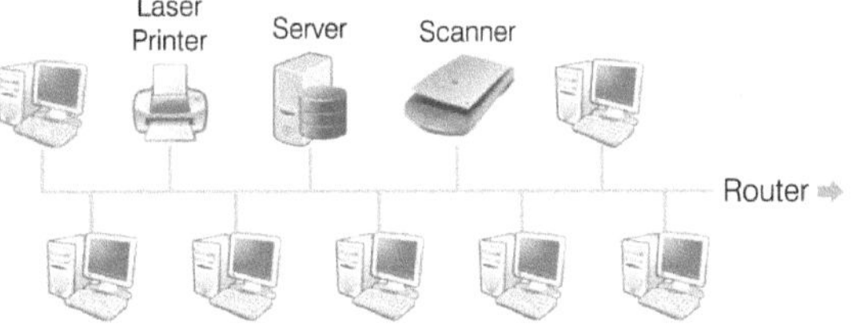

9. Which is the name of the network topology in which there are bi-directional links between each possible node?
(a) Ring   (b) Mesh
(c) Tree   (d) None of these

Ans. (b) In mesh topology, every node has a dedicated point-to-point link to every other node, that is why bi-directional links are possible.

10. Suggest the most suitable type of network topology he should use in order to maximise speed and make each computer independent of network breakdowns.   **[CBSE Question Bank 2021]**
(a) Bus topology   (b) Star topology
(c) Ring topology   (d) Mesh topology

Ans. (*b*) Start Topology allows several types of cables in same network, which increases speed. Failure of single system will not bring down the entire network and all system are connected to the central hub.

11. In order to allow data transfer from server to only the intended computers which network device is required in the lab to connect the computers?

[CBSE Question Bank 2021]

(a) Switch   (b) Hub
(c) Router   (d) Gateway

Ans. (*a*) Switch forwards a data packet to a specific route by establishing a temporary connection between the source and the destination.

12. .... network device is known as an intelligent hub.   [CBSE Question Bank 2021]

(a) Switch   (b) Hub
(c) Router   (d) Gateway

Ans. (*a*) A hub forward each incoming packet (data) to all the hub ports, while a switch forwards each incoming packet to the specified recipient.

13. Which of the following topology contains a backbone cable running through the whole length of the network?

(a) Star   (b) Bus   (c) Mesh   (d) Tree

Ans. (*b*) A bus topology is an arrangement in which the computers and the peripheral devices are connected to a common single data line.

14. Computer connected to a star topology fails, the entire network will

(a) also fail   (b) work unaffectedly
(c) only server will work   (d) None of these

Ans. (*b*) In star topology, each communicating device is connected to a central node which is a networking device like a hub or a switch. So, when the hub fails the whole network goes down.

But when any computer in the star topology fails, the other computers in the network continue to work unaffectedly.

15. Network device that sends the data over optimising paths through connected loop is

(a) gateway   (b) hub
(c) router   (d) bridge

Ans. (*c*) Network device that sends the data over optimising paths through connected loop is router.

16. In specific, if systems use separate protocols, which one of the following devices is used to link two systems?

(a) Repeater   (b) Gateway
(c) Bridge   (d) Hub

Ans. (*b*) If the system used separate protocols, gateway device is used to link two systems.

17. If all devices are connected to a central hub, then topology is called

(a) bus topology   (b) ring topology
(c) star topology   (d) tree topology

Ans. (*c*) If all devices are connected to a central hub, then topology is called star topology.

18. The WWW is made up of the set of interconnected .... that are linked together over the Internet.

(a) electronic documents   (b) web pages
(c) files   (d) All of these

Ans. (*b*) Web pages are the HTML documents which are linked with each other and together known as website or WWW.

19. In URL, http://www.arihant.com/index.htm, which component identifies the path of a web page?

(a) http
(b) www.arihant.com
(c) /index.htm
(d) All of the above

Ans. (*c*) The most general form of a URL syntax is as follows

```
protocol://domain name/<directory
path>/<object name>
```

So, here we can see /<directory path>/<object name> is the path.

20. Which of the following statement(s) is/are true about URL?

(a) URL stands for Uniform Resource Locator.
(b) You can enter URL into address bar.
(c) Both (a) and (b)
(d) It is not necessary for URL to be unique.

Ans. (*c*) URL stands for Uniform Resource Locator. It is the global address of documents and other resources on the World Wide Web and the resources can be searched through writing resource name on the browser address bar.

21. A website is a collection of

(a) web server   (b) web page
(c) web browser   (d) WWW

Ans. (*b*) A group of related web pages that follow the same theme and are connected together with hyperlinks is called a website.

22. Home page helps viewers to find out what they can find on the particular site. Home page is the

(a) first page of a website   (b) index page
(c) about page   (d) None of these

Ans. (*a*) Home page is the first page of a website.

23. Which of the following website is not used for job search?

(a) monster.com   (b) recruitment.com
(c) naukri.com   (d) Myspace

Ans. (*d*) Myspace is not used for searching job and rest all websites mentioned are used to search job.

24. Web page is created using language
(a) XML (b) Java (c) C (d) HTML

Ans. (*d*) The HyperText Markup Language or HTML is the standard markup language for documents designed to be displayed in a web browser.

25. By default, web pages are saved in the .... folder.
(a) Download (b) Document
(c) Picture (d) Music

Ans. (*b*) Documents is the default location for all downloaded web pages.

26. A browser is a program, which is used to
(a) connect to Internet
(b) create websites
(c) view sites on web
(d) All of the above

Ans. (*d*) A browser is a program, which is used to connect to Internet, create websites and view sites on web. Browsers are primarily intended to use the World Wide Web, they can also be used to access information provided by web servers in private networks or files in file systems.

27. Which of the following is developed by Apple Incorporation?
(a) Lynx (b) Opera
(c) Safari (d) Mozilla Firefox

Ans. (*c*) Safari is a graphical web browser developed by Apple Incorporation, which based primarily on open-source software properties notably including WebKit. It was first introduced on Mac OS X Panther in 2003, and was later incorporated to the iPhone and iPod Touch with iPhone OS 1 in 2007.

• Case Based MCQs

28. Direction *Read the case and answer the following questions.*

Beauty lines fashion incorporation is a fashion company with design unit and market unit at Bangalore 135m away from each other. The company recently connected their LANs using Ethernet cable to share the stock related information. But after joining their LAN's they are not able to show the information due to loss of signal in between.

(i) Which device out of the following should you suggest to be installed for a smooth communication?
(a) Modem (b) Repeater
(c) UPS (d) None of these

(ii) Which network is suitable to connect computers across different cities?
(a) WAN (b) MAN
(c) PAN (d) LAN

(iii) The company wants to increase their bandwidth and speed for communication at any cost. Which of the following cable(s) is/are suitable for that?
(a) Coaxial Cable (b) Optical Fibre
(c) Both (a) and (b) (d) None of these

(iv) What will be the best possible connectivity out of the following? You will suggest to connect the new set up of offices in Bangalore with its London based office.
(a) Satellite Link (b) Infrared
(c) Ethernet (d) None of these

(v) Which of the following device will be suggested by you to connect each computer in each of the buildings?
(a) Switch (b) Modem
(c) Gateway (d) None of these

Ans. (i) (*b*) They should use repeater. As repeater is a device used to amplify the signals.

(ii) (*b*) **MAN** It is a computer network that connects computers within a metropolitan area, which could be a single large city, multiple cities and towns.

(iii) (*b*) **Optical Fibre** They are designed for long-distance, high-performance data networking and telecommunications. Compared to wired cables, fiber optic cables provide higher bandwidth and transmit data over longer distances.

(iv) (*a*) **Satellite Link** Through satellites communication across countries is easily possible.

(v) (*a*) Switch is a networking hardware that connects devices on a computer network to receive and forward data to the destination device. Therefore, switch will help in communication between each of the buildings.

29. Web server is a special computer system running on HTTP through web pages. The web page is a medium to carry data from one computer system to another. The working of the web server starts from the client or user. The client sends their request through the web browser to the web server. Web server takes this request, processes it and then sends back processed data to the client. The server gathers all of our web page information and sends it to the user, which we see on our computer system in the form of a web page. When the client sends a request for processing to the web server, a domain name and IP address are important to the web server. The domain name and IP address are used to identify the user on a large network.

(i) Web servers are
   (a) IP addresses
   (b) computer systems
   (c) web pages of a site
   (d) a medium to carry data from one computer to another

(ii) What does the web server need to send back information to the user?
   (a) Home address
   (b) Domain name
   (c) IP address
   (d) Both (b) and (c)

(iii) What is the full form of HTTP?
   (a) HyperText Transfer Protocol
   (b) HyperText Transfer Procedure
   (c) Hyperlink Transfer Protocol
   (d) Hyperlink Transfer Procedure

(iv) The .... translates Internet domain and host names to IP address.
   (a) domain name system
   (b) routing information protocol
   (c) Internet relay chart
   (d) network time protocol

(v) Computer that requests the resources or data from another computer is called as ....
   (a) server
   (b) client
   (c) Both (a) and (b)
   (d) None of the above

Ans. (i) (*b*) Web servers are computer systems.

That means a web server is computer software and hardware that accepts requests *via* HTTP, the network protocol created to distribute web content or its secure variant HTTPs.

(ii) (*d*) Domain name and IP address need to send back information to the user.

(iii) (*a*) HTTP stands for HyperText Transfer Protocol. It specifies how to transfer hypertext (linked web documents) between two computers.

(iv) (*a*) Domain name system is the way the Internet domain names are stored and translated to IP addresses. The domain names systems matches the name of website to IP addresses of the website.

(v) (*b*) Computer that requests the resources or data from other computer is known as client. Client computer always make use of the software or hardware in which the service is made by the server.

PART 2
Subjective Questions

• Short Answer Type Questions

1. Write the name of benefits of networking.

Ans. Some of the benefits of networking are
   (i)   File sharing
   (ii) Hardware sharing
   (iii) Application sharing
   (iv) User communication
   (v)   Access to remote database

2. Write any two uses of Internet.

Ans. Two uses of Internet are as follows:
   (i) Internet is used for communication and information sharing.
   (ii) Business use the Internet to provide access to complex databases.

3. Differentiate between the terms Internet and Intranet.

Ans. Differences between Internet and Intranet are as follows

Internet	Intranet
Access by an individual with dial-up access.	Access by only authorised employees.
Information on Internet could be general, public and advertisement.	Information on Intranet could be specific, corporate and proprietary.

4. What is the difference between message switching and packet switching?

Ans. In message switching, data packets are stored on the disk while in packet switching, all the packets of fixed size are stored in main memory making it more efficient as compared to other switching techniques.

5. What is the use of baud rate?

Ans. Baud rate is a measure of the number of symbols (signals) transferred or line changes every second. It may represent more than one binary bit.

Every symbol can represent or convey one or several bits of data. For a binary signal of 20 Hz, this is equivalent to 20 baud.

6. A company wants to form a network on their five computers to a server within the company premises. Represent star and ring topologies diagrammatically for this network.

Ans.

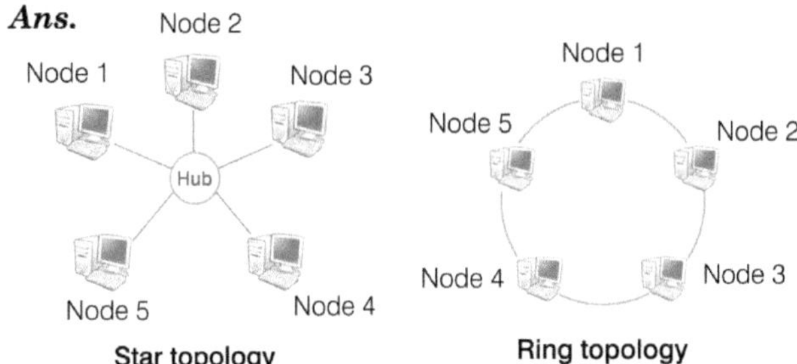

7. Explain the term

(i) Bandwidth   (ii) Broadband

Ans. (i) **Bandwidth** It is the communication capacity of a network. It refers to the data carrying capacity of a channel or medium.

(ii) **Broadband** It is a wide bandwidth data transmission with an ability to simultaneously transport multiple signals and traffic types.

8. In twisted pair cable, two insulated wires are twisted around each other which provides protection against noise. Explain.

Ans. Twisting the cables keep them close together so that, any external magnetic fields must cross both cable at the same time, so the interference created in one cable is cancelled by the almost exact opposite amount of interference in the other.

9. Explain the three main parts of an optical fibre cable.

Ans. The three main parts of an optical fibre cable are as follows

(i) **Core** It is the section through which the data travel in the form of light.

(ii) **Cladding** It is the covering part of core. Its function is to reflect back the light into the core, as it is a denser medium.

(iii) **Protective Coating** It is the outer cover of cladding for the protection of optical fibre from damage and moisture.

10. Write one advantage and one disadvantage of using optical fibre cable.

Ans. **Advantage of using optical fibre cable** It is immune to electrical and magnetic interference, i.e. the data does not get disturbed and pure data is retrieved on the other end.

Disadvantage of using optical fibre cable Connecting either two fibres together or a light source to a fibre is a difficult process.

11. Write two advantages of using an optical fibre cable over an ethernet cable to connect two service stations, which are 190 m away from each other.

Ans. **Low power** Because signals in optical fibres degrade less, lower power transmitters can be used.

Higher data rate Due to higher bandwidth, data rate of optical fibre is more than the data rate of ethernet cable (upto 1 Gbps).

12. Compare and contrast the two wireless transmission media : bluetooth and infrared.

Ans. Bluetooth and infrared both are short range wireless transmission media. This is the only point at which both these data transmission technologies look similar but there is a lot of differences between the two. Infrared is mostly used in TV remotes and there must be a direct line-of-sight between the transmitter and the receiver while on the other hand bluetooth uses a radio frequency which allows transmission through walls and other objects.

13. Explain two problems that can occur during transmission of data.

Ans. Two problems that can occur during transmission of data are as follows

(i) **Crosstalk** Disturbance caused by the electric or magnetic fields of one signal in an adjacent signal.

(ii) **Attenuation** During transmission, the signal strength is reduced, this phenomenon is called attenuation.

14. Write down any two points of differences between LAN, MAN and WAN.

Ans. Two major points of differences among LAN, MAN and WAN are as follows

Basics	LAN	MAN	WAN
Geographical Area Distance	Generally within a building Upto 5 km	Within a city Upto 160 km	Across the continents Unlimited

15. Write the difference between LAN and MAN.

Ans. Differences between LAN and MAN are as follows

LAN	MAN
LAN stands for Local Area Network	MAN stands for Metropolitan Area Network.
LAN's ownership is private	MAN's ownership can be private or public.
The speed of LAN is high.	The speed of MAN is average.
There is more fault tolerance in LAN	There is less fault tolerance.
LAN's design and maintenance is easy	MAN's design and maintenance is difficult than LAN
LAN's cost is high but less than MAN.	MAN's cost is higher than LAN

16. Which device is used to connect dissimilar networks?

Ans. A gateway is a device, which is used to connect dissimilar networks. The gateway establishes an intelligent connection between a local network and external network, which are completely different in structure. Gateway also serve as proxy server and a firewall system that prevents the unauthorised access.

17. Identify the following devices

(i) An intelligent device that connects several nodes to form a network and redirects the received information only to intended node(s).

(ii) A device that regenerates (amplifies) the received signal and re-transmits it to its destinations.

Ans. (i) Switch (ii) Repeater

18. Identify the following devices

(i) A device that is used to connect different types of networks. It performs the necessary translation so that the connected networks can communicate properly.

(ii) A device that converts data from digital bit stream into an analog signal and vice-versa.

Ans. (i) Router (ii) Modem

19. Mr. GopiNath Associate Manager of Unit Nations corporate recently discovered that the communication between his company's accounts office and HR office is extremely slow and signals drop quite frequently. These offices are 120 metre away from each other and connected by an Ethernet cable.

(i) Suggest him a device which can be installed in between the office for smooth communication.

(ii) What type of network is formed by having this kind of connectivity out of LAN, MAN and WAN?

Ans. (i) The device that can be installed between the office for smooth communication is repeater.

(ii) The type of network is Local Area Network (LAN).

20. Write one advantage of bus topology of network. Also, illustrate how four computers can be connected with each other using star topology of network?

Ans. **Advantage of bus topology** In bus topology, computers can be connected with each other using server (host) along a single length of cable.

Four computers can be connected with each other using star topology in the following way:

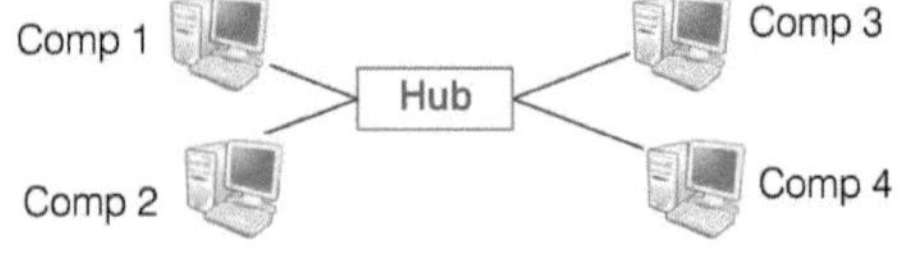

21. What is the difference between star topology and bus topology of network?

Ans. Differences between star topology and bus topology are as follows :

Star Topology	Bus Topology
All the nodes are directly connected with the central node or server.	There is a single length of transmission medium on which various nodes are attached and the server can be anywhere in the transmission cable.
Easy to detect faults.	Faults cannot be easily detected.
It is fast in transmission	Becomes slow with increase in node.

22. Define tree topology. Also, write down its two limitations.

Ans. A tree topology is an extension and variation of bus topology. Its basic structure is like an inverted tree, where the root acts as a server.

Limitations

- Long cables are required for this kind of topologies.
- There is the dependence on the root node.

23. What is the significance of HTTP?

Ans. HTTP is a protocol used on Internet. It works in combination with WWW. It allows us to access hypertext documents on WWW. Since, WWW allow us to access or use multimedia files on the Internet and the hypertext files supports multimedia.

24. What is protocol? Which protocol is used to copy a file from/to a remote server?

Ans. Protocol is a set of rules that two or more computers must follow to communication on network. FTP (File Transfer Protocol) is used to copy a file from/to a remotely located server.

25. In which communication, the computers in a network are connected through wire or cable? Explain its types, if any.

Ans. Wired communication is the communication in which the wires or cables are used for connecting different devices in a network.

There are three types of wired communication.

(i) **Twisted pair cable** Two identical wires are wrapped together and twisted around each other.

(ii) **Co-axial cable** It consists of a core wire surrounded by foil shields or conducting braid or wire mesh.

(iii) **Optical fibre cable** It consists of thin threads made up of glass like substance, which are capable of carrying light signal from one end to another.

Optical fibre consists of the following parts

- Core
- Cladding
- Protective coating

26. How is co-axial cable different from optical fibre?

Ans. Differences between co-axial cable and optical fibre.

Co-axial cable	Optical fibre
It is used to transmit the signal in electrical form.	It is used to transmit the signal in light form.
Co-axial cable is made of plastics, copper wires etc.	Optical fibre is made of plastics and glasses.
The cost of co-axial cable is less.	The cost of optical fibre is high.
Installation and implementation of co-axial cable is easy.	Installation and implementation of optical fibre is difficult.
Co-axial cables are less affected due to the external magnetic field.	These cables are not affected due to external magnetic field.

27. Explain wireless technology and give a brief note on the following

(i) Bluetooth   (ii) Radiowave

Ans. Wireless technology is also known as unguided media. This media does not use any wires or cable for its connectivity in the network. It uses electromagnetic waves. Some of the wireless technologies are :

(i)   Bluetooth   (ii) Radiowave
(iii) Infrared   (iv) Microwave
(v) Satellite communication

(i) **Bluetooth** It is used for exchanging data over a short distance from fixed and mobile devices. This type of media comes under PAN (Personal Area Network).

(ii) **Radiowave** When two terminals are connected by using radio frequencies, then such type of communication is known as radiowave transmission. Radiowave transmission set-up has two parts.

- **Transmitter** Devices, which transmit signals are termed as transmitter.
- **Receiver** Devices, which receive signals are known as receiver.

28. Write a short note on LAN and PAN.

Ans. **LAN** A Local Area Network is a computer network covering a small geographical area like a home, office or small group of building such as building in a school. Computer connected to a LAN can share information and peripheral equipments.

PAN It stands for Personal Area Network. It is a computer network used for communication among computer and different technological devices close to it. Technologies such as bluetooth and infrared communication form a wireless PAN around the device.

29. In networking, what is WAN? How is it different from LAN?

Ans. The network which connects the different countries is known as WAN.

Differences between LAN and WAN are as follows

LAN	WAN
LAN stands for Local Area Network.	WAN stands for Wide Area Network.
The speed of LAN is high.	The speed of WAN is slower than LAN.
There is less congestion in LAN.	There is more congestion in WAN.
There is more fault tolerance in LAN.	There is less fault tolerance in WAN.
LAN's design and maintenance is easy.	WAN's design and maintenance is difficult than LAN.
LAN covers small area i.e. within the building.	WAN covers large geographical area.
Transmission medium used in LAN is co-axial or UTP cable.	WAN uses satellite link as a transmission or communication medium.

30. Define hub and write its functions and types.

Ans. A hub connects several computers together and acts as a central node or server.

Function of a hub

- Interconnects number of computers or users.
- All the incoming data packets received by the hub are send to all hub ports and from their, the data is sent to all the computers, connected in a hub network.

Hub are of two types

(i) **Active hub** It acts as repeater. It amplifies the signal as these move from one device to another.

(ii) **Passive hub** It simply passes the signal from one connected device to another.

31. What are the functions of the following devices?

(i) Repeater   (ii) Switch

Ans. (i) **Repeater** It is a network device, that amplifies and restores signals for long distance transmission.

It interconnects identical network. Useful for long distance transmission, as they assure that there is no loss of data packets on the way.

(ii) **Switch** It is a device used to segment networks into different subnetworks, called subnets or LAN segments. This prevents traffic overloading. Switches are responsible for filtering, i.e. transforming data in a specific way and forwarding packets.

32. Define repeaters with its two types.

Ans. Repeaters are used to amplify the signals, when they are transported over a long distance.

Repeaters are of two types

(i) **Amplifier** It amplifies or boosts the incoming signals. So, it amplifies both the signal and any concurrent noise.

(ii) **Signal repeater** It only amplifies the signal and filters out the noise signals. So, we get only the clear signal at the receiver end.

33. When the computer network uses telephone lines as communication channel then MODEM is used as a data communication device. Now, explain the working of MODEM.

Ans. MODEM performs the task of modulation at sender's site and DEModulation at the receiver's site. Basically, our computer generates data in the form of digital signals, which need to be forwarded to the receiver through telephone lines. Since, telephone lines can carry only analog signals. So, digital signals need to be converted to analog signals at sender's site, this is called modulation. At receiver's site, again analog signals should be converted back to the original digital signals, then this is called demodulation.

34. Write one advantage of star topology over bus topology and one advantage of bus topology over star topology.

Ans. **Advantage of star topology over bus topology** The star topology is the most reliable as there is a direct connection of every nodes in the network with the central node, so any problem in any node will affect the particular node only. While in bus topology, if problem exists in common medium, it will affect the entire node.

Advantage of bus topology over star topology Extension of network is very easy in bus topology. We can connect new node along its length. While in star topology, it is difficult to expand, as the new node has to connect all the way to central node and there is not available port in central node.

35. Differentiate between XML and HTML.

Ans. XML was designed to describe data and to focus on what data is. HTML was designed to display data and to focus on how data looks.

HTML is about displaying information while XML is about describing information.

36. What is the difference between domain name and IP address?

Ans. IP address is an identifier for a computer or device on a TCP/IP network.

e.g. 1.160.10.240 could be an IP address.

A domain name is a name that identifies one or more IP addresses.

e.g. The domain name microsoft.com represents about a dozen IP addresses.

37. Write a short note on IP address and give its characteristics.

Ans. Internet internally follows number based addressing system. Numeric address of a computer is called IP address by a scheme called Domain Name System (DNS).

The IP address consists of four numbers from 0 to 255 separated by dots.

The characteristics of an IP address are as follows

(i) IP addresses are unique.

(ii) IP addresses are global and standardised.

38. Distinguish between website and web browser.

Ans. Website is a place on the net servers to keep web pages. Web browser is a software application for retrieving, presenting and traversing information on the world wide web.

39. Discuss the functioning of a web browser and web server.

Ans. Web browsers became such a pervasive way to access information that users and organisations desired to access. So, web servers had to be extended to allow software application development and access to database.

A web server provides four major functions

(i) Surfing web pages.

(ii) Running gateway programs and returning output.

(iii) Controlling access to the server.

(iv) Monitoring and logging server access statistics.

• Long Answer Type Questions

40. Trine Tech Corporation (TTC) is a professional consultancy company. The company is planning to set up their new offices in India with its hub at Hyderabad. As a network adviser, you have to understand their requirement and suggest them the best available solutions. Their queries are mentioned as (i) to (v) below.

Physical locations of the blocks of TTC

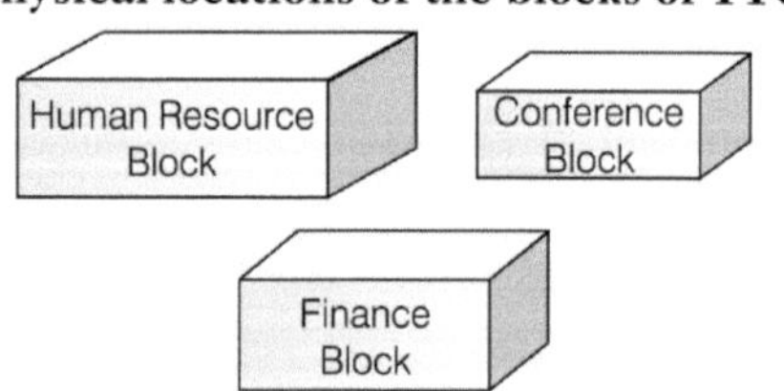

Block to block distance (in m)

Block (From)	Block (To)	Distance
Human Resource	Conference	110
Human Resource	Finance	40
Conference	Finance	80

Expected number of computers

Block	Computers
Human Resource	25
Finance	120
Conference	90

(i) Which will be the most appropriate block, where TTC should plan to install their server?

(ii) Draw a block to block cable layout to connect all the buildings in the most appropriate manner for efficient communication.

(iii) What will be the best possible connectivity out of the following, you will suggest to connect the new set up of offices in Bengalore with its London based office.
- Satellite Link
- Infrared
- Ethernet

(iv) Which of the following device will be suggested by you to connect each computer in each of the buildings?
- Switch
- Modem
- Gateway

(v) Company is planning to connect its offices in Hyderabad which is less than 1 km. Which type of network will be formed?

Ans. (i) TTC should install its server in finance block as it is having maximum number of computers.

(ii)

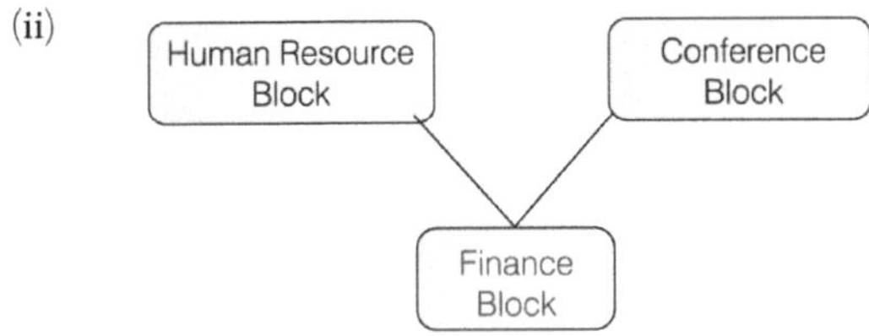

The layout is based on minimum cable length required, which is 120 metres in the above case.

(iii) Satellite Link.   (iv) Switch.

(v) LAN

41. Granuda consultants are setting up a secured network for their office campus at Faridabad for their day-to-day office and web based activities. They are planning to have connectivity between 3 buildings and the head office situated in Kolkata. Answer the questions (i) to (v) after going through the building positions in the campus and other details, which are given below.

Distance between various buildings

Building RAVI to Building JAMUNA	120 m
Building RAVI to Building GANGA	50 m
Building GANGA to Building JAMUNA	65 m
Faridabad Campus to Head Office	1460 km

Number of computers

Building RAVI	25
Building JAMUNA	150
Building GANGA	51
Head Office	10

(i) Suggest the most suitable place (i.e. block) to house the server of this organisation. Also, give a reason to justify your suggested location.

(ii) Suggest a cable layout of connections between the building inside the campus.

(iii) Suggest the placement of the following devices with justification:
(a) Switch   (b) Repeater

(iv) The organisation is planning to provide a high speed link with its head office situated in the Kolkata using a wired connection. Which of the following cable will be most suitable for this job?
(a) Optical fibre   (b) Co-axial cable
(c) Ethernet cable

(v) Consultancy is planning to connect its office in Faridabad which is more than 10 km from Head office. Which type of network will be formed?

Ans. (i) The most suitable place to house the server is JAMUNA because it has maximum number of computers.

(ii)

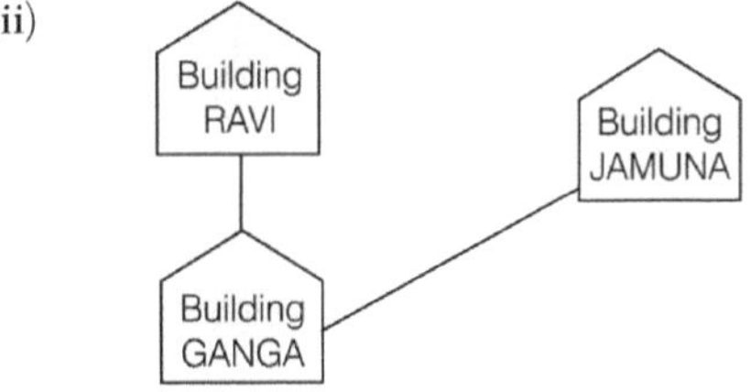

(iii) (a) Switches are needed in every building to share bandwidth in every building.

(b) Repeaters may be skipped as per above layout, (because distance is less than 100 m) however, if building RAVI and building JAMUNA are directly connected, we can place a repeater there as the distance between these two buildings is more than 100 m.

(iv) (b) Co-axial cable.

(v) MAN

42. Freshminds University of India is starting its first campus in Ana Nagar of South India with its centre admission office in Kolkata. The university has three major blocks comprising of Office block, Science block and Commerce block is in 5 km area campus.

As a network expert, you need to suggest the network plan as per (i) to (v) to the authorities keeping in mind the distance and other given parameters.

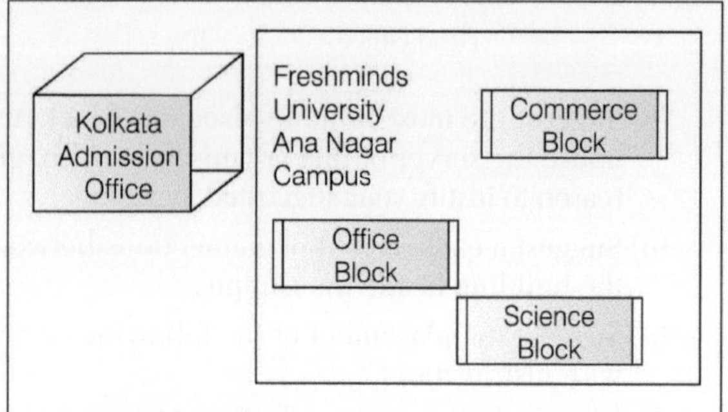

Expected wire distancebetween various locations

Office Block to Science Block	90 m
Office Block to Commerce Block	80 m
Science Block to Commerce Block	15 m
Kolkata Admission Office to Ana Nagar Campus	450 km

Expected number of computers to be installed at various locations in the university are as follows:

Office Block	10
Science Block	140
Commerce Block	30
Kolkata Admission Office	8

(i) Suggest the authorities, the cable layout amongst various blocks inside university campus for connecting the blocks.

(ii) Suggest the most suitable place (i.e. block) to house the server for this university with a suitable reason.

(iii) Suggest an efficient device form the following to be installed in each of the block to connect all the computers.

(a) Modem   (b) Switch   (c) Gateway

(iv) Suggest the most suitable (very high speed) service to provide data connectivity between admission office located in Kolkata and the campus located in Ana Nagar form the following options:

- Telephone line
- Fixedline dial-up connection

- Co-axial cable network
- GSM
- Leased line
- Satellite connection.

(v) University is planning to connect its campus in Kolkata which is more than 100 km. Which type of network will be formed?

Ans. (i)

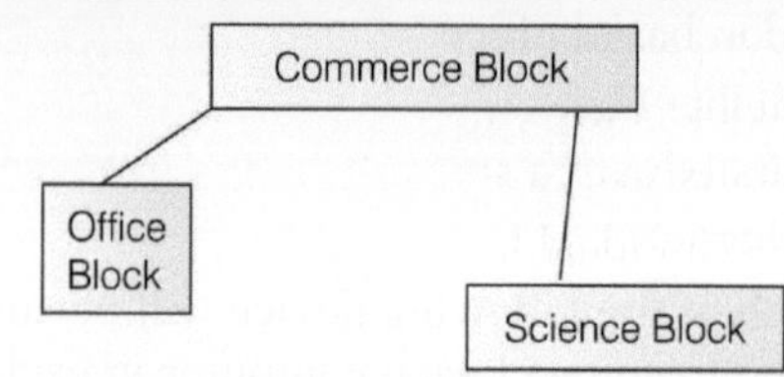

(ii) The most suitable place to house the server is Science Block as it has maximum number of computers. Thus, reducing the cabling cost and increases efficiency of network.

(iii) (b) Switch is the device to be installed in each of the blocks to connect all the computers.

(iv) Satellite connection.

(v) MAN

43. Quick Learn University is setting up its academic blocks at Prayag Nagar and planning to set up a network. The university has three academic blocks and one human resource centre as shown in the diagram below:

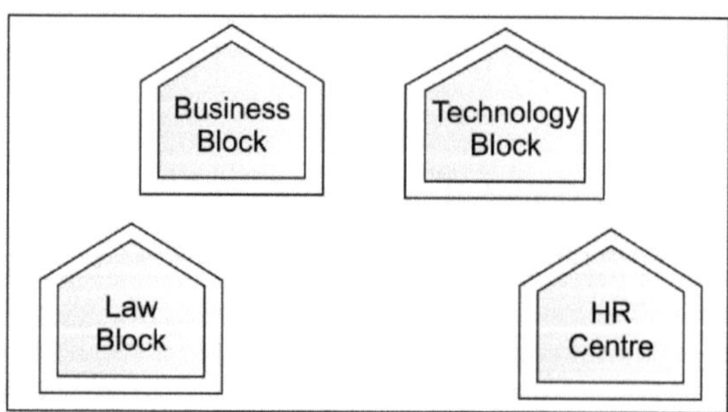

Centre to centre distance between various blocks/centre is as follows

Law Block to Business Block	40 m
Law Block to Technology Block	80 m
Law Block to HR Centre	105 m
Business Block to Technology Block	30 m
Business Block to HR Centre	35 m
Technology Block to HR Centre	15 m

Number of computers in each of the blocks/centre are as follows

Law Block	15
Technology Block	40
HR Centre	115
Business Block	25

(i) Suggest the most suitable place (i.e. block/centre) to install the server of this university with a suitable reason.

(ii) Suggest an ideal layout for connecting these block/centre for a wired connectivity.

(iii) Which device you will suggest to be placed/installed in each of these blocks/centre to efficiently connect all the computers with in these blocks/centre ?

(iv) The university is planning to connect its admission office in the closest big city, which is more than 250 km from university, which type of network out of LAN, MAN or WAN will be formed? Justify your answer.

(v) Expand the following

   • LAN   • WAN

Ans. (i) HR centre as it has maximum number of computers.

(ii)

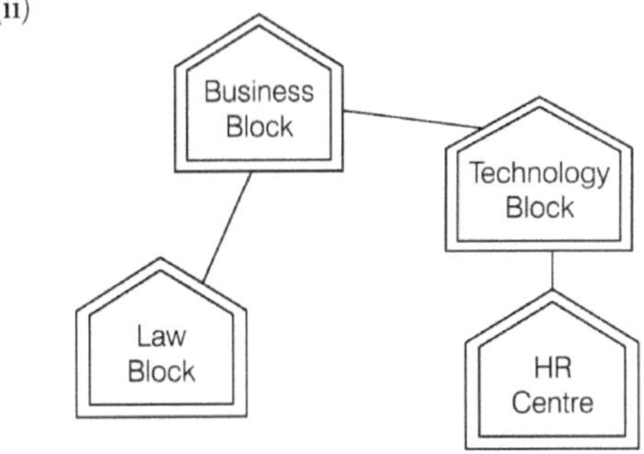

(iii) Switch.

(iv) WAN as it is another city.

(v) • Local Area Network
    • Wide Area Network

44. Tech Up Corporation (TUC) is a professional consultancy company. The company is planning to set up their new offices in India with its hub at Hyderabad. As a network adviser, you have to understand their requirement and suggest to them the best available solutions. Their queries are mentioned as (i) to (v) below.

Physical locations of the blocks of TUC

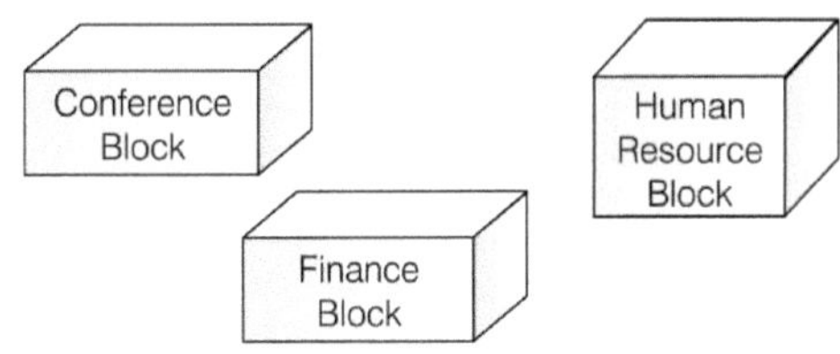

Block to block distances (in metre)

Block (From)	Block (To)	Distance
Human Resource	Conference	60
Human Resource	Finance	120
Conference	Finance	80

Expected number of computers to be installed in each block

Block	Computers
Human Resource	125
Finance	25
Conference	60

(i) What will the most appropriate block, where TUC should plan to install their server?

(ii) Draw a block to block cable layout to connect all the buildings in the most appropriate manner for efficient communication.

(iii) What will be the best possible connectivity out of the following, you will suggest to connect the new setup of offices in Bengalore with its London based office?

   • Infrared

   • Satellite Link

   • Ethernet Cable

(iv) Which of the following devices will be suggested by you to connect each computer in each of the buildings?

   • Gateway

   • Switch

   • Modem

(v) Company is planning to connect its Block in Hyderabad which is more than 20 km. Which type of network will be formed?

Ans. (i) TUC should install its server in Human Resource Block as it has maximum number of computers.

(ii)

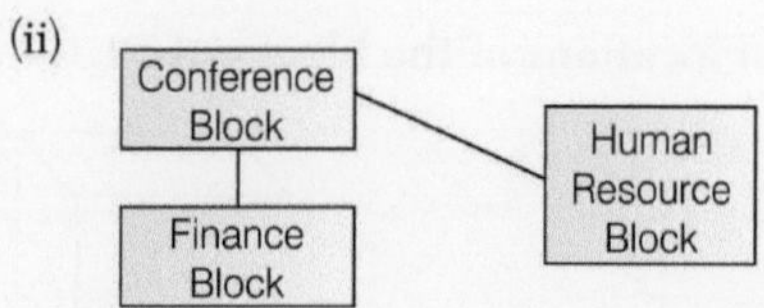

The above layout is based on the minimum length of cable required, i.e. 140 m.

(iii) Satellite Link.

(iv) Switch.

(v) MAN

45. G.R.K International Inc. is planning to connect its Bengaluru Office Setup with its Head Office in Delhi. The Bengaluru Office G.R.K. International Inc. is spread across an area of approx. 1 square kilometres consisting of 3 blocks. Human Resources, Academics and Administration. You as a network expert have to suggest answers to the four queries (i) to (v) raised by them.

Note Keep the distances between blocks and number of computers in each block in mind, while providing them the solutions.

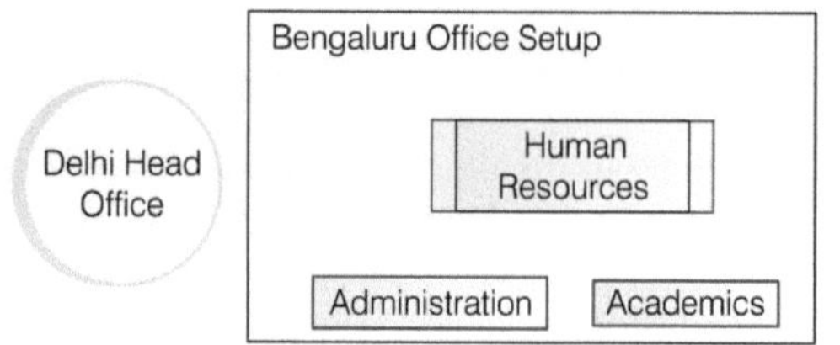

Shortest distances between various blocks

Human Resources to Administration	100m
Human Resources to Academics	65m
Academics to Administration	110m
Delhi Head Office to Bengaluru Office Setup	2350 km

Number of computers installed at various blocks

Block	Number of Computers
Human Resources	155
Administration	20
Academics	100
Delhi Head Office	20

(i) Suggest the most suitable block in the Bengaluru Office Setup to host the server. Give a suitable reason with your suggestion.

(ii) Suggest the cable layout among the various blocks within the Bengaluru Office Setup for connectiing the blocks.

(iii) Suggest a suitable networking device to be installed in each of the blocks essentially required for connecting computers inside the blocks with fast and efficient connectivity.

(iv) Suggest the most suitable media to provide secure, fast and reliable data connectivity between Delhi Head Office and the Bengaluru Office Setup.

(v) Expand the following

  • WAN

  • LAN

Ans. (i) Human Resources, because it has maximum number of computers.

(ii)

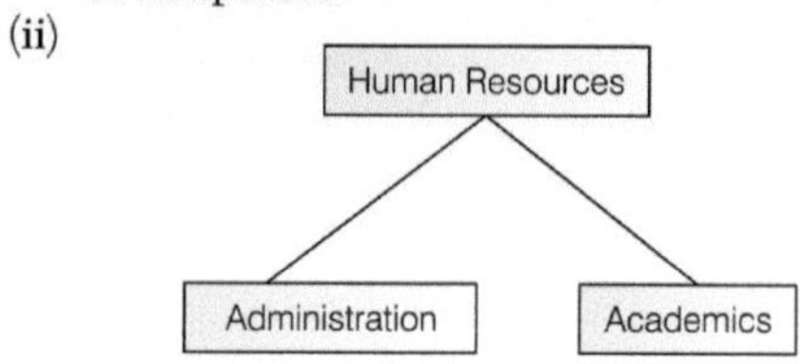

(iii) Hub/Switch.

(iv) Satellite.

(v) • Wide Area Network

  • Local Area Network

46. Expertia Professional Global (EPG) in an online corporate training provider company for IT related courses. The company is setting up their new campus in Mumbai. You as a network expert have to study the physical locations of various buildings and the number of computers to be installed. In the planning phase, provide the best possible answers for the queries (i) to (v) raised by them.

Physical locations of the buildings of EPG

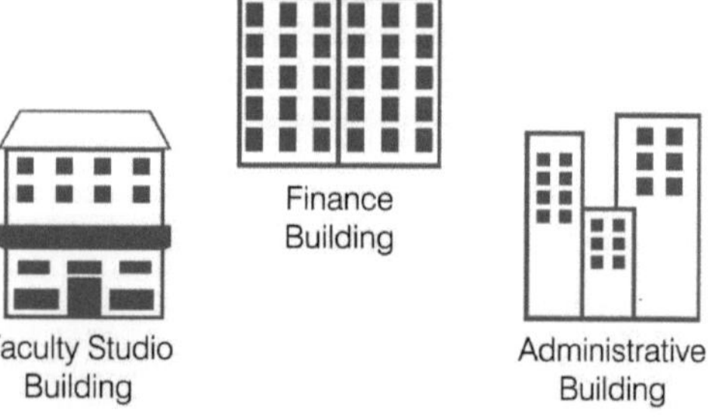

Building to building distance (in metre)

From	To	Distance
Administrative Building	Finance Building	60
Administrative Building	Faculty Studio Building	120
Finance Building	Faculty Studio Building	70

Expected computers to be installed
in each building

Buildings	Computers
Administrative Building	20
Finance Building	40
Faculty Studio Building	120

(i) Suggest the most appropriate building, where EPG should plan to install the server.

(ii) Suggest the most appropriate building to building cable layout to connect all three buildings for efficient communication.

(iii) Which type of network out of the following is formed by connection the computers of these three buildings?

(a) LAN

(b) MAN

(c) WAN

(iv) Which wireless channel out of the following should be opted by EPG to connect to students of all over the world?

(a) Infrared

(b) Microwave

(c) Satellite

(v) Expand the following

- WAN
- MAN

Ans. (i) EPG should install the server in the Faculty Studio Building as it has maximum number of computers.

(ii)

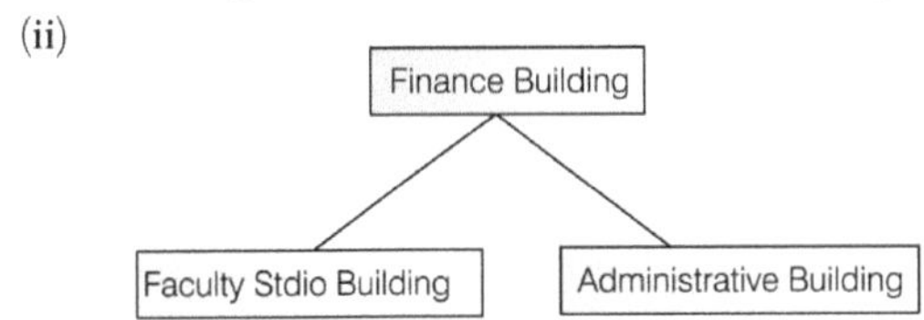

(iii) (a) LAN (Local Area Network).

(iv) (c) Satellite.

(v) • Wide Area Network

  • Metropolitan Area Network

47. Workalot consultants are setting up a secured network for their office campus of Gurgaon for their day-to-day office and web based activities. They are planning to have connectivity between 3 buildings and the head office situated in Mumbai.

Answer the questions (i) to (v) after going through the building positions in the campus and other details, which are given below:

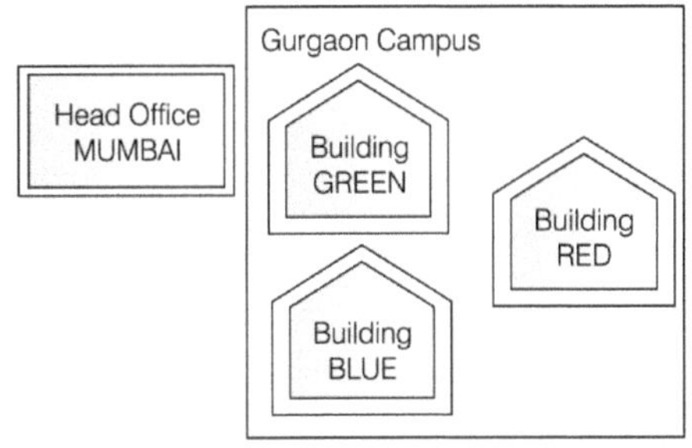

Distance between various buildings

Building GREEN to Building RED	110 m
Building GREEN to Building BLUE	45 m
Building BLUE to Building RED	65 m
Gurgaon Campus to Head Office	1760 km

Number of computers

Building GREEN	32
Building RED	150
Building BLUE	45
Head Office	10

(i) Suggest the most suitable place (i.e. building) to house the server of this organisation. Also, give a reason to justify your suggested location.

(ii) Suggest a cable layout of connections between the buildings inside the campus.

(iii) Suggest the placement of the following devices with justification :

(a) Switch (b) Repeater

(iv) The organisation is planning to provide a high speed link with its head office situated in the Mumbai using a wired connection. Which of the following cables will be most suitable for this job?

(a) Optical fibre (b) Co-axial cable

(c) Ethernet cable

(v) What is the use of firewall in network?

Ans. (i) Building RED is the suitable place to house the server because it has maximum number of computers.

(ii)

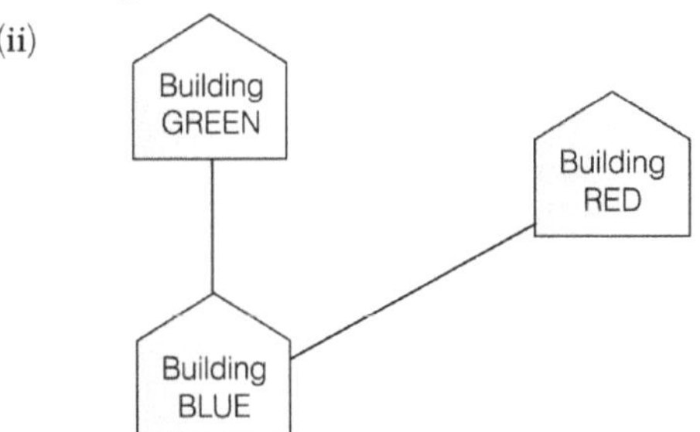

(iii) (a) **Switches** are needed in every building as they help share bandwidth in every building.

(b) **Repeaters** may be skipped as per above layout (because distance is less than 100 m), however if building GREEN and building RED are directly connected, we can place a repeater there as the distance between these two buildings is more than 100 m.

(iv) (b) Co-axial cable.

(v) Firewall prevents the unauthorised access in the network.

48. Learn Together is an educational NGO. It is setting up its new campus at Jabalpur for its web-based activities. The campus has four compounds as shown in the diagram below:

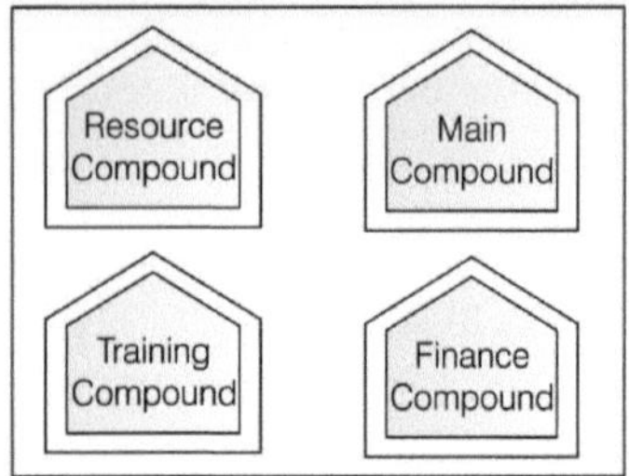

Centre to centre distance between various compounds as per architectural drawing (in m) is as follows

Main Compound to Resource Compound	110 m
Main Compound to Training Compound	115 m
Main Compound to Finance Compound	35 m
Resource Compound to Training Compound	25 m
Resource Compound to Finance Compound	135 m
Training Compound to Finance Compound	100 m

Expected number of computers in each compound are as follows

Main Compound	5
Resource Compound	15
Training Compound	150
Finance Compound	20

(i) Suggest a cable layout of connections between the compounds.

(ii) Suggest the most suitable place (i.e. compound) to house the server for this NGO. Also, provide a suitable reason for your suggestion.

(iii) Suggest the placement of the following devices with justification:

(a) Repeater   (b) Hub/Switch

(iv) The NGO is planning to connect its international office situated in Mumbai, which out of the following wired communication link, will you suggest for a very high speed connectivity?

(a) Telephone analog line   (b) Optical fibre

(c) Ethernet cable.

(v) Expand the following

- LAN   - PAN

Ans. (i)

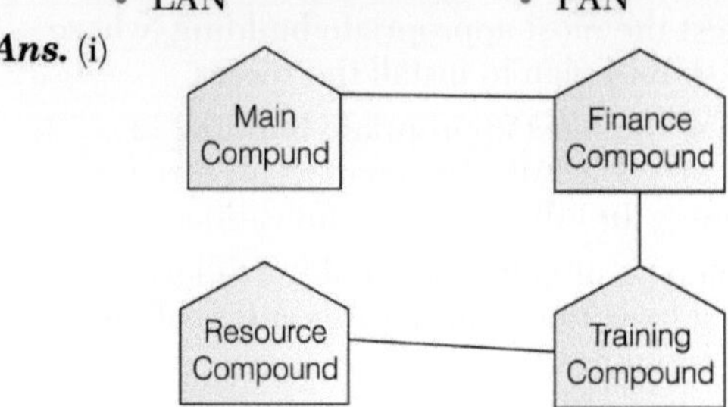

(ii) The most suitable place to house the server is Training Compound as it has maximum number of computers.

(iii) (a) **Repeater** As per one layout (shown in (i)), the repeater can be avoided as all distances between the compounds are <=100 m.

(b) **Hub/Switch** Training compound as it is hosting the server.

(iv) (b) Optical fibre.

(v) - Local Area Network
- Personal Area Network

49. Vidya for All is an educational NGO. It is setting up its new campus at Jaipur for its web-based activities. The campus has four buildings as shown in the diagram below:

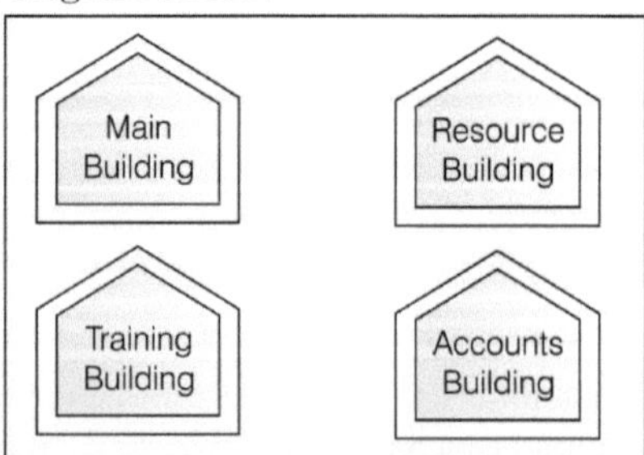

Centre to centre distance between various buildings as per architectural drawing (in m) is as follows

Main Building to Resource Building	120 m
Main Building to Training Building	40 m
Main Building to Accounts Building	135 m
Resource Building to Training Building	125 m
Resource Building to Accounts Building	45 m
Training Building to Accounts Building	110 m

Expected number of computers in each building are as follows

Main Building	15
Resource Building	25
Training Building	250
Accounts Building	10

(i) Suggest a cable layout of connection between the buildings.

(ii) Suggest the most suitable place (i.e. building) to house the server for this NGO. Also, provide a suitable reason for your suggestion.

(iii) Suggest the placement of the following devices with justification:

   (a) Repeater   (b) Hub/Switch.

(iv) The NGO is planning to connect its international office situated in Delhi. Which out of the following wired communication links, will you suggest for a very high speed connectivity?

   (a) Telephone analog line   (b) Optical fibre
   (c) Ethernet cable.

(v) Expand the MODEM.

Ans. (i)

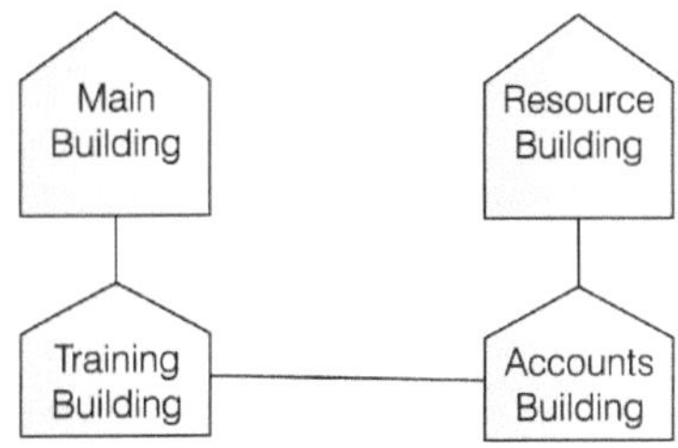

(ii) The most suitable place to house the server for this NGO is Training Building because it has the maximum number of computers.

(iii) (a) **Repeater** As per one layout (shown in (i)), the repeater can be avoided as all distances between the compounds are <= 100 m.

   (b) **Hub/Switch** Training building as it is hosting the server.

(iv) (b) Optical fibre. (v) Modulator Demodulator

50. Eduminds University of India is starting its campus in a small town Parampur of Central India with its centre admission office in Delhi. The university has three major buildings comprising of Admin building, Academic building and Research building in 5 km area campus.

As a network expert, you need to suggest the network plan as per (i) to (v) to the authorities keeping in mind the distances and other given parameters.

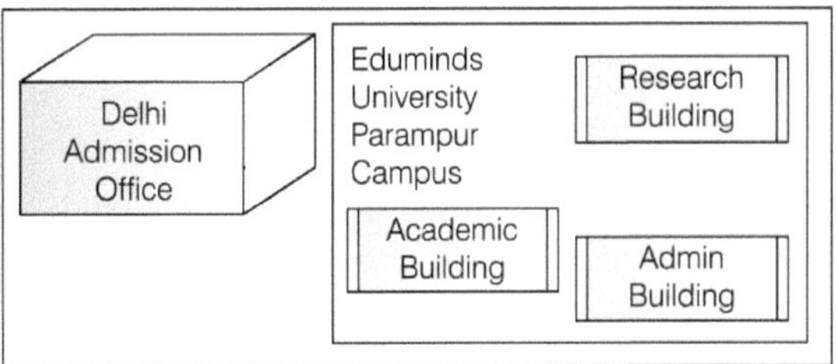

Expected wire distance between various locations

Research Building to Admin Building	90 m
Research Building to Academic Building	80 m
Academic Building to Admin Building	15 m
Delhi Admission Office to Parampur Campus	1450 km

Expected number of computers to be installed at various locations in the university are as follows

Research Building	20
Academic Building	150
Admin Building	35
Delhi Admission Office	5

(i) Suggest the authorities, the cable layout amongst various buildings inside the university campus for connecting the buildings.

(ii) Suggest the most suitable place (i.e. building) to house the server of this organisations with a suitable reason.

(iii) Suggest an efficient device for the following to be installed in each of the building to connect all the computers

   (a) Gateway

   (b) Modem

   (c) Switch

(iv) Suggest the most suitable (very high speed) service to provide data connectivity between admission building located in Delhi and the campus located in Parampur form the following options:

- Telephone line
- Fixedline dial-up connection
- Co-axial cable network
- GSM
- Leased line
- Satellite connection.

(v) University is planning to connect its campus in Delhi which is less than 100 km. Which type of network will be formed?

Ans. (i)

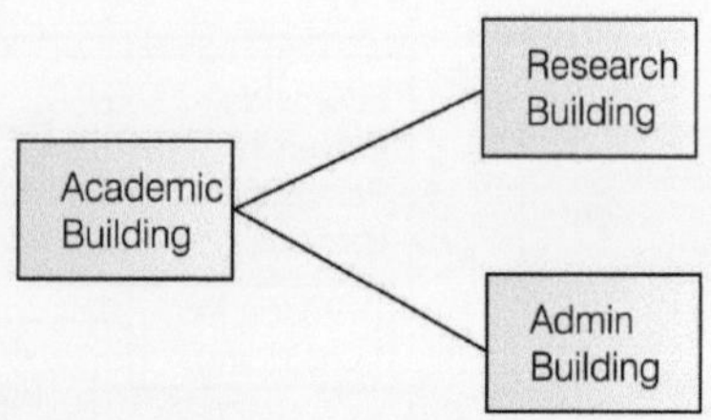

(ii) The most suitable place to house the server is Academic Building as it has maximum number of computers. Thus, it decreases the cabling cost and increase efficiency of network.

(iii) (c) Switch is to be installed in each of building to connect all the computers.

(iv) Satellite connection.

(v) MAN

51. Institute of Distance Learning is located in Pune and is planning to go in for networking of four wings for better interaction. The details are shown below:

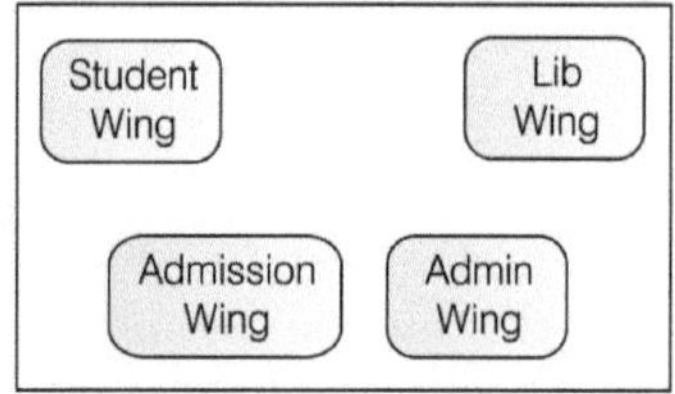

The distance between various wings

Student Wing to Admin Wing	150 m
Student Wing to Admission Wing	100 m
Student Wing of Lib Wing	325 m
Admission Wing to Admin Wing	100 m
Admission Wing to Lib Wing	125 m
Admin Wing to Lib Wing	90 m

Number of computers

Student Wing	225
Admission Wing	50
Admin Wing	10
Lib Wing	25

(i) Suggest the type of networking (LAN, MAN, WAN) for connecting Lib Wing to Admin Wing. Justify your answer.

(ii) Suggest the most suitable place (i.e. wing) to house the server, with a suitable reason.

(iii) Suggest and placement of the following devices with reasons.

    (a) Repeater   (b) Switch

(iv) The Institute is planning to link its study centre situated in Delhi. Suggest an economic way to connect it with reasonably high speed. Justify your answer.

(v) Expand the following

- PAN

- WAN

Ans. (i) Since, the distance between Lib Wing and Admin Wing is small. So type of networking is small, i.e. LAN.

(ii) Since, maximum number of computers are in Student Wing, so suitable place to house the server is Student Wing.

(iii) (a) Repeater should be installed between Student Wing and Admin Wing as distance is more than 60 m.

    (b) Switch should be installed in each wing to connect several computers.

(iv) Broadband connection as it is between economical and speedy.

(v) • Personal Area Network
    • Wide Area Network

52. Bias Methodologies is planning to expand their network in India, starting with three cities in India to build infrastructure for research and development of their chemical products. The company has planned to set up their main office in Pondicherry at three different locations and have named their offices as Back Office, Research Lab and Development Unit. The company has one more research office namely Corporate Unit in Mumbai. A rough layout of the same is as follows:

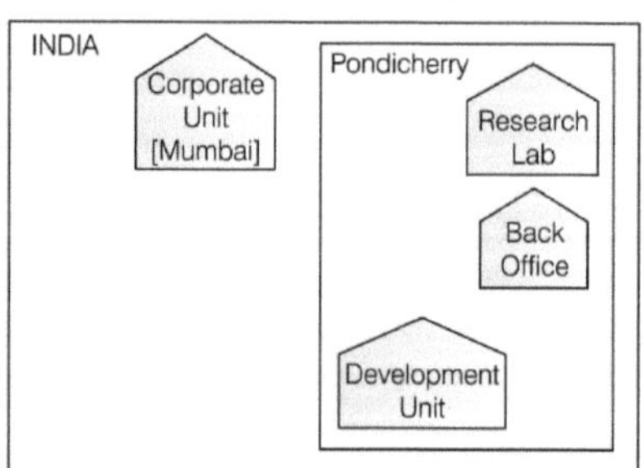

Approximate distance between these offices are as follows

From	To	Distance
Research Lab	Back Office	110 m
Research Lab	Development Unit	16 km
Research Lab	Corporate Unit	1800 km
Back Office	Development Unit	13 km

In continuation of the above, the company experts have planned to install the following number of computers in each of their offices

Research Lab	158
Back Office	79
Development Unit	90
Corporate Unit	51

(i) Suggest the type of network required (out of LAN, MAN, WAN) for connecting each of the following office units.

- Research Lab and Back Office
- Research Lab and Development Unit.

(ii) Which one of the following device, will you suggest for connecting all the computers with in each of their office units?

- Switch/Hub
- Modem
- Telephone.

(iii) Which of the following communication medium, will you suggest to be procured by the company for connecting their local office units in Pondicherry for very effective (high speed) communication?

- Telephone cable
- Optical fibre
- Ethernet cable.

(iv) Suggest a cable/wiring layout for connecting the company's local office units located in Pondicherry. Also, suggest an effective method/technology for connecting the company's office unit located in Mumbai.

(v) Which building is suitable to install the server with suitable reason?

Ans. (i) LAN and MAN.

(ii) Switch/Hub.

(iii) Optical fibre.

(iv) 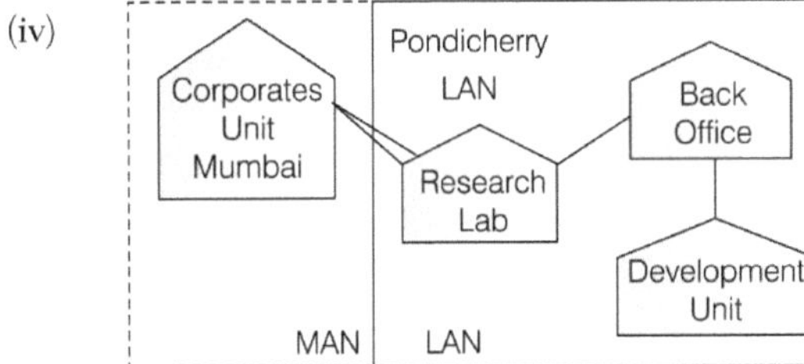

An effective method/technology for connecting the company's offices–unit located in Mumbai is dial-up or broadband.

(v) Research lab is suitable to install the server because it has maximum number of computers.

53. China Middleton Fashion is planning to expand their network in India, starting with two cities in India of provide infrastructure for distribution of their product. The company has planned to set up their main office units in Chennai at the different locations and have named their offices as Production Unit, Finance Unit and Media Unit. The company has its Corporate Unit in Delhi. A rough layout of the same is as follows:

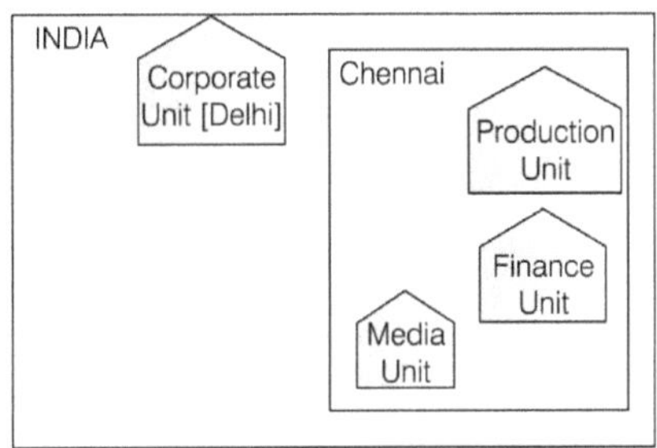

Approximate distance between these units are as follows

From	To	Distance
Production Unit	Finance Unit	70 m
Production Unit	Media Unit	15 km
Production Unit	Corporate Unit	2112 km
Finance Unit	Media Unit	15 km

In continuation of the above, the company experts have planned to install the following number of computers in each of their office units

Production Unit	150
Finance Unit	35
Media Unit	10
Corporate Unit	30

(i) Suggest the kind of network required (out of LAN, MAN, WAN) for connecting each of the following office units:

- Production Unit and Media Unit
- Production Unit and Finance Unit.

(ii) Which one of the following device will you suggest for connecting all the computers with in each of their office units?

- Switch/Hub
- Modem
- Telephone.

(iii) Which of the following communication media, will you suggest to be procured by the company for connecting their local office units in Chennai for very effective (high speed) communication?

- Telephone cable
- Optical fibre
- Ethernet cable.

(iv) Suggest a cable/wiring layout for connecting the company's local office units located in Chennai. Also, suggest an effective method/technology for connecting the company's office unit located in Delhi.

(v) Suggest the most suitable place to install the server with reason.

Ans. (i) MAN and LAN.

(ii) Switch/Hub.

(iii) Optical fibre.

(iv)

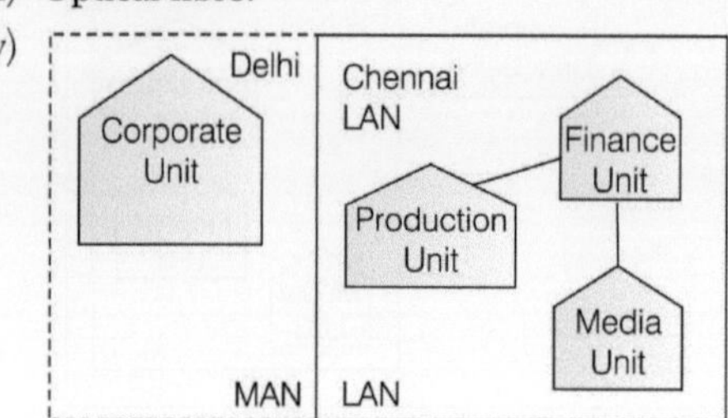

An effective method/technology for connecting the company's office in Delhi and Chennai is broadband connection.

(v) Production unit is suitable to install the server because it has maximumk number of computers.

54. Gargi Education Service Ltd. is an educational organisation. It is planning to set up its India campus at Nepal with its head office at Mumbai. The Nepal campus has 4 main buildings– ADMIN, ENGINEERING, BUSINEES and MEDIA.

You as a network expert have to suggest the best network related solutions for their problems raised in (i) to (v), keeping in mind the distance between the buildings and other given parameters.

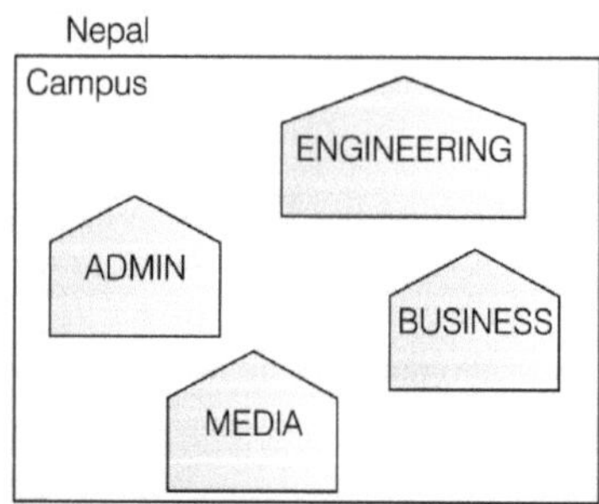

Shortest distance between various buildings

ADMIN To ENGINEERING	50 m
ADMIN To BUSINESS	80 m
ADMIN To MEDIA	45 m
ENGINEERING To BUSINEES	60 m
ENGINEERING To MEDIA	50 m
BUSINESS To MEDIA	45 m
Mumbai Head Office To Nepal Campus	2175 m

Number of computers installed at various buildings are as follows

ADMIN	110
ENGINEERING	75
BUSINEES	40
MEDIA	10
Mumbai Head Office	20

(i) Suggest the most appropriate location of the server inside the Nepal Campus (out of 4 buildings), to get the best connectivity for maximum number of computers. Justify your answer.

(ii) Suggest and draw the cable layout to efficiently connect various buildings within the Nepal Campus for connecting the computers.

(iii) Which hardware device will you suggest to be procured by the company to be installed to protect and control the Internet uses within the campus.

(iv) Which of the following will you suggest to establish the online face-to-face communication between the people in the ADMIN office of Nepal Campus and Mumbai Head Office?

(a) Cable TV   (b) E-mail

(c) Video Conferencing   (d) Text Chat

(v) Expand the following

- MAN
- PAN

Ans. (i) ADMIN is the most appropriate location of the Nepal Campus because it has maximum number of computers.

(ii)

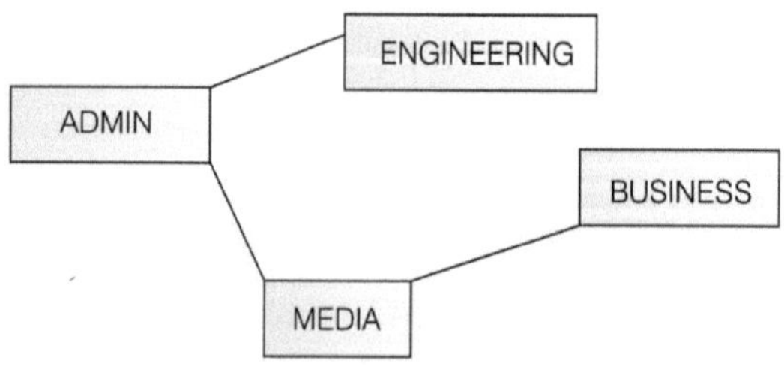

(iii) Firewall.

(iv) (c) Video Conferencing.

(v)   • Metropolitan Area Network
      • Personal Area Network

Chapter Test

Multiple Choice Questions

1. Which of the following is not a feature of networking?   [CBSE 2011]

   (a) Resource sharing
   (b) Uninterrupted Power Supply (UPS)
   (c) Reduced cost
   (d) Reliability

2. What is the use of bridge in the network?

   (a) To connect LANs
   (b) To amplify signals
   (c) To control network speed
   (d) All of these

3. Data is converted in a form so as to travel over telephone lines using this device.

   (a) Modem
   (b) Hub
   (c) Switch
   (d) Router

4. If a Lawyer sharing the case files *via* bluetooth from his phone to the client's phone, considered as which of the network type?

   (a) LAN
   (b) PAN
   (c) MAN
   (d) CAN

Short Answer Type Questions

5. What is the purpose of switch in a network?

6. Give two examples of PAN and LAN type of networks.   [Delhi 2016]

7. Illustrate the layout for connecting five computers in a bus and a star topology of networks.   [CBSE 2015]

Long Answer Type Questions

8. Trine Tech Corporation (TTC) is a professional consultancy company. The company is planning to set up their new offices in India with its hub at Hyderabad. As a network adviser, you have to understand their requirement and suggest them the best available solutions. Their queries are mentioned as (i) to (v) below.

Block to block distance (in metre)

Block (From)	Block (To)	Distance
Human Resource	Conference	110
Human Resource	Finance	40
Conference	Finance	80

Expected number of computers to be in each block

Block	Computers
Human Resource	25
Finance	120
Conference	90

  (i) Which will be the most appropriate block, where TTC should plan to install their server?

  (ii) Draw a block to block cable layout to connect all the buildings in the most appropriate manner for efficient communication.

  (iii) Which of the following device will be suggested by you to connect each computer in each of the buildings?

     (a) Switch
     (b) Modem
     (c) Gateway

  (iv) The company is planning to connect its admission office in Hyderabad which is more than 1000 km from company. Which type of network will be formed?

9. Granuda consultants are setting up a secured network for their office campus at Faridabad for their day-to-day office and web based activities. They are planning to have connectivity between three buildings and the head office situated in Kolkata.

Answer the questions (i) to (iv) after going through the building positions in the campus and other details, which are given below

Distance between various buildings

Building RAVI to Building JAMUNA	120 m
Building RAVI to Building GANGA	50 m
Building GANGA to Building JAMUNA	65 m
Faridabad Campus to Head Office	1460 km

Number of Computers

Building RAVI	25
Building JAMUNA	150
Building GANGA	51
Head Office	10

(i) Suggest the most suitable place (i.e. block) to house the server of this organisation. Also, give a reason to justify your suggested location.

(ii) Suggest a cable layout of connections between the building inside the campus.

(iii) Suggest the placement of the following devices with justification:

(a) Switch   (b) Repeater

(iv) Consultancy is planning to connect its office in Faridabad which is more than 10 km from head office. Which type of network will be formed?

Answers

For Detailed Solutions

Scan the code

CHAPTER 03

Database Concepts

In this Chapter...

- Database Management System (DBMS)
- Working of Databse
- View of Data (Data Abstraction)
- Data Models
- Relational Database
- Keys

A database can be defined as a collection of information organized in such a way that a computer program can be used to retrieve data quickly. You can think of a database as an electronic filing system.

The contents of a database are obtained by combining the data from all the different sources in an organization. This data forms the base for all further activities such as performing logical, mathematical and other operations and maintains any information that may be necessary to the decision-making processes involved in the management of that organization.

A database has the following properties

- It is a collection of data elements representing real-world information.
- It is logical, coherent and internally consistent.

For example, consider the names, telephone numbers and addresses of the relatives. You may have recorded this data in an indexed address book or you may have stored it on a hard drive, using application software such as Microsoft Access or Excel. This collection of related data with an implicit meaning is known as a **Database**.

Database Management System (DBMS)

A Database Management System is a software system that enables users to define, create and maintain the database and provides controlled access to this database.

The primary goal of a DBMS is to provide a way to store and retrieve database information that is both convenient and efficient. Data in a database can be added, deleted, changed, sorted or searched, all using a DBMS.

Application program accesses the data stored in the database by sending request to the DBMS. *For example,* MySQL, INGRES, MS-ACCESS etc.

The purpose of a Database Management System is to bridge the gap between information and data. The data stored in memory or on disk must be converted to usable information.

The basic processes that are supported by a DBMS are

(i) Specification of data types, structures and constraints to be considered in an application.
(ii) Storing the data itself into persistent storage.
(iii) Manipulation of the database.
(iv) Querying the database to retrieve desired information.
(v) Updating the content of the database.

Advantages of DBMS

(i) Reduced data redundancy
(ii) Elimination of inconsistency
(iii) Data sharing
(iv) Data integrity
(v) Data security
(vi) Backup and recovery

Limitations of DBMS

  (i) High cost
  (ii) Database failure
  (iii) Data quality
  (iv) Confidentiality, privacy and security

Need of Database System

The need of database systems arose in the early 1960s in response to the **traditional file processing system**. In the file processing system, the data is stored in the form of files, and a number of application programs are written by programmers to add, modify, delete, and retrieve data to and from appropriate files.

New application programs are added to the system as the need arises. *For example*, suppose a saving bank decides to offer current accounts. As a result, the bank creates new permanent files that contain information about all the current accounts maintained in the bank, and it may have to write new application programs to deal with situations that do not arise in saving accounts, such as overdrafts. Thus, as time goes by, the system acquires more files and more application programs.

However, the file processing system has a number of disadvantages, which are given below

- Some information may be duplicated in several files.
- The file processing system lacks the insulation between program and data.
- Handling new queries is difficult, since it requires change in the existing application programs or requires a new application program.
- In this system, all the integrity rules need to be explicitly programmed in all application programs, which are using that particular data item.
- This system lacks security features. To overcome these problems, database system was designed.

Components of Database System

A database system is composed of four components- User, Hardware, Software and Data, which coordinate with one another to form an effective database system.

The major components of a database system are described below

  (i) **User** The users are the people who manage the database and perform different operations on it.

    Basically, users are those persons who need the information from the database to carry out their primary business responsibilities i.e. personnel, staff, clerical etc.

There are mainly three kinds of people who plays different roles in database system. They are **application programmers**, who develop the application programs, the **end-users** access the database from a terminal using a query language provided by database system and **database administrator**, who is responsible for the design, construction and maintenance of a database system.

Database Administrator (DBA)

The person having the central control over the system is called Database Administrator. The DBA has many different responsibilities but the overall goal of a DBA is to maintain the database system and to provide users with access to the required information when they need it. The DBA makes sure that the database is protected.

Some responsibilities of DBA are as follows

- Ensuring regular and accurate update of the database.
- Identifying and resolving user's problem.
- Schema and physical organization modification.
- Storage structure and access method definition.
- Processing and maintaining database.

  (ii) **Hardware** The hardware consists of various secondary storage devices, such as magnetic tapes, hard disks, floppy disks, CD-ROM's etc, on which data is stored and the input/output devices, such as mouse, keyboard, lightpen, printers, scanners etc., which are used for storing (by providing commands) and retrieving the required data in an efficient manner.

    Since database can range from those of a single user with a desktop computer to those on mainframe computers with thousands of users, therefore proper care should be taken for choosing appropriate hardware devices for a required database.

  (iii) **Software** This is the most important component of database. It acts as an interface between the user and the database. In other words, software interacts with the users, application programs, and database of a particular storage media to insert, update, delete and retrieve data.

    For performing these operations such as insertion, deletion and updation we can either use the query languages like SQL, QUEL or application softwares such as Visual Basic, etc.

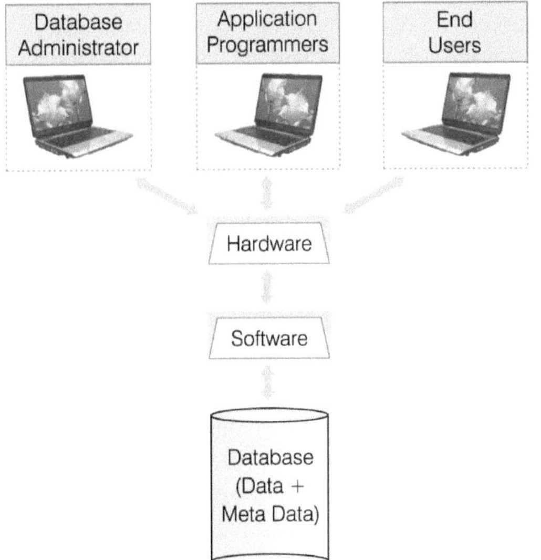

(iv) **Data** It is an important component of database. Most of the organizations generate, store and process large amount of data. The data act as a bridge between the hardware, software and the users.

A database contains various types of data

- **User Data** It contains a table of data in the form of rows (records) and columns (fields).

- **Meta Data** It means 'data about data' i.e. a logical description of the structure of a data.

- **Application Data** It contains the structure and format queries, reports and other application components.

Working of Database

Databases are created to operate on large quantities of information by input, store, retrieve, and manage the information.

Database is a centralized location which provides an easy way to access the data by several users. It does not keep the separate copies of a particular data file still a number of users can access the same data at the same time.

As the below diagram shows, to perform any operation in the presence of a Database Management System (DBMS).

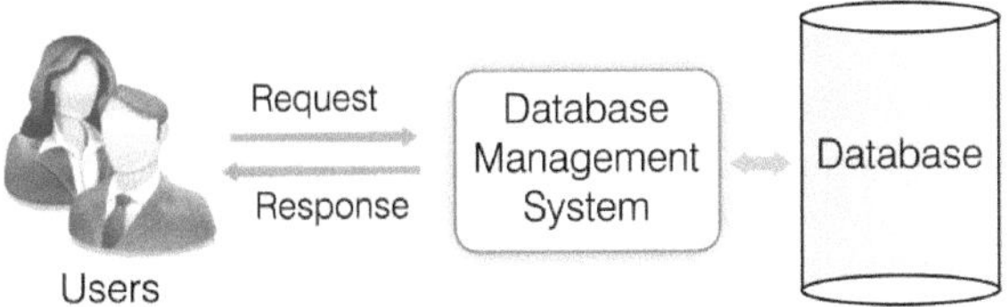

Here, DBMS works as an interface between the user and the centralized database. First, a request or query is forwarded to a DBMS which works (i.e., a searching process is started on the centralized database) on the received query with the available data and if the result is obtained, is forwarded to the user. If the output does not completely fulfill the requirements of the user then a rollback (again search) is done and again search process is performed until the desired output is obtained.

DBMS *versus* **File Processing System**

Database Management System	File Processing System
A database management system co-ordinates both the physical and the logical access to the data.	File processing system co-ordinates only the physical access.
A database management system is a bundle of applications, i.e. dedicated for managing data stored in a database.	A file processing system is a collection of raw data files stored in the hard drive of a system.
A database management system is designed to allow flexible access to data (i.e. queries).	File processing system is designed to allow predetermined access to data (i.e. compiled programs).
A database management system is designed to co-ordinate multiple users accessing the same data at the same time.	A file processing system is usually designed to allow one or more programs to access different data files at the same time.

View of Data (Data Abstraction)

The major purpose of a database system is to provide users with an abstract view of data. That is, the system hides certain details of how the data are stored and maintained.

For the system to be usable, it must retrieve data efficiently. The need for efficiency has led designers to use complex data structures to represent data in the database.

Since many database system users are not computer trained, developers hide the complexity from users through several levels of abstraction, to simplify user's interactions with the system. This concept is known as data abstraction.

Several levels of abstraction are described below

(i) **Internal Level** It is the lowest level of abstraction that describes how the data is physically stored and organised on storage medium. It describes complex low-level data structures and access method to be used by the database. It is also known as **physical level**.

(ii) **Conceptual Level** The conceptual level presents a logical view of the entire database and thus, it is also known as **logical level**.

It describes the type data is stored in the database, the relationships among the data and complete view of user's requirements without any concern for physical implementation.

It allows the user to bring all the data in the database together and see it in consistant manner. It hides the complexity of physical storage structures. Database administrator, who must decide what information to keep in the database, uses the logical level of abstraction.

(iii) **External Level** It is the highest level of database abstraction and also known as **view level**. The external level describes a part of database for a particular group of users. In general, most of the users do not require the entire data stored in database, instead, they need to access only a part of the database.

The view level of abstraction exists to simplify their interaction with the system. It provides a powerful and flexible security mechanism by hiding parts of database from certain users.

The user is not aware of the existance of other information that is missing from the view. It permits users to access data in a way that is customized to their needs, so that the same data can be seen by different users in different ways, at the same time.

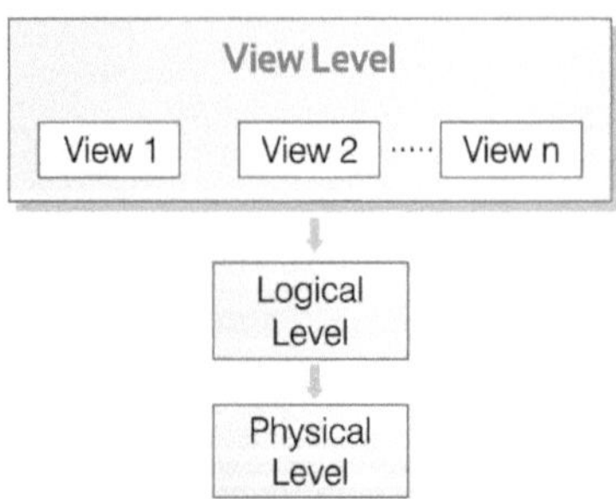

Three Levels of Data Abstraction

To understand the concept of data abstraction, consider the example of the database of a banking organization.

- On the internal level, we find all of the files that store data used by the banking organization, *i.e.*, data of clients, employees of the bank, clients' accounts, pay slips, etc. On this level, we also find the information about the location of data (*For example*, disk location, block, index, etc.)

- On the conceptual level, we find all the data description used, *for example*, the concept of client will be defined by a list of the types of information characterising each client– a code, a last name, a first name, an address, etc., and the content (*For example*, the client accounts.)

- On the external level, we find selections from or categorizations of the database needed by the different users, *for example*, the personnel who prepare the pay slips only have to access to the parts of the database concerning the employees of the bank. They cannot access client accounts.

Data Models

Data model can be defined as an integrated collection of concepts for describing and manipulating data, relationship between data and constraints on the data in an organisation.

A data model provides a way to describe the design of a database at the internal, conceptual and external level.

A data model comprises of three components, which are given below

- A **structural part,** consisting of a set of rules according to which databases can be constructed.

- A **manipulative part,** defining the types of operations that are allowed on the data (this includes the operations that are used for updating or retrieving data from the database and for changing the structure of the database).

- Possibly a set of **integrity rules**, which ensures that the data is accurate.

The purpose of a data model is to represent data and to make the data understandable. The different data models that are used for database management system are:

Hierarchical Data Model

In hierarchical data model, data is organised in a tree-like structure. There is a hierarchy of parent and child data segments. It comprises a set of records connected to one another through links. The link is an association between two or more records. To create links between these records, the hierarchical model uses parent child relationship.

In a hierarchical database, the parent child relationship is One to Many. This restricts a child segment to having only one parent segment but a parent segment can have one or more child segments. Top of the structure consists of a single segment and known as **root segment**. The operations that can be performed on hierarchical model are retrieval, insertion, deletion and modification of records.

Network Data Model

In network data model, data is represented by collection of records and relationships among data are represented by links like hierarchical data model.

The only difference is that in the network model, records are organized as arbitrary graphs rather than trees. In this model, the parent child relationship is Many to Many, i.e. one child segment can have multiple parent segments.

Relational Data Model

In a relational data model, data is stored in different tables with relationship to each other. These tables are called **relations**. These tables communicate and show information which facilitates data search ability, organisation and reporting.

Relational Database

A tabular database in which data is defined so that it can be reorganized and accessed in a number of different ways.

In a relational database, data is stored in different tables with relationships to each other. These tables communicate and share information, which facilitates data search ability, organization and reporting.

Various terms related to relational database are as follows

  (i) **Relation** A relation is a table with columns and rows which represent the data items and relationships among them. Relations have three important properties a name, cardinality and a degree.

     These properties help us to further define and describe relations

- **Name** The first property of a relation is its name, which is represented by the title or the entity identifier.
- **Cardinality** The second property of a relation is its cardinality, which refers to the number of tuples (rows) in a relation.
- **Degree** The third property of a relation is its degree, which refers to the number of attributes (columns) in each tuple.

  (ii) **Domain** A domain is a collection of all possible values from which the values for a given column or an attribute is drawn. A domain is said to be atomic if elements are considered to be indivisible units.

Relational Database Management System (RDBMS)

A Relational Database Management System (RDBMS) is a database management system. It is developed by Dr. E.F. Codd, of IBM's San Jose Research Laboratory.

RDBMS stores data in the form of related tables. RDBMS are powerful because they require few assumptions about how data is related or how it will be extracted from the database.

An important feature of relational database is that a single database can be spread across several tables. Today, popular commercial for large databases include Oracle, Microsoft SQL server, Sybase, MySQL.

  (iii) **Attributes** The heading columns of a table are known as attributes. Each attribute of a table has a distinct name.

  (iv) **Tuples** The rows in a relation are also known as tuples. Each row or tuple has a set of permitted values for each attribute.

Attributes	Emp_Id	Emp_Name	Emp_Salary	Years
	100	Jim	20000	2
Tuples	101	James	21000	1
	102	Anne	21001	3

Differences between DBMS and RDBMS

DBMS	RDBMS
In DBMS, relationship between two tables or files are maintained programmatically.	In RDBMS, relationship between two tables or files can be specified at the time of table creation.
DBMS does not support client-server architecture.	Most of the RDBMS support client-server architecture.
DBMS does not support distributed databases.	Most of the RDBMS support distributed databases.
In DBMS, there is no security of data.	In RDBMS, there are multiple levels of security such as command level, object level.
Each table is given an extension in DBMS.	Many tables are grouped in one database in RDBMS.

Keys

The key is defined as the column or attribute or a combination of attributes that is used to identify records of the database table. Sometimes we might have to retrieve data from more than one table, in those cases we require to join tables with the help of keys.

A key is also used to arrange the records either in ascending or descending order. It also controls and maintains the integrity of information store in the database.

There are various types of keys, which are as follows

Primary Key

The primary key of a relational table uniquely identifies each record in the table. In some tables, combination of more than one attributes is declared as primary key. In that case, primary key is known as composite key.

Every relation does have a primary key.

For example, in the given table StudentId works as a primary key because it contains Id's, which are unique for each student.

Candidate Key

The set of all attributes which can uniquely identify each tuple of a relation are known as candidate keys. Each table may have one or more candidate keys and one of them will become the primary key. *For example*, column StudentId and the combination of FirstName and LastName work as the candidate keys for the given table.

A candidate key must possess the following properties

(i) For each row the value of the key must uniquely identify that row.

(ii) No attribute in the key can be discarded without destroying the property of unique identification.

Alternate Key

From the set of candidate keys after selecting one of the key as primary key, all other remaining keys are known as alternate keys. These keys are also unique but they allow nulls. *For example*, from the candidate keys (StudentId, FirstName and LastName), StudentId chosen as a primary key then the FirstName and LastName column work as a alternate keys.

Foreign Key

A foreign key is a non-key attribute whose value is derived from the primary key of another table. The relationship between two tables is established with the help of foreign key. A table may have multiple foreign keys, and each foreign key can have different referenced table. Foreign keys play an essential role in database design, when tables are broken apart then foreign keys make it possible for them to be reconstructed.

For example, CourseId column of Student table work as a foreign key for student table, as well as a primary key for Course table (referenced table).

Referential Integrity

It concerns the concept of a foreign key. The referential integrity rules states that any foreign key value can only be in one of two states. The usual state of affairs is that the foreign key value refers to a primary key value of some table in the database.

Occasionally and this well depend on the rules of the data owner, a foreign key value can be null.

In this case, we are explicitly saying that either there is no relationship between the objects represented in the database or that this relationship is unknown.

StudentId	FirstName	LastName	CourseId
L0002345	Jim	Black	C002
L0001254	James	Harradine	A004
L0002349	Amanda	Holiand	C002
L0001198	Simon	McCloud	S042
L0023487	Peter	Murray	P301
L0018453	Anne	Norris	S042

Student table

CourseId	CourseName
A004	Accounts
C002	Computing
P301	History
S042	Short Course

Course table

Chapter Practice

Objective Questions

• Multiple Choice Questions

1. DBMS stands for
 (a) Database Microsoft System
 (b) Database Migration System
 (c) Database Management System
 (d) None of the above

Ans. (c) DBMS is the short form of Database Management System. It refers to a category of softwares that store and manage bulk volumes of data.

2. A table can have .... primary key(s).
 (a) 1 (b) 2
 (c) 3 (d) multiple

Ans. (a) A table can have only a single primary key to identify the records.

3. Which of the following is not a DBMS?
 (a) MS-Word
 (b) MySQL
 (c) Oracle
 (d) Microsoft SQL Server

Ans. (a) MySQL , Oracle and Microsoft SQL Server are all DBMS but MS-Word is a documentation software.

4. The total number of columns in a table is called
 (a) cardinality (b) degree
 (c) spreadsheet (d) relation

Ans. (b) The term degree refers to the total number of columns in a table.

5. Tables can be linked by
 (a) primary key (b) candidate key
 (c) alternate key (d) foreign key

Ans. (d) A foreign key is a common field found in two tables and it links the two tables.

6. The total number of rows in a table is called
 (a) domain (b) tuple
 (c) field (d) cardinality

Ans. (d) The total number of rows in a table is called cardinality.

7. If we delete an attribute of a table
 (a) degree increases
 (b) cardinality increases
 (c) degree and cardinality increase
 (d) degree decreases

Ans. (d) Degree is the total number of attributes/columns in a table , so if a column is deleted the degree decreases.

8. Raj wants to make EmpNo and PFNo columns of his table as the primary key. Is it possible?
 (a) Yes
 (b) No
 (c) Yes , possible as a comination of columns
 (d) None of the above

Ans. (c) Two columns cannot be primary key. But a combination of the columns can be primary key.

9. Software that is used to create , manipulate , maintain a relational database management system is called **(NCERT)**
 (a) documentation software
 (b) spreadsheet software
 (c) RDBMS
 (d) designing software

Ans. (c) A Relational Database Management System (RDBMS) is a software that can be used to maintain , manipulate and create large volumes of data in relations/tables and relationships between them.

10. In a relational data model, a data structure that organises the information about a single topic into rows and columns is
 (a) block (b) record (c) tuple (d) table

Ans. (d) The tables stores the individual domains of data of a database system and thus stores the data and organises it.

11. Which of the following is the drawback of DBMS?
 (a) Improvement in data
 (b) Backup and recovery
 (c) Complexity
 (d) Maintenance of data integrity

Ans. (c) The complex structure of tables , the relationships between them , other database objects and their management is what makes database systems complex and specialised software and people to manage. Database systems are complex, difficult and time-consuming to design.

12. Which of the following component of database system consists of various secondary storage devices on which data is stored?

(a) Hardware   (b) User   (c) Data   (d) Software

Ans. (a) The permanent or secondary storage device is the hard disk or any kind of disk storage that resides in the hardware unit.

13. In files, there is a key associated with each record which is used to differentiate among different records. For every file, there is atleast one set of keys that is unique. Such a key is called

(a) unique key   (b) prime attribute

(c) index key   (d) primary key

Ans. (d) A primary key carries unique values and hence is used to identify the records uniquely.

• Case Based MCQs

Direction *Read the case and answer the following questions.*

14. Anita has created a table "Players" to store the details of players who play in her sports academy . She has planned to create the following table with columns :

PlayerId, PlayerName , Game, Type , AadharNo

Table : Players

PlayerId	PlayerName	Game	Type	AadharNo
P01	Becker	Tennis	Indoor	333444657
P02	Robin	Tennis	Indoor	192900877
P03	Sunetra	Football	Outdoor	214567432
P04	Rakhi	Cricket	Outdoor	111231896

Answer the following questions, which based on the given information.

(i) Which column can she make the primary key?

(a) PlayerId   (b) PlayerName

(c) Game   (d) Type

(ii) Which column(s) can act as candidate key?

(a) Only PlayerId   (b) Only AadharNo

(c) Both (a) and (b)   (d) Type

(iii) Which column is the foreign key in the table?

(a) PlayerName   (b) Type

(c) Game   (d) None of these

(iv) What is the degree of the table?

(a) 1   (b) 2   (c) 3   (d) 5

(v) What will be the cardinality of the table, if two columns are added to the table?

(a) 7   (b) 6

(c) 4   (d) None of these

Ans. (i) (a) The PlayerId column stores unique and non-blank values , hence it can serve as primary key.

(ii) (c) All the field combinations that can serve as primary key for unique identification of records in a table are called candidate keys. Here PlayerId and AadharNo can serve as primary key.

So, these fields can act as candidate keys.

(iii) (d) The concept of foreign key is relevant only when there are multiple tables.

(iv) (d) Degree of a table is the total number of columns, i.e. 5.

(v) (c) The total number of rows in a table is its cardinality, i.e. 4. Adding columns to table increases its degree not cardinality.

15. Mr. Sharma is a new user of database systems . He has created a table storing the details of staff in his office. He is confused about some of the terms related to tables and databases. Help him solving his confusions.

Table : Staff

StaffId	StaffName	Dept	Salary	PF AcNo
1	Mrs. Fernandes	Accts	19500	UP/1108
2	Mr. Das	Sales	45000	WB/6777
3	Ms. Sunita	IT	65000	CH/0097
4	Mr. Roy	Accts	25000	WB/4567

(i) The vertical set storing the departments under the heading "Dept" is called

(a) field   (b) attribute

(c) column   (d) All of these

(ii) What is the cardinality of the table?

(a) 2   (b) 3   (c) 4   (d) 1

(iii) Can "StaffName" column serve as primary key?

(a) No

(b) Yes, only if it stores non-blank and distinct names

(c) Yes, only if it stores only distinct names

(d) Yes

(iv) A tuple carries

(a) a single value

(b) double values

(c) a row of multiple values as a record

(d) None of the above

(v) An attribute which can uniquely identify tuples of the table but is not defined as primary key of the table is called   **(NCERT)**

(a) primary key   (b) alternate key

(c) forign key   (d) None of these

Ans. (i) (d) The vertical columns of table are also called fields or attributes.

(ii) (c) Cardinality means the number of rows in a table, i.e. 4.

(iii) (b) The primary key of a table has to be unique and NOT NULL .

(iv) (c) A tuple is a horizontal row or record storing all the details of an entity.

(v) (*b*) All the candidate key fields that are not primary key are alternate keys. In a table there can be multiple such fields who can serve as primary key. Such fields are called candidate keys. Among these any one serves as primary key. The rest of the candidate keys are called alternate keys.

PART 2
Subjective Questions

• Short Answer Type Questions

1. What do you understand by the term database?

Ans. A database is a huge collection of data accumulating in a particular system. It comprises of historical data, operational and transactional data. The database grows everyday with the transactions dealing with it.

A database has the following properties
  (i) It is a collection of data elements representing real-world information.
  (ii) It is logical, coherent and internally consistent.

2. What is a DBMS? Expand and explain in short.

Ans. A Database Management System is a software system that enables users to define, create and maintain the database and provides controlled access to this database.

The primary goal of a DBMS is to provide a way to store and retrieve database information that is both convenient and efficient. Data in a database can be added, deleted, changed, sorted or searched, all using a DBMS.

3. What is a table? Also, write the other name of table.

Ans. Table is also called a relation, it is a diagrammatically a matrix of rows and columns that store the data of a particular system. A table is just like a sheet in Excel, that stores data in some columns and rows. The data is arranged under some fields, where each field stores similar kind of data.

4. What do you mean by fields of a table? Give examples.

Ans. A field of a table is simply a vertical column of the table. A field is also called an attribute. It stores similar kind of data. e.g. Name, Class, Marks etc., can be fields of student table, EmpId, Empname, Dept can be fields of Employee table. Each field derives its values from a pool of data which is called as the domain. All the values in a single field will be of same data type.

5. What are records? Also, write the other name of record.

Ans. A record is a horizontal row of a table storing complete data of one entity. It is also called a tuple.
e.g.

2	Mr. Das	Sales	45000

The above record of Mr. Das carries all the information about him. Similarly other records of the table carry data about other employees.
All the records together make up the data of the table.

6. What do you understand by the term degree of a table? Can it change?

Ans. The term degree refers to the total number of columns in a table. Yes the degree changes with addition or deletion of columns.
e.g. If a table "Product" stores the data in columns "PNo, PName, Qty, Price", there are 4 columns, hence the degree will be 4.

7. What do you understand by the term cardinality of a table? How can it be modified?

Ans. The total number of rows of a table is called the cardinality. It gets modified by the addition or deletion of rows. If rows are added to the table the cardinality increases. If rows are deleted the cardinality decreases.

8. What is a primary key? How many primary keys can be there in a table?

Ans. It is a combination of one or more fields in a table that can uniquely identify a record. There can be only one primary key in a table. It plays an important role in identifying the records, because it is the primary key who carries unique values. The criteria for a field to become primary key is : It must be carrying unique and NOT NULL values.

9. What is candidate key?

Ans. All the field combinations that can serve as primary key for unique identification of records in a table are called candidate keys.
For example, If a student table carries "RollNo., Name, Class, AadharNo., AdmissionNo" columns, then columns RollNo., AadharNo. and AdmissionNo can become the candidate keys since all carry unique values.

10. Can we have multiple candidate keys in a table? Give example.

Ans. Yes, we can have multiple candidate primary keys.
e.g. In an Employee table, ENo and AadharNo both can serve as primary key, hence both are candidate keys. Only primary key in a table will be a single field , candidate keys can be multiple.

11. Which fields are regarded as alternate keys?

Ans. All the candidate key fields that are not primary key are alternate keys.
e.g. If a table Employee carries columns "ENo, EName, PFNo, VoterId", then "ENo" is set as primary key and the other candidate keys "PFNo" and "VoterId" will be the alternate keys.

12. Why foreign keys are allowed to have NULL values?   (NCERT)

Ans. A foreign key is a field that links two tables . A table may have links to multiple tables . Each link is supported by a value that is common in the two tables . If there is a missing foreign key value for a record , it means the link is missing and no matching values are present. This is perfectly a valid situation, not an error .

13. How many foreign keys can be there in a table?

Ans. A table can have multiple foreign keys depending on the number of tables to which the mother table has links.

Multiple tables can be linked by the foreign key which will be common in all of them . It is by the foreign key that the corresponding values will be obtained from the tables.

14. Write names of few softwares used as DBMS.

Ans. MySQL, Oracle , DB/2, Ingres softwares obey certain common rules of relational algebra. Like they all support most of the codd's rules and support SQL . Some of these softwares like MySQL are free and some like Oracle is proprietary, that it has to be bought.

15. What do you understand by the term domain?

Ans. Domain refers to the pool or set of values from which a field of a table derives its values. e.g. The RollNo field derives its values from the set of integers from 1-100 (approx.). The "Dept" field derives its values from the domain of possible departments and the "Marks" field derives its values from the range of marks in an examination.

16. Give suitable example of a table with sample data and illustrate primary and candidate keys in it.

Ans. **Candidate Key** It is a set of all attributes that uniquely identifies records in a table. Each table may have one or more candidate keys.

Table : Student

AdmNo	RollNo	Name	Class	Marks
2715	1	Rame	12	90
2816	2	Shyeam	11	95
2404	3	Ajay	10	92
2917	4	Tarun	12	94

e.g. In Student table, AdmNo and RollNo both can identify records uniquely. So, both are candidate key.

Primary Key It is a set of one or more attributes that can uniquely identify each tuple of a relation. A relation can have only one primary key.

e.g. In Student table, AdmNo of all students are different. So, we have created AdmNo as primary key.

17. List some commonly used DBMS software packages.

Ans. Some commonly used DBMS software packages are

(i) MySQL	(ii) Oracle
(iii) Postgre	(iv) DB2
(v) MS-SQL	(vi) Sybase

18. Differentiate between an attribute and a tuple with an example.

Ans. The columns of a table are referred to as attributes. It is also known as field which is reserved for a specific piece of data. The rows of a table are referred to as tuples.

Attributes

S.No.	Name	Class
1	Raj	10
2	Ajay	12
3	Rahul	11

Tuples

19. What is the difference between degree and cardinality of a table? What is the degree and cardinality of the following table?

Eno	Name	Salary
101	John Fedrick	45000
103	Raya Mazumdar	50600

Ans. **Degree** The number of attributes or columns in a table is called the degree of the table.

The degree of the given table is 3.

Cardinality The number of rows or records in a table is called the cardinality of the table. The cardinality of the given table is 2.

20. Mention atleast three limitations of DBMS.

Ans. Some limitations of DBMS are given below

(i) **High Cost** DBMS requires various software, hardware and highly intelligent people for operating and maintaining the database system. It increases its cost.

(ii) **Database Failure** If database is corrupted due to power failure or any other reason, our valuable data may be lost or whole system stops.

(iii) **Data Quality** With increased number of users accessing data directly. There are enormous opportunities for users to damage data. So, it is not easy to provide a strategy to support multiple users to update data simultaneously.

• Long Answer Type Questions

21. Explain the role of database management system in maintaining huge volumes of data of different domains. Explain your views using an example.

Ans. A database management system is a specialised software that helps maintain large volumes of data pertaining to a real life system . Examples of such systems include business houses , transport systems, libraries , schools etc.

It not only stores bulk data in structured way but also helps to add , modify ,search , update and delete data from such databases. Examples of DBMS softwares are MySQL , Microsoft SQL Server , Oracle etc.

Application program accesses the data stored in the database by sending request to the DBMS.

For example, MySQL, INGRES, MS-ACCESS etc.

The purpose of a Database Management System is to bridge the gap between information and data. The data stored in memory or on disk must be converted to usable information.

22. A table "Sports" exists with 3 columns and 5 rows. What is its degree and cardinality? 2 rows are added to the table and 1 column deleted. What will be the degree and cardinality now?

Ans. The term degree refers to the total number of columns in a table. The term cardinality refers to the total number of rows in a table.

Initially, Sports table has 3 columns and 5 rows, so

Degree : 3

Cardinality : 5

After operations, 2 rows are added to the table and 1 column deleted.

Now, degree : 2 cardinality : 7.

23. Differentiate the terms primary key and candidate key.

Ans. Differences between primary key and candidate key are

Primary key	Candidate key
A primary key is a single field in a table that is used to identify the records uniquely.	A candidate key is a set of columns who are eligible for unique identification of records.
Only one field among the candidate keys is selected as primary key.	A table can have multiple candidate keys.
Primary key of a table is used in linking the data of the table to another table.	Candidate keys do not have such role.

24. Explain by an example how foreign key is useful for bringing data from multiple tables?

Ans. Consider the two tables given below

Table : Student

RollNo	Name	Class	Marks	AddressID
1	Rohan	12ScA	78.5	A1
2	Smita	11ComC	67.7	A2
3	Priya	12HumA	82.6	A3

Table : Address

AddressID	Place	State	Contact
A1	Pahargunj	Delhi	9876745655
A2	Kolkata	WB	9434566778
A3	Barnala	Punjab	9433534038

Referring to the above tables , if we look for Place to which "Priya" belongs" , we can link the tables by the foreign key "AddressID" of the Student table to get place as "Barnala" by the AddressID "A3". So, a foreign key helps in bringing data from multiple tables.

Chapter Test

Multiple Choice Questions

1. The other name for a table is
  (a) database   (b) relation
  (c) domain   (d) degree

2. A DBMS is used for
  (a) designing   (b) image merging
  (c) compression of file   (d) None of these

3. Special value that is stored when actual data value is unknown for an attribute. **(NCERT)**
  (a) None   (b) NULL
  (c) NaN   (d) None of these

4. The foreign key of a table
  (a) has unique values
  (b) has integer type values
  (c) has a linking column in another table
  (d) None of the above

5. The number of rows of a table is
  (a) limited
  (b) not limited
  (c) can be restricted while table creation
  (d) None of the above

Short Answer Type Questions

6. What is the use of foreign key field?

7. What are the components of a database system?

8. Can a primary key be alternate key?

9. While creating a table Rahul has restricted duplicate values in one of the columns. Can he make the column as primary key? Justify your answer.

10. Explain the term relation.

Long Answer Type Questions

11. Considering the following tables

Table : STUDENT

RollNo	Name	Class	Section	Registration_ID
11	Mohan	XI	1	IP-101-15
12	Sohan	XI	2	IP-104-15
21	John	XII	1	CS-103-14
22	Meena	XII	2	CS-101-14
23	Juhi	XII	2	CS-101-10

Table : PROJECT

ProjectNo	PName	Submission_Date
101	Airline Database	12/01/2018
102	Library Database	12/01/2018
103	Employee Database	15/01/2018
104	Student Database	12/01/2018
105	Inventory Database	15/01/2018
106	Railway Database	15/01/2018

Table : PROJECT ASSIGNED

Registration_ID	ProjectNo
IP-101-15	101
IP-104-15	103
CS-103-14	102
CS-101-14	105
CS-101-10	104

Answer the questions, which based on above information.

(i) Name primary key of each table.

(ii) Find foreign key(s) in table PROJECT ASSIGNED.

(iii) Is there any alternate key in table STUDENT? Give justification for your answer.

(iv) Can a user assign duplicate value to the field RollNo of STUDENT table? Jusify.

12. An organisation wants to create a database EMP_DEPENDENT to maintain following details about its employees and their dependent.

EMPLOYEE(AadharNumber, Name, Address, Department,EmployeeID)

DEPENDENT(EmployeeID, DependentName, Relationship)

(i) Name the attributes of EMPLOYEE, which can be used as candidate keys.

(ii) The company wants to retrieve details of dependent of a particular employee. Name the tables and the key which are required to retrieve this detail.

(iii) What is the degree of EMPLOYEE and DEPENDENT relation?

13. What are the major components of a database system?

14. Differentiate the terms DBMS and RDBMS.

15. In a multiplex, movies are screened in different auditoriums. One movie can be shown in more than one auditorium. In order to maintain the record of movies, the multiplex maintains a relational database consisting of two relations *viz*. CINEMA and PEOPLE respectively as shown below:

CINEMA(Movie_ID, MovieName, ReleaseDate)

PEOPLE(AudiNo, Movie_ID, Seats, ScreenType, TicketPrice)

(i) Is it correct to assign Movie_ID as the primary key in the CINEMA relation? If no, then suggest an appropriate primary key.

(ii) Is it correct to assign AudiNo as the primary key in the PEOPLE relation? If no, then suggest appropriate primary key.

(iii) Is there any foreign key in any of these relations?

Answers

Multiple Choice Questions

1. (b)   *2. (d)*   *3. (b)*   *4. (c)*   *5. (b)*

For Detailed Solutions

Scan the code

CHAPTER 04

Structured Query Language

In this Chapter...

- SQL Statements
- SQL Data Types
- DDL Statements/Commands
- DML Statements/Commands
- Operator in SQL
- Working with NULL Values
- Aggregate Functions
- GROUP BY Statement
- HAVING Clause
- Join

Structured Query Language (SQL) is the most popular query language used by major relational database management systems such as MySQL, ORACLE, SQL Server, etc. SQL is easy to learn as the statements comprise of descriptive english words and are not case sensitive.

SQL provides statements for defining the structure of the data, manipulating data in the database, declaring constraints and retrieving data from the database in various ways, depending on your requirements.

SQL provides variety of tasks such as

- Querying data.
- Creating, replacing, altering and dropping tables.
- Inserting, updating and deleting rows in a table.
- Controlling access to the database.
- Guaranteeing database consistency and integrity.

Advantages of SQL

(i) **SQL is portable** It is not platform dependent, it can be used in all types of devices; PCs, laptops and even mobile phones also.

(ii) **High speed** SQL queries can be used to retrieve large amount of records from a database quickly and efficiently.

(iii) **Easy to learn and understand** SQL generally consists of english language statements and it is very easy to learn and understand.

(iv) **SQL is used for relational database** SQL is widely used for relational database.

(v) **SQL acts as both programming language and interactive language** SQL can do both the jobs of being a programming language as well as an interactive language at the same time.

(vi) **Client/server language** SQL provides client-server architecture. It is used for linking front end computers and back end databases.

(vii) **Supports object based programming** With the emergence of object based programming, object storage capabilities are extended to relational database.

Disadvantages of SQL

(i) **Difficulty in interfacing** Interfacing a SQL database is more complex than adding a few lines of code.

(ii) **More features implemented in proprietary way** Although SQL databases confirm to ANSI and ISO standards, some databases go for proprietary extensions to standard SQL to ensure vendor lock-in.

SQL Statements

SQL command or statement is a special kind of sentence that contains clauses and all end with a semicolon(;) just as a sentence ends with a period.

There are four types of SQL statements

DDL (Data Definition Language)

It provides statements for creation and deletion of the database tables, views, etc. The DDL provides a set of definitions to specify the storage structure in a database system.

Some DDL statements are as follows

(i) **CREATE** used to create new table in the database.

(ii) **DROP** used to delete tables from the database.

(iii) **ALTER** used to change the structure of the database table. This statement can add up additional column, drop existing, and even change the data type of columns involved in a database table.

(iv) **RENAME** used to rename a table.

DML (Data Manipulation Language)

It provides statements for manipulating the database objects. It is used to query the databases for information retrieval.

Some DML statements are as follows

(i) **INSERT** used to insert data into a table.

(ii) **SELECT** used to retrieve data from a database.

(iii) **UPDATE** used to update existing data within a table.

(iv) **DELETE** used to delete all records from a table.

DCL (Data Control Language)

It is used to assign security levels in database, which involves multiple user setups. They are used to grant defined role and access privileges to the users.

Some DCL statements are as follows

(i) **GRANT** used to give user's access privileges to database.

(ii) **REVOKE** used to withdraw access privileges given with grant command.

TCL (Transaction Control Language)

It is used for controlling the transactions in a database system. These are also used to manage the changes made by DML.

Some TCL statements are as follows

(i) **COMMIT** used to save the work done.

(ii) **SAVEPOINT** used to identify a point in a transaction to which you can later rollback.

(iii) **ROLLBACK** used to restore database to original since the last COMMIT.

(iv) **SET TRANSACTION** establishes properties for the current transactions.

In this chapter, we will discuss only DDL and DML statements.

Rules for SQL commands

Rules for SQL commands are given below

(i) SQL statements can be typed in lowercase or uppercase letter. SQL statements are not case sensitive.

(ii) The statements can be typed in single line or multiple lines.

(iii) A semicolon (;) is used to terminate the SQL statements.

(iv) The statements may be distributed across the line but keywords cannot be.

(v) A comma (,) is used to separate parameters without a clause.

(vi) Characters and date constants or literals must be enclosed in single quotes ('A').

(vii) A command can be typed either full or first four characters.

SQL Data Types

Data types are declared to identify the type of data that will be stored in a particular field or variable.

The following list of general SQL data types are given below

Data Type	Syntax	Explanation (if applicable)
INTEGER	INTEGER or INT	A 32-bit signed integer value and its range from −2147483648 to 2147483647.
SMALLINT	SMALLINT	A 16-bit signed integer value and its range from −32768 to 32767.
NUMERIC	NUMERIC (p,s)	Where, p is a precision value and s is a scale value. e.g. numeric (6,2) is a 6 digit number that has 4 digit before the decimal and 2 digit after the decimal.
DECIMAL	DECIMAL (p,s)	Where, p is a precision value and s is a scale value. (same as NUMERIC)
REAL	REAL	Single-precision floating point number.
DOUBLE PRECISION	DOUBLE PRECISION	Double-precision floating point number.
FLOAT	FLOAT(p)	Where, p is a precision value.
CHARACTER	CHAR(x)	Where, x is the number of characters to be stored. This data type will occupy space for NULL values. It can hold atmost 255 characters.
CHARACTER VARYING	VARCHAR(x)	Where, x is the number of characters to be stored. It will occupy space for NULL values. It can hold atmost 2000 characters and used in ANSI standard.
CHARACTER VARYING	VARCHAR2 (x)	Where, x is the number of characters to be stored. It can hold 4000 bytes of characters and used only in Oracle.
DATE	DATE	Stores year, month and day values.
TIME	TIME	Stores hour, minute and second values.

SQL Command Basics

SQL database is a way of organizing a group of tables and table stores the data in the form of rows and columns.

To create a bunch of different tables that share a common theme, you would group them into one database to make the management process easier. So, for manipulating data, we need to know about database commands, which are described below

Creating and Using a Database

Create a database   Creating database is an easier task. You need to just type the name of the database in a CREATE DATABASE command.

Syntax
```
CREATE DATABASE [IF NOT
EXISTS]<database_name>;
```

Here, **CREATE DATABASE** command will create an empty database with the specified name and would not contain any table.

IF NOT EXISTS is an optional part of this statement which prevents you from an error if there exists a database with the given name in the database catalog.

For example, `mysql>CREATE DATABASE BOOK;`

Output `Query OK, 1 row affected <0.01 sec>`

Select a Database

Creating database is not enough for use. Before working with tables, first you have to select the database. The only thing need to be considered before selecting a database is that it must already exist. To select a database **USE** command is used.

Syntax `USE <database_name>;`

For example, `mysql>USE ENGBOOK;`

where, **USE** command makes the specified database as a current working database and **EGNBOOK** is the database name.

Output `Database changed`

Show Databases

To check the names of the existing databases on the server you need to use the SHOW command. This will provide you the information about databases and the contents available in it.

Syntax `SHOW DATABASES;`

For example, `mysql>SHOW DATABASES;`

Output
```
+----------+
| Database |
+----------+
| BOOK     |
| SCHOOL   |
| COPIES   |
| STUDENT  |
+----------+
```

Dropping a Database

Database can be removed or deleted using DROP command. But before deleting a database make sure that you do not need the data stored in different tables of a database because when you delete a database, all its tables also gets removed along with it.

Syntax `DROP DATABASE <database_name>;`

For example,
```
mysql>DROP DATABASE SCHOOL;
```

Output
```
Query OK, 1 row affected (0.04 sec)
```

DDL Statements/Commands

Some DDL statements are as follows

CREATE Statement

The CREATE statement is used to create a table in a database. In this command, we need to give information about table like number of columns, rows and its types and constraints.

Syntax
```
CREATE TABLE <table_name>
(
    <column_name1><data_type>[(<size>)]
                        [constraints],
    <column_name2><data_type>[(<size>)]
                        [constraints],
    <column_name3><data_type>[(<size>)]
                        [constraints],
    ....
)
```

The data type specifies what type of data, the column can hold and the size or constraint is optional.

e.g. If we want to create a table PERSONS that contains five columns: P_Id, FirstName, LastName, Address and City.

We use the following CREATE statement:
```
CREATE TABLE PERSONS
(
    P_Id INT Primary Key,
    FirstName VARCHAR(25)NOT NULL,
    LastName VARCHAR(25),
    Address VARCHAR(30),
    City VARCHAR(25)
);
```

Constraints

Constraints are the conditions that the table must satisfy. These can be enforced on the attributes of a relation. These can be specified at the time of creating table. They are used to ensure integrity of a relation, hence named as integrity constraints.

Some types of constraints are:

- **NOT NULL Constraint** It ensures that a column cannot store NULL value.
- **UNIQUE Constraint** It is used to uniquely identify each record in a database.
- **PRIMARY KEY Constraint** It ensures that a column have an unique identity, which helps to find a particular record in a table and no column that is part of the primary key constraint can contain a NULL value.
- **FOREIGN KEY Constraint** It designates a column or combination of columns as a foreign key and establishes its relationship with a primary key in different tables.
- **CHECK KEY Constraint** It is used to define condition, which column in each row must satisfy.
- **DEFAULT Constraint** It inserts default value into a column.

Show Statement

The show or list table is very important when we have many databases that contain various tables. Sometimes the table names are the same in many databases. In that case, this query is very useful. We can get the number of table information of a database using the following statement.

```
mysql>
```

e.g.

Suppose we have database Company in which Department, Accountant, Wages are tables. To show the name of all the tables present in database Company, so following command is used

```
mysql>Use Company; Database changed
mysql>SHOW TABLES;
```

Output

```
+-------------------+
| Tables_in_Company |
+-------------------+
| Department        |
| Accountant        |
| Wages             |
+-------------------+
```

DESCRIBE Statement

DESCRIBE or DESC   command is used to verify the structure of a table that you have created.

This command display the column names, available data items with their data types.

Syntax   `DESCRIBE <table_name>;`

or

`DESC <table_name>;`

For example, `DESC PERSONS;`

Output

```
+-----------+-------------+------+-----+---------+-------+
| Field     | Type        | Null | Key | Default | Extra |
+-----------+-------------+------+-----+---------+-------+
| P_Id      | Int         | NO   | PRI |         |       |
| FirstName | varchar(25) | NO   |     |         |       |
| LastName  | varchar(25) | YES  |     |         |       |
| Address   | varchar(30) | YES  |     |         |       |
| City      | varchar(25) | YES  |     |         |       |
+-----------+-------------+------+-----+---------+-------+
```

DROP Statement

The DROP statement is used to remove the table definition and all data, constraints and permission specified for that table.

You have to be careful while using the DROP command because once the table is deleted, then all the information available in the table would be lost forever. But there is a condition for dropping a table; it must be empty. A table with rows in it cannot be dropped.

Syntax `DROP TABLE table_name;`

e.g.   `DROP TABLE EMPLOYEE;`

The above query will delete the table EMPLOYEE and after this, no table with Employee name would exist.

We cannot even rollback after dropping a table.

ALTER Statement

The ALTER statement is used to add, delete or modify columns and constraints in the existing table.

To ADD a Column

Syntax

```
ALTER TABLE table_name ADD column_name
data_type;
```

e.g. `ALTER TABLE STUDENT ADD Section CHAR;`

The above query will add column Section to STUDENT table, whose data type is character.

To DROP Column

Syntax `ALTER TABLE table_name DROP COLUMN column_name;`

e.g. `ALTER TABLE STUDENT DROP COLUMN location;`

The above query will delete a column location from STUDENT table.

To MODIFY Column Data Type

Syntax `ALTER TABLE table_name MODIFY column_name data_type;`

e.g. `ALTER TABLE STUDENT MODIFY Fee NUMBER(15,2);`

The above query will modify the data type of Fee column, of STUDENT table.

To DELETE a Constraint

Syntax
```
ALTER TABLE table_name DROP
Constraint_Name;
```
e.g. `ALTER TABLE STUDENT DROP Primary Key;`

The above query will delete the primary key constraint from STUDENT table.

RENAME Statement

The RENAME statement is used to rename a table.

Syntax
```
RENAME old_table_name TO new_table_name;
```
e.g. `RENAME STUDENT TO CANDIDATE;`

The above query will rename STUDENT table to CANDIDATE.

DML Statements/Commands

Some DML statements are as follows

INSERT Statement

The INSERT statement is used to insert a new row/data in a table.

Syntax
```
INSERT INTO table_name VALUES
                (value1, value2, value3,...);
```
or
```
INSERT INTO table_name(column1, column2,
column3,...)VALUES(value1, value2,
value3,...);
```

e.g. If we have the following PERSONS table

P_Id	LastName	FirstName	Address	City
1	Hansen	Ola	Timoteivn 10	Sandnes
2	Svendson	Tove	Borgvn 23	Sandnes
3	Pettersen	Kari	Storgt 20	Stavanger

and we want to insert a new row in the PERSONS table.

We use the following SQL statement
```
INSERT INTO PERSONS VALUES (4,'Nilsen',
Johan', 'Bakken 2', 'Stavanger');
```
The PERSONS table will now look like this

P_Id	LastName	FirstName	Address	City
1	Hansen	Ola	Timoteivn 10	Sandnes
2	Svendson	Tove	Borgvn 23	Sandnes
3	Pettersen	Kari	Storgt 20	Stavanger
4	Nilsen	Johan	Bakken 2	Stavanger

Insert Data Only in Specified Columns

It is also possible to add data only in specific columns.

e.g. The following SQL statement will add a new row, but add data only in the P_Id, LastName and the FirstName columns.

We use the following SQL statement
```
INSERT INTO PERSONS(P_Id, LastName,
            FirstName)
VALUES(5, 'Tjessem', 'Jakob');
```
The PERSONS table will now look like this

P_Id	LastName	FirstName	Address	City
1	Hansen	Ola	Timoteivn10	Sandnes
2	Svendson	Tove	Borgvn 23	Sandnes
3	Pettersen	Kari	Storgt 20	Stavanger
4	Nilsen	Johan	Bakken 2	Stavanger
5	Tjessem	Jakob	NULL	NULL

SELECT Statement

The SELECT statement is used to select data from a database or view table information. The result is stored in a result table, called the result set.

Syntax

To select some specify columns
```
SELECT column_name(s) FROM table_name;
```
or
To select all columns
```
SELECT * FROM table_name;
```

SQL is not case sensitive. SELECT is the same as select. The asterisk (*) is a quick way of selecting all columns.

In SQL, SELECT clause is used to list the attributes desired in the result of a query and FROM clause is used to list the relations from which such columns are to be extracted.

e.g. If we want to select the content of the columns named LastName and FirstName from the PERSONS table.

We have to use the following SELECT statement
```
SELECT LastName,FirstName FROM PERSONS;
```
The result set will look like this

LastName	FirstName
Hansen	Ola
Svendson	Tove
Pettersen	Kari

e.g. If we want to select all the columns from the PERSONS table.

We have to use the following SELECT statement
```
SELECT * FROM PERSONS;
```

The result set will look like this

P_Id	LastName	FirstName	Address	City
1	Hansen	Ola	Timoteivn 10	Sandnes
2	Svendson	Tove	Borgvn 23	Sandnes
3	Pettersen	Kari	Storgt 20	Stavanger

Column Alias

Column alias is used to temporarily rename a table's column for the purpose of a particular query. This renaming is a temporary change and the actual column name does not change in the database.

Syntax `SELECT <column_name1> AS <Alias_name> FROM <table_name>;`

Alias_name specifies the reference name of the specified column.

For example, to select the DOJ of all the employees referenced as Joining_Date from the table COMPANY the query would be like

```
mysql> SELECT DOJ AS Joining_Date FROM COMPANY;
```

Query produces the following output

```
+-------------------+
|   Joining_Date    |
+-------------------+
|    2012-02-06     |
|    2002-12-04     |
|    2004-08-06     |
|    2007-09-06     |
|    2001-07-06     |
|    2012-05-06     |
|    2001-02-06     |
+-------------------+
7 rows in set (0.00 sec)
```

Operators in SQL

SQL supports different types of operators, some of them are described below

Arithmetic Operators

These operators are used to perform mathematical calculations, such as addition, subtraction, multiplication, division and remainder.

Some most important arithmetic operators used in SQL are

OPERATOR	DESCRIPTION
+ (Addition)	Add the two arguments together
− (Subtraction)	Subtract the second argument from the first argument
* (Multiplication)	Multiplies the two arguments
/ (Division)	Divide the first argument by the second argument
% (Modulo)	Divide the first argument from the second argument and provides the remainder of that operation

Syntax

```
SELECT  <Expression1> <arithmetic operator>
     <Expression2>
     [FROM <table_name>]
     [WHERE <Condition>];
```

For example, query to display **EMP_NAME, EMP_DEPT_NO** and 20% of **EMP_SALARY** for each employee for social fund.

```
mysql>  SELECT EMP_NAME, EMP_DEPT_NO,
     EMP_SALARY*0.20
     FROM COMPANY;
```

Above query produces the following output

```
+--------------+-------------+----------------+
| EMP_NAME     | EMP_DEPT_NO | EMP_SALARY*0.20|
+--------------+-------------+----------------+
| Rahul Sharma |     D05     |      5120      |
| Vikas Mittal |     D03     |      5200      |
| Puneet Jain  |     D05     |      4200      |
| Sachin Vats  |     D02     |      4700      |
| Uday Singh   |     D03     |      5200      |
| Ravi Shukla  |     D01     |      4700      |
| Vinay Rana   |     D03     |      4800      |
+--------------+-------------+----------------+
7 rows in set (0.00 sec)
```

Arithmetic operators can be implemented through simple SELECT statement without any table. This acts like a function.

For example,

```
SELECT 35*2+5;
```

Above query produces the following output

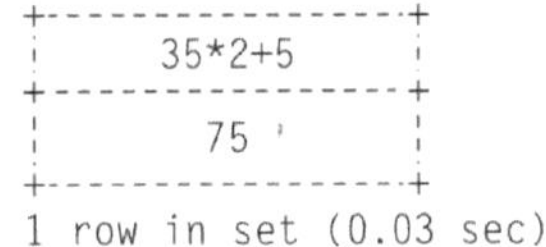

```
+-------------+
|   35*2+5    |
+-------------+
|     75      |
+-------------+
1 row in set (0.03 sec)
```

Comparison Operators

These operators are used to test or compare the value of two operands, *i.e.*, between two variables or between a variable and a constant.

If the condition is false, then the result is zero (0) and if the condition is true, then the result is non-zero. These operators are also called **relational operators.**

Some of the comparison/relational operators used in SQL are as follows

OPERATOR	DESCRIPTION
=	Equal to
>	Greater than
<	Less than
>=	Greater than or equal to
<=	Less than or equal to

OPERATOR	DESCRIPTION
<> or !=	Not equal to (not ISO standard)
!<	Not less than (not ISO standard)
!>	Not greater than (not ISO standard)

Syntax

```
SELECT <column name>|*|expression
FROM <table name> WHERE<expression>
<comparison operator> <expression>;
```

For example, query to display **EMP_NAME** and **EMP_SALARY** for those employees whose salary is greater than or equal to 25000.

```
mysql>  SELECT EMP_NAME,EMP_SALARY
        FROM COMPANY
        WHERE EMP_SALARY> = 25000;
```

Query produces the following output

```
+--------------+--------------+
| EMP_NAME     | EMP_SALARY   |
+--------------+--------------+
| Rahul Sharma |    25600     |
| Vikas Mittal |    26000     |
| Uday Singh   |    26000     |
+--------------+--------------+
3 rows in set (0.00 sec)
```

When we use relational operators with character data type, < means earlier in the alphabet and > means later in the alphabet 'Bangalore '<' 'Brajil' as 'a' comes before 'r' in alphabet.

Logical Operators

The logical operators compare two conditions at a time to determine whether a row can be selected for the output. Logical operators are also called **boolean operators**, because these operators return a boolean data type value as TRUE, or FALSE.

When retrieving data using a SELECT statement, you can use these operators in the WHERE clause, which allows you to combine more than one condition.

Some of the Boolean/Logical operators used in SQL are as follows

OPERATOR	DESCRIPTION
AND	Logical AND compares two expressions and return true, when both expressions are true
OR	Logical OR compares two expressions and return true, when atleast one of the expressions is true
NOT	NOT takes a single expression as an argument and changes its value from false to true or from true to false. You can use an exclamation point (!) in place of this operator

Syntax

```
SELECT <column name>|*|<expression>
FROM <table name>
WHERE <expressions> <boolean operator>
<expressions>;
```

For example, query to display **EMP_CODE** and **EMP_NAME** for those employees whose **EMP_DEPT_NO** is D05 and **EMP_SALARY** is greater than 22000.

```
mysql>  SELECT EMP_CODE,EMP_NAME
        FROM COMPANY
        WHERE (EMP_DEPT_NO='D05'AND
        EMP_SALARY >22000);
```

Query produces the following output

```
+-----------+--------------+
| EMP_CODE  | EMP_NAME     |
+-----------+--------------+
| 100       | Rahul Sharma |
+-----------+--------------+
1 rows in set (0.00 sec)
```

For example, query to display **EMP_CODE** and **EMP_NAME** for those employees whose **EMP_DEPT_NO** is D05 or '**EMP_SALARY**' is greater than 22000.

```
mysql>  SELECT EMP_CODE, EMP_NAME
        FROM COMPANY
        WHERE(EMP_DEP_NO = 'D05' OR
        EMP_SALARY>22000);
```

Above query produces the following output

```
+-----------+--------------+
| EMP_CODE  | EMP_NAME     |
+-----------+--------------+
|    100    | Rahul Sharma |
|    101    | Vikas Mittal |
|    102    | Puneet Jain  |
|    103    | Sachin Vats  |
|    104    | Uday Singh   |
|    105    | Ravi Shukla  |
|    106    | Vinay Rana   |
+-----------+--------------+
7 rows in set (0.00 sec)
```

For example, query to display **EMP_CODE** and **EMP_NAME** for the employee whose **EMP_SALARY** is not greater than 22000.

```
mysql>  SELECT EMP_CODE, EMP_NAME
        FROM COMPANY
        WHERE(NOT EMP_SALARY>22000);
                    or
mysql>  SELECT EMP_CODE, EMP_NAME
        FROM COMPANY
        WHERE !(EMP_SALARY>22000);
```

Above query produces the following output

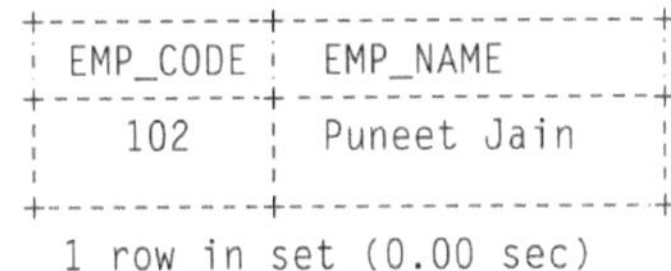

```
+----------+---------------+
| EMP_CODE | EMP_NAME      |
+----------+---------------+
|   102    | Puneet Jain   |
+----------+---------------+
1 row in set (0.00 sec)
```

DISTINCT Keyword

In a table, some of the columns may contain duplicate values. This is not a problem, however, sometimes you may want to list only the different (distinct) values in a table.

The DISTINCT keyword can be used to return only distinct (different) values in a particular column or a whole table.

Syntax
```
SELECT DISTINCT column_name(s)
FROM table_name;
```

e.g. If we want to select only the distinct values from the column named "City" from the PERSONS table.

We have to use the following SELECT statement
```
SELECT DISTINCT City FROM PERSONS;
```

The result set will look like this

City
Sandnes
Stavanger

ALL Keyword

ALL clause result just the same as that when you do not specify DISTINCT. It will give values of selected attribute from every row of table without considering the duplicate records.

Syntax
```
SELECT ALL column_name FROM table_name;
```

WHERE Clause

The WHERE clause is used to extract only those records that fulfill a specified criteria.

Syntax
```
SELECT column_name(s) FROM table_name
WHERE condition;
```

e.g. If we want to select only the persons living in the city "Sandnes" from the table PERSONS.

We use the following SELECT statement
```
SELECT * FROM PERSONS
WHERE City='Sandnes';
```

The result set will look like this

P_Id	LastName	FirstName	Address	City
1	Hansen	Ola	Timoteivn 10	Sandnes
2	Svendson	Tove	Borgvn 23	Sandnes

Operators Allowed in the WHERE Clause

(i) **BETWEEN Operator** selects a range of data between two values. The values can be numbers, text or dates.

Syntax
```
SELECT column_name(s)
FROM table_name
WHERE column_name
BETWEEN value1 AND value2;
```

e.g. If we want to select the persons with a last name alphabetically between "Hansen" and "Pettersen" from the table PERSONS.

We use the following SELECT statement
```
SELECT * FROM PERSONS
WHERE LastName
BETWEEN 'Hansen' AND 'Pettersen';
```

The result set will look like this

P_Id	LastName	FirstName	Address	City
1	Hansen	Ola	Timoteivn 10	Sandnes
3	Pettersen	Kari	Storgt 20	Stavanger

(ii) **NOT BETWEEN Operator** selects the data outside the range of data between two values. The values can be text, numbers or dates.

Syntax
```
SELECT column_name(s)
FROM table_name
WHERE column_name
NOT BETWEEN value1 AND value2;
```

e.g. To display the persons outside the range in the previous example, use NOT BETWEEN operator.

We use the following SELECT statement
```
SELECT * FROM PERSONS
WHERE LastName
NOT BETWEEN 'Hansen' AND 'Pettersen';
```

The result set will look like this

P_Id	LastName	FirstName	Address	City
2	Svendson	Tove	Borgvn 23	Sandnes

(iii) **LIKE Operator** is used to match a value similar to specific pattern in a column using % and _. The % sign represents zero, one or multiple characters, while _ represents a single character. It is useful when you want to search rows to match a specific pattern, or when you do not know the entire value.

Syntax
```
SELECT column_name FROM table_name
WHERE column_name LIKE "condition";
```

e.g. To display the FirstName that start with letter "T".

We use the following SELECT statement
```
SELECT FirstName FROM PERSONS
WHERE FirstName LIKE "T%";
```

The result set will look like this

FirstName
Tove

e.g. If we want to display the all records, where the LastName's second letter is 'a'.

We use the following SELECT statement

```
SELECT * FROM PERSONS
WHERE LastName LIKE"_a%";
```

The result set will look like this

P_Id	LastName	FirstName	Address	City
1	Hansen	Ola	Timoteivn 10	Sandnes

(iv) **IN Operator** checks a value within a set of values separated by commas and retrieve the rows from the table which are matching.

The IN operator allows you to specify multiple values in a WHERE clause.

Syntax

```
SELECT column_name(s)
FROM table_name
WHERE column_name IN (value1,value2,...);
```

e.g. If we want to select the persons with a last name equal to "Hansen" or "Pettersen" from the table PERSONS.

We use the following SELECT statement

```
SELECT * FROM PERSONS
WHERE LastName IN
    ('Hansen','Pettersen');
```

The result set will look like this

P_Id	LastName	FirstName	Address	City
1	Hansen	Ola	Timoteivn 10	Sandnes
3	Pettersen	Kari	Storgt 20	Stavanger

ORDER BY Clause

The ORDER BY keyword is used to sort the result set along a specified column with the SELECT command. The ORDER BY keyword sorts the records in ascending order by default. If you want to sort the records in a descending order, you can use the DESC keyword.

Syntax
```
SELECT column_name(s)
    FROM table_name
    ORDER BY column_name(s)ASC/DESC;
```

e.g. If we want to select all the persons from the table PERSONS, however, we want to sort the persons by their last name in ascending order.

We use the following SELECT statement
```
SELECT * FROM PERSONS
ORDER BY LastName ASC;
```

The result set will look like this

P_Id	LastName	FirstName	Address	City
1	Hansen	Ola	Timoteivn 10	Sandnes
3	Pettersen	Kari	Storgt 20	Stavanger
2	Svendson	Tove	Borgvn 23	Sandnes

UPDATE Statement

The UPDATE statement is used to update existing records in a table.

The WHERE clause in the UPDATE statement specifies, which record or records that should be updated. If you omit the WHERE clause, all records will be updated.

Note Expressions are also used in the SET clause of the UPDATE command to manipulate the values.

Syntax
```
UPDATE table_name
    SET column1=value1, column2=value2,...
    WHERE <condition>;
```

e.g. If we want to update the person "Ola Hansen" in the PERSONS table.

We use the following SQL statement
```
UPDATE PERSONS
SET Address='Nissestien 67',
City ='Sandnes'
WHERE LastName='Hansen' AND
FirstName='Ola';
```

The PERSONS table will now look like this

P_Id	LastName	FirstName	Address	City
1	Hansen	Ola	Nissestien 67	Sandnes
2	Svendson	Tove	Borgvn 23	Sandnes
3	Pettersen	Kari	Storgt 20	Stavanger

SQL UPDATE Warning

Be careful when updating records. If we omit the WHERE clause in the example above, like this:
```
UPDATE PERSONS
SET Address='Nissestien 67',
City='Sandnes';
```

The PERSONS table would have looked like this

P_Id	LastName	FirstName	Address	City
1	Hansen	Ola	Nissestien 67	Sandnes
2	Svendson	Tove	Nissestien 67	Sandnes
3	Pettersen	Kari	Nissestien 67	Sandnes

DELETE Statement

The DELETE statement is used to delete rows in a table. The WHERE clause in the DELETE statement specifies, which records to be deleted. If you omit the WHERE clause, all records will be deleted.

Syntax `DELETE FROM table_name WHERE <condition>;`

e.g. If we want to delete the person "Kari Pettersen" in the PERSONS table.

We use the following SQL statement

```
DELETE FROM PERSONS
WHERE LastName='Pettersen'
AND FirstName='Kari';
```

The PERSONS table will now look like this

P_Id	LastName	FirstName	Address	City
1	Hansen	Ola	Timoteivn 10	Sandnes
2	Svendson	Tove	Borgvn 23	Sandnes

Delete All Rows

It is possible to delete all rows in a table without deleting the table. This means that the table structure, attributes and indexes will be intact.

Syntax `DELETE FROM table_name;`

Working with NULL Values

In SQL, the empty values are represented as NULL in a table. If a table having null values, then you can display columns with null values or without null values and you can replace NULL values with another value.

To handle NULL values in SQL, you should use the following commands

IS NULL Clause

If we want to search the column whose value is NULL in a table, then we use IS NULL clause.

Syntax

```
SELECT<column_name> FROM <table_name>
WHERE <column_name> IS NULL;
```

e.g. Let us consider the following table Teacher:

T_No	T_Name	T_Salary	DOJ
T01	Aradhna	17000	2013-01-08
T02	Ritika	NULL	2013-12-14
T03	Ravindra	NULL	2013-11-23
T04	Dushyant	16000	2014-01-10
T05	Swati	19000	2014-02-10

Query to display column whose value is NULL.

We use the following SQL statement

```
SELECT * FROM Teacher
WHERE T_Salary IS NULL;
```

Above query produces the following output

T_No	T_Name	T_Salary	DOJ
T02	Ritika	NULL	2013-12-14
T03	Ravindra	NULL	2013-11-23

IS NOT NULL Clause

If we want to search the column whose value is not NULL in a table then we use IS NOT NULL clause.

Syntax
```
SELECT<column name> FROM <table_name>
WHERE <column_name> IS NOT NULL;
```

e.g. Consider the above table Teacher. Query to display column whose value is not NULL.

We use the following SQL statement

```
SELECT * FROM Teacher
WHERE T_Salary IS NOT NULL;
```

Above query produces the following output

T_No	T_Name	T_Salary	DOJ
T01	Aradhna	17000	2013-01-08
T04	Dushyant	16000	2014-01-10
T05	Swati	19000	2014-02-10

Aggregate Functions

Aggregate functions are also known as **group functions**. Aggregate functions return a result only in single row based on group of rows, rather than on single row. It always appears in SELECT command and in ORDER BY and HAVING clauses. They are commonly used with the GROUP BY clause in a SELECT statement. Some of the aggregate functions are MIN, MAX, SUM, AVG, COUNT. The SQL aggregate functions return a single value, calculated from values in a column.

There are different types of aggregate functions

AVG()

This function returns the average value of a specified column.

Syntax
```
SELECT AVG(column_name)
FROM table_name;
```

e.g. Consider the following table PAYMENTS:

Empid	Emp_Name	Salary	Department
1	Ridhi	20000	D1
2	Rohit	25000	D2
3	Rakesh	20000	D2
4	Roshan	44000	D1
5	Rohini	15000	D3
6	Radha	14000	D1

To display the average of employees salary from PAYMENTS table.

```
SELECT AVG(Salary) FROM PAYMENTS;
Output
```

AVG(Salary)
23000

COUNT( )

This function returns the total number of values or rows of the specified field or column. COUNT (*) is a special function, as it returns the count of all rows in a specified table. It includes all the null and duplicate values.

Syntax
```
SELECT COUNT(*) FROM table_name;
```
e.g. To count the total number of employees from PAYMENTS table.
```
SELECT COUNT(*) "Employees" FROM PAYMENTS;
Output
```

Employees
6

DISTINCT Clause with COUNT( ) Function

The DISTINCT keyword helps us in removing the duplicate value from the result. When it is used with aggregate function COUNT, it returns the number of distinct rows in a specified table.

Syntax
```
SELECT COUNT(DISTINCT column_name)
    FROM table_name;
```
e.g. To count total number of rows in Department column from PAYMENTS table.
```
SELECT COUNT(Department) "Deptid"
FROM PAYMENTS;
Output
```

Deptid
6

e.g. To count distinct values of column Department from PAYMENTS table.
```
SELECT COUNT(DISTINCT Department) "Deptid"
FROM PAYMENTS;
```
Output

Deptid
3

MAX( )

This function returns the largest value from the selected column.

Syntax
```
SELECT MAX(column_name)
    FROM table_name;
```
e.g. To find the maximum salary of employee from PAYMENTS table.
```
SELECT MAX(Salary) "Maximum"
FROM PAYMENTS;
```
Output

Maximum
44000

MIN( )

This function returns the smallest value from the selected column.

Syntax
```
SELECT MIN(column_name)
    FROM table_name;
```
e.g. To display the minimum salary of employee from PAYMENTS table.
```
SELECT MIN(Salary) "Minimum"
FROM PAYMENTS;
```
Output

Minimum
14000

SUM( )

This function returns the sum of values in the specified column. The SUM works on numeric fields only. Null values are excluded from the result returned.

Syntax
```
SELECT SUM(column_name)
    FROM table_name;
```
e.g. To count sum of employee's salary from PAYMENTS table.
```
SELECT SUM(Salary) "Salary"
FROM PAYMENTS;
```
Output

Salary
138000

GROUP BY Statement

The GROUP BY statement is used with the aggregate functions to group the result set by one or more columns.

Syntax
```
SELECT column_name,
    aggregate_function(column_name)
    FROM table_name
    WHERE condition
    GROUP BY column_name;
```
Consider the following ORDERS table

TABLE: ORDERS

O_Id	OrderDate	OrderPrice	Customer
1	2008/11/12	1000	Hansen
2	2008/10/23	1600	Nilsen
3	2008/09/02	700	Hansen
4	2008/09/03	300	Hansen
5	2008/08/30	2000	Jensen
6	2008/10/04	100	Nilsen

e.g. If we want to find the total sum (OrderPrice) of each customer from table ORDERS.

We use the following SQL statement

```
SELECT Customer, SUM(OrderPrice)
FROM ORDERS
GROUP BY Customer;
```

The result set will look like this

Customer	SUM(OrderPrice)
Hansen	2000
Nilsen	1700
Jensen	2000

Let's see what happens if we omit the GROUP BY statement:

```
SELECT Customer,SUM(OrderPrice)
FROM ORDERS;
```

The result set will look like this

Customer	SUM(OrderPrice)
Hansen	5700

In the above case, SELECT statement cannot be used, because the SELECT statement above has two columns specified (Customer and SUM(OrderPrice)). The "SUM(OrderPrice)" returns a single value (that is the total sum of the `"OrderPrice" column), while "Customer" returns 6 values (one value for each row in the "ORDERS" table). This will therefore not give us the correct result. However, you have seen that the GROUP BY statement solves this problem.

HAVING Clause

The HAVING clause is used with GROUP BY clause to place condition because the WHERE keyword could not be used with aggregate functions.

Syntax

```
SELECT column_name,
aggregate_function(column_name)
FROM table_name
WHERE condition
GROUP BY column_name
HAVING aggregate_function(column_name)
                        <condition>;
```

e.g. If we want to find any of the customers have a total order of less than 2000 from table ORDERS.

We use the following SQL statement

```
SELECT Customer,SUM(OrderPrice)
FROM ORDERS
GROUP BY Customer
HAVING SUM(OrderPrice)<2000;
```

The result set will look like this

Customer	SUM(OrderPrice)
Nilsen	1700

e.g. If we want to find the customers 'Hansen' or 'Jensen' have a total order of more than 1500.

We add an ordinary WHERE clause to the SQL statement

```
SELECT Customer,SUM(OrderPrice)
FROM ORDERS
WHERE Customer='Hansen' OR
Customer='Jensen'
GROUP BY Customer
HAVING SUM(OrderPrice)>1500;
```

The result set will look like this

Customer	SUM(OrderPrice)
Hansen	2000
Jensen	2000

Join

A join is a query that combines rows from two or more tables. In a join query, more than one tables are listed in FROM clause. The function of combining data from multiple tables is called joining. SQL can obtain data from several related tables by performing either a physical or virtual join on the tables.

Joins are used when we have to select data from two or more tables. Joins are used to extract data from two (or more) tables, when we need a relationship between certain columns in these tables.

The SQL Join condition is always used in the WHERE clause of SELECT, UPDATE and DELETE statements.

There are different kind of SQL joins

Equi Join

Equi join is a simple SQL join condition that uses equal sign as a comparison operator.

Syntax
```
SELECT col1, col2, col3
FROM table1, table2
WHERE table1.col1 = table2.col1;
```

Consider the following tables PERSON and ORDERS

Table : PERSON

P_Id	Last_Name	First_Name	City
1	Sharma	Abhay	Mumbai
2	Gupta	Mohan	Delhi
3	Verma	Akhil	Mumbai

Table : ORDERS

O_Id	Order_No	P_Id
1	10050	3
2	25000	3
3	5687	1
4	45000	1
5	35000	15

e.g. To join two tables PERSON and ORDERS using a condition (i.e. P_Id of PERSON table is equal to the P_Id of ORDERS table).

We use the following SQL statement

```
SELECT Last_Name, First_Name, Order_No
FROM PERSON, ORDERS
WHERE PERSON.P_Id=ORDERS.P_Id
ORDER BY PERSON.Last_Name;
```

The query will give us the below result

Last_Name	First_Name	Order_No
Sharma	Abhay	5687
Sharma	Abhay	45000
Verma	Akhil	10050
Verma	Akhil	25000

SQL equi joins are further classified into two categories

(i) Inner Join

The inner join using either of the equivalent queries gives the intersection of two tables, i.e. it returns us the rows, which are common in both the tables.

Syntax

```
SELECT col1, col2
FROM table1 INNER JOIN table2
ON table1.column_name=table2.column_name;
```

e.g. To perform INNER JOIN on two tables PERSON and ORDERS.

We use the following SQL statement

```
SELECT Last_Name, First_Name FROM
PERSON INNER JOIN ORDERS ON
PERSON.P_Id=ORDERS.P_Id;
```

The result set will look like this

Last_Name	First_Name
Verma	Akhil
Verma	Akhil
Sharma	Abhay
Sharma	Abhay

(ii) Outer Join

The outer join include rows in a joined result even when they have no match in the joined table. An outer join returns all rows that satisfy the join condition and also returns those rows from one table for which no rows from the other satisfy the join condition.

Left Outer Join The left outer join returns all the rows from the left table, even if there are no matches in the right table.

Syntax

```
SELECT column 1, column 2
FROM table1 LEFT JOIN table2 ON
table1.column_name = table2.column_name;
```

e.g. To perform LEFT OUTER JOIN on two tables PERSON and ORDERS.

We use the following SQL statement

```
SELECT P.Last_Name,
P.First_Name,O.Order_No
FROM PERSON P
LEFT JOIN ORDERS O
ON P.P_Id = O.P_Id ORDER BY
P.First_Name;
```

The query will give us the below result

Last_Name	First_Name	Order_No
Sharma	Abhay	5687
Sharma	Abhay	45000
Verma	Akhil	25000
Verma	Akhil	10050
Gupta	Mohan	

Right Outer Join The right outer join returns all the rows from the right table, even if there are no matches in the left table.

Syntax

```
SELECT column1, column2
FROM table1 RIGHT JOIN table2
ON table1.column_name=table2.column_name;
```

e.g. To perform RIGHT OUTER JOIN on two tables PERSON and ORDERS.

We use the following SQL statement

```
SELECT P.Last_Name, P.First_Name,
O.Order_No FROM PERSON P RIGHT JOIN ORDERS
ON P.P_Id = O.P_Id
ORDER BY P.Last_Name;
```

The query will give us the below result

Last_Name	First_Name	Order_No
Sharma	Abhay	45000
Sharma	Abhay	5687
Verma	Akhil	25000
Verma	Akhil	10050
		35000

Self Join

A self join is a join, where we join a particular table to itself. Here in this case, it is necessary to ensure that the join statement defines an ALIAS name for both the copies of the tables to avoid column ambiguity. Consider the following table COURSE:

Table : COURSE

Course_Id	Course_Name	Pre_Course
1	C	NULL
2	C++	1
3	Java	2
4	C#	3
5	VB.NET	3

e.g. To perform SELF JOIN on COURSE table.

We use the following SQL statement

```
SELECT a.Course_Name AS COURSE,
b.Course_Name AS Prerequisite_Course
FROM COURSE a, COURSE b
WHERE a.Pre_Course = b.Course_Id;
```

The result set will look like this

COURSE	Prerequisite_Course
C++	C
Java	C++
C#	Java
VB.NET	Java

Non-Equi Join

Non-equi join is used to return the result from two or more tables, where exact join is not possible. The SQL non-equi join uses comparison operators instead of, the equal sign like $>, <, >=, <=$ alongwith conditions.

Syntax

```
SELECT * FROM table1, table2
WHERE table1.column > table2.column;
```

Consider the following tables

Table: EMP

empno	ename	sal	date
110	Priya	7000	11-11-2010
111	Seema	14000	15-02-2014
151	Sachin	30000	18-04-2015
142	Deepa	25000	20-05-2015

Table : SALGRADE

empno	city	lowsal	hisal	grade
110	Delhi	5000	10000	2
111	NCR	11000	13000	1
142	Meerut	10000	20000	5

e.g. To perform NON-EQUI JOIN on two tables EMP and SALGRADE.

We use the following SQL statement

```
SELECT e.empno, e.ename, e.sal, s.grade
FROM EMP e, SALGRADE s
WHERE e.sal BETWEEN s.lowsal AND s.hisal;
```

The result set will look like this

empno	ename	sal	grade
110	Priya	7000	2
111	Seema	14000	5

Natural Join

The natural join is a type of equi join and is structured in such a way that, columns with same name of associated tables will appear once only.

Syntax

```
SELECT * FROM table1
NATURAL JOIN table2;
```

Consider the following tables

Table : FOODS

Item_Id	Item_Name	Item_Unit	Company_Id
1	Chex Mix	Pcs	16
6	Cheez-it	Pcs	15
2	Biscuit	Pcs	15
3	Munch	Pcs	17
4	Rice	Pcs	15
5	Cake	Pcs	18
7	Snake	Pcs	NULL

Table : COMPANY

Company_Id	Company_Name	Company_City
18	Order All	Boston
15	Jack Hill Ltd	London
16	Akas Foods	Delhi
17	Foodies	London
19	Sip_n_Bite	New York

e.g. To fetch all the unique columns from 'FOODS' and 'COMPANY' tables, after joining these tables.

We use the following SQL statement

```
SELECT * FROM FOODS NATURAL JOIN COMPANY
WHERE FOODS.Company_Id=COMPANY.Company_Id;
```

The result set will look like this

Item_ Id	Item_ Name	Item_ Unit	Company_ Id	Company_ Name	Company_ City
1	Chex Mix	Pcs	16	Akas Foods	Delhi
6	Cheez-it	Pcs	15	Jack Hill Ltd	London
2	Biscuit	Pcs	15	Jack Hill Ltd	London
3	Munch	Pcs	17	Foodies	London
4	Rice	Pcs	15	Jack Hill Ltd	London
5	Cake	Pcs	18	Order All	Boston

Chapter Practice

Objective Questions

• Multiple Choice Questions

1. Which of the following is/are advantage(s) of SQL?
   (a) High speed   (b) Client/server language
   (c) Easy to learn   (d) All of these

Ans. (d) High speed, client/server language, easy to learn and understand are advantages of SQL. It is portable and used for relational database.

2. Which of the following command is used to remove the table definition and all data?
   (a) CREATE   (b) SELECT
   (c) DROP   (d) None of these

Ans. (c) DROP command is used to remove the table definition and all data.

3. Which of the following is a correct syntax to add a column in SQL command?
   (a) `ALTER TABLE table_name ADD column_name data_type;`
   (b) `ALTER TABLE ADD column_name data_type;`
   (c) `ALTER table_name ADD column_name data_type;`
   (d) None of the above

Ans. (a) Syntax to add a column in SQL command is
   `ALTER TABLE table_name ADD column_name data_type;`

4. Which keyword can be used to return only different values in a particular column or a whole table?
   (a) WHERE   (b) DISTINCT
   (c) ALL   (d) BETWEEN

Ans. (b) DISTINCT keyword can be used to return only different values in a particular column or a whole table.

5. The .... keyword sorts the records in ascending order by default.
   (a) LIKE   (b) UPDATE
   (c) ORDER   (d) ORDER BY

Ans. (d) ORDER BY keyword sorts the records in ascending order by default.

6. The clause used to check NULL values is
   (a) IS NULL
   (b) IS NOT NULL
   (c) Both (a) and (b)
   (d) None of the above

Ans. (a) The IS NULL clause is used to check NULL values in a field.

7. The .... operator is used for pattern matching.
   (a) BETWEEN   (b) LIKE
   (c) IN   (d) LOOKSLIKE

Ans. (b) The LIKE operator is used to match patterns in a field.

8. To delete all the records from a table "Product" the command will be
   (a) `DEL FROM Product;`
   (b) `DELETE FROM Product;`
   (c) `REMOVE ALL FROM Product;`
   (d) `DELETE ALL;`

Ans. (b) To delete all the records from a table "Product" the command will be
   `DELETE FROM Product;`

9. The .... character displays all the columns of a table in a SELECT query.
   (a) #   (b) @   (c) *   (d) /

Ans. (c) The * character displays all the columns in a SELECT query.

10. The .... command removes a table completely.
   (a) DELETE   (b) REMOVE
   (c) DROP   (d) UPDATE

Ans. (c) The DROP command removes a table completely along with its data.

11. The "SET" clause is used along with .... command.
   (a) DELETE   (b) DESCRIBE
   (c) CREATE   (d) UPDATE

Ans. (d) The UPDATE command updates data of a table . It uses the "SET" clause to specify the field to be updated.

12. What is true about the following SQL statement?

```
mysql> SELECT*FROM Student;          (NCERT)
```

(a) Displays contents of table 'Student'.
(b) Displays column names and contents of table 'Student'.
(c) Results in error as improper case has been used.
(d) Displays only the column names of table 'Student'.

Ans. (b) The command displays entire contents of the table along with column names.

13. Which operator is used to compare a value to a specified list of values?

(a) ANY   (b) BETWEEN
(c) ALL   (d) IN

Ans. (d) The IN operator easily tests the expression, if it matches any value in a specified list of value.

14. Which of the following is the correct order of a SQL statement?

(a) SELECT, GROUP By, WHERE, HAVING
(b) SELECT, WHERE, GROUP BY, HAVING
(c) SELECT, HAVING, WHERE, GROUP BY
(d) SELECT, WHERE, HAVING, GROUP BY

Ans. (b) In SQL statement, the WHERE clause always comes before GROUP BY and HAVING clause always comes after GROUP BY. Hence, option (b) is correct.

15. …… provides statements for creation and deletion of the database tables, views.

(a) DDL   (b) DCL
(c) DML   (d) TCL

Ans. (a) DDL (Data Definition Language) provides statements for creation and deletion of database tables, views.

16. Which of the following is not an aggregate function?

(a) AVG()   (b) ADD()
(c) MAX()   (d) COUNT()

Ans. (b) There is no aggregate function named ADD() but SUM() is an aggregate function which performs mathematical sum of multiple rows having numerical values.

17. Which aggregate function returns the count of all rows in a specified table?

(a) SUM()   (b) DISTINCT()
(c) COUNT()   (d) None of these

Ans. (c) COUNT() function returns the total number of values or rows of the specified field or column.

18. In which function, NULL values are excluded from the result returned?

(a) SUM()   (b) MAX()
(c) MIN()   (d) All of these

Ans. (d) NULL values are excluded from the result returned by all the aggregate functions.

19. The AVG() function in MySQL is an example of

(a) Math function   (b) Text function
(c) Date function   (d) Aggregate function

Ans. (d) The AVG() function returns the average value from a column or multiple-rows.

So, the AVG ( ) function in MySQL is an example of aggregate function.

20. Which of the following function count all the values except NULL?

(a) COUNT(*)
(b) COUNT(column_name)
(c) COUNT(NOT NULL)
(d) COUNT(NULL)

Ans. (a) All aggregate functions exclude NULL values while performing the operation and COUNT(*) is an aggregate function.

21. What is the meaning of "GROUP BY" clause in MySQL?

(a) Group data by column values
(b) Group data by row values
(c) Group data by column and row values
(d) None of the mentioned

Ans. (a) Through GROUP BY clause we can create groups from a column of data in a table.

22. Which clause is similar to "HAVING" clause in MySQL?

(a) SELECT   (b) WHERE
(c) FROM   (d) None of the mentioned

Ans. (b) HAVING clause will act exactly same as WHERE clause. i.e. filtering the rows based on certain conditions.

23. Which clause is used with an "aggregate functions"?

(a) GROUP BY   (b) SELECT
(c) WHERE   (d) Both (a) and (c)

Ans. (a) "GROUP BY" is used with an aggregate functions.

24. Which of the following join gives the intersection of two tables?

(a) Outer join   (b) Inner join
(c) Equi join   (d) None of these

Ans. (b) Inner join gives the intersection of two tables.

25. ……… is a simple SQL join condition that uses equal sign as a comparison operator.

(a) Equi join   (b) Non-equi join
(c) Both (a) and (b)   (d) None of the above

Ans. (a) Equi join is a simple SQL join condition that uses equal sign as a comparison operator.

• Case Based MCQs

26. Direction *Read the case and answer the following questions.*

Ronita wants to store the data of some products in a table product as follows

Table : Product

PNo	PName	Qty	Date_Of_Mfg
P01	Pencil	20	2020-09-01
P02	Eraser	5	1990-09-11
P03	Book	16	2000-04-03
P04	Notebook	15	2016-12-11
P05	Color	10	2015-02-04

She also wants to perform some operations and manipulations on the table . Help her to find the solutions of following questions.

(i) A command that displays the details of all the products will be

(a) `SELECT * FROM Product;`

(b) `SHOW * FROM Product;`

(c) `DISPLAY * FROM Product;`

(d) `SELECT ALL details FROM Product;`

(ii) The default date format in which date has to be stored in MySQL is

(a) DD-MM-YYYY   (b) DD-YY-MM

(c) MM-YY-DD   (d) YYYY-MM-DD

(iii) Which command she can use to add a new column to the table?

(a) INSERT   (b) UPDATE

(c) ADD COLUMN   (d) ALTER

(iv) Suggest her a proper data type for the "PName" column.

(a) Varchar

(b) Double

(c) Float

(d) Integer

(v) She is confused whether she has to use the "COLUMN" clause with the ALTER TABLE command to add a column to the table. What should she do ?

(a) COLUMN clause is must.

(b) COLUMN clause is optional.

(c) COLUMN clause is must for adding integer columns only.

(d) None of the above

Ans. (i) (*a*) `SELECT * FROM Product;`

(ii) (*d*) By default, MySQL stores date in YYYY-MM-DD format.

(iii) (*d*) The ALTER command can be used to make any changes to the structure of a table.

(iv) (*a*) The varchar is a variable length data type that can used for columns storing string/character type of data.

(v) (*b*) With the ALTER TABLE command the COLUMN clause is optional, in adding columns to a table.

27. Table: Book_Information

Column Name
Book_ID
Book_Title
Price

Table: Sales

Column Name
Store_ID
Sales_Date
Sales_Amount

Basis on above table information, answer the following questions.

(i) Which SQL statement allows you to find the highest price from the table Book_Information?

(a) `SELECT Book_ID,Book_Title,MAX(Price) FROM Book_Information;`

(b) `SELECT MAX(Price) FROM Book_Information;`

(c) `SELECT MAXIMUM(Price) FROM Book_Information;`

(d) `SELECT Price FROM Book_Information ORDER BY Price DESC;`

(ii) Which SQL statement allows you to find sales amount for each store?

(a) `SELECT Store_ID, SUM(Sales_Amount) FROM Sales;`

(b) `SELECT Store_ID, SUM(Sales_Amount) FROM Sales ORDER BY Store_ID;`

(c) `SELECT Store_ID, SUM(Sales_Amount) FROM Sales GROUP BY Store_ID;`

(d) `SELECT Store_ID, SUM(Sales_Amount) FROM Sales HAVING UNIQUE Store_ID;`

(iii) Which SQL statement lets you to list all store name whose total sales amount is over 5000 ?

(a) `SELECT Store_ID, SUM(Sales_Amount) FROM Sales GROUP BY Store_ID HAVING SUM(Sales_Amount) > 5000;`

(b) `SELECT Store_ID, SUM(Sales_Amount) FROM Sales GROUP BY Store_ID HAVING Sales_Amount > 5000;`

(c) `SELECT Store_ID, SUM(Sales_Amount) FROM Sales WHERE SUM(Sales_Amount) > 5000 GROUP BY Store_ID;`

(d) `SELECT Store_ID, SUM(Sales_Amount) FROM Sales WHERE Sales_Amount > 5000 GROUP BY Store_ID;`

(iv) Which SQL statement lets you find the total number of stores in the SALES table?

(a) `SELECT COUNT(Store_ID) FROM Sales;`

(b) `SELECT COUNT(DISTINCT Store_ID) FROM Sales;`

(c) `SELECT DISTINCT Store_ID FROM Sales;`

(d) `SELECT COUNT(Store_ID) FROM Sales GROUP BY Store_ID;`

(v) Which SQL statement allows you to find the total sales amount for Store_ID 25 and the total sales amount for Store_ID 45?

(a) `SELECT Store_ID, SUM(Sales_Amount) FROM Sales WHERE Store_ID IN ( 25, 45) GROUP BY Store_ID;`

(b) `SELECT Store_ID, SUM(Sales_Amount) FROM Sales GROUP BY Store_ID HAVING Store_ID IN ( 25, 45);`

(c) `SELECT Store_ID, SUM(Sales_Amount) FROM Sales WHERE Store_ID IN (25,45);`

(d) `SELECT Store_ID, SUM(Sales_Amount) FROM Sales WHERE Store_ID = 25 AND Store_ID =45 GROUP BY Store_ID;`

Ans. (i) (*b*) `SELECT MAX(Price) FROM Book_Information;`

(ii) (*c*) `SELECT Store_ID, SUM(Sales_Amount) FROM Sales GROUP BY Store_ID;`

(iii) (*a*) `SELECT Store_ID, SUM(Sales_Amount) FROM Sales GROUP  BY Store_ID HAVING SUM(Sales_Amount) > 5000;`

(iv) (*d*) `SELECT COUNT(Store_ID) FROM Sales GROUP BY Store_ID;`

(v) (*b*) `SELECT Store_ID, SUM(Sales_Amount) FROM Sales GROUP BY  Store_ID HAVING Store_ID IN ( 25, 45);`

PART 2
Subjective Questions

• Short Answer Type Questions

1. Differentiate between ALTER and UPDATE commands in SQL. **(NCERT)**

Ans. Differences between ALTER and UPDATE commands in SQL are

ALTER command	UPDATE command
It belongs to DDL category.	It belongs to DML category.
It changes the structure of the table.	It modifies data of the table.
Columns can be added, modified , deleted etc.	Data can be changed, updated with values and expressions.

2. How is char data type different from varchar data type? **(NCERT)**

Ans. Differences between char data type and varchar data type are

Char	Varchar
It is fixed length.	It is variable length.
Wastage of memory.	Memory usage only as per data size.
Less useful.	Better data type.

3. Explain the use of ORDER BY clause.

Ans. The ORDER BY clause is used to arrange the records in ascending or descending order. Data present in a table can be arranged as per requirement on a specific field in ascending or descending order. The default is ascending order. To arrange in descending order the DESC clause is to be used. To arrange in ascending order ASC may be used.

e.g. `SELECT * FROM Employee ORDER BY EMP_SALARY DESC;`

The above command arranges the records in descending order of salary.

4. Write the queries for the following questions using the table Product with the following fields.

(P_ Code, P_Name, Qty, Price)

(i) Display the price of product having code as P06.

(ii) Display the name of all products with quantity greater than 50 and price less than 500.

Ans. (i) `SELECT Price FROM Product WHERE P_Code="P06";`

The criteria of the records that are to be displayed can be specified with WHERE clause of SQL.

(ii) `SELECT P_Name FROM Product WHERE Qty>50 AND Price<500;`

The criteria of the records that are to be displayed can be specified with WHERE clause of SQL. Here, the condition is quantity > 50 and price<500 .

5. Is it compulsory to provide values for all columns of a table while adding records? Give an example.

Ans. No it is not compulsory to provide values for all columns of a table while adding records. We can use NULL values wherever values are missing.

e.g. `INSERT INTO Employee VALUES (1,NULL,"Sales",89000);`

6. Amit wrote the command to create a table "Student" as :

`CREATE TABLE Student(RollNo integer, Name varchar(20), Marks float(8,2));`

What does (8,2) mean here?

Ans. While specifying float columns in a table the width and the number of decimals have to be specified. Here 8 is the total width and 2 is the number of decimal places for the Marks column.

7. Rakesh wants to increase the price of some of the products by 20% , of his store whose price is less than 200. Assuming the following structure , what will be the query?

PNo	PName	Quality	Price

Ans.
```
UPDATE ITEM SET Price=Price + Price *
0.2 WHERE Price<200 ;
```
The UPDATE command updates data of a table . While updating, the expression for update value can be assigned to the updating field. The records to be updated can be specified as WHERE condition.

8. Write the use of LIKE clause and a short explanation on the two characters used with it.

Ans. This operator is used to search a specified pattern in a column. It is useful when you want to search rows to match a specific pattern or when you do not know the entire value.The SQL LIKE clause is used to compare a value to similar values using wildcard characters.

We describe patterns by using two special wildcard characters, given below:

(i) The per cent sign (%) is used to match any substring.

(ii) The underscore (_) is used to match any single character.

The symbols can also be used in combinations.

9. Given the command below.
```
DELETE FROM Toys WHERE ToyName LIKE "S_t%";
```
Which records will be deleted by the above command?

Ans. The command has a LIKE clause with "S_t%" which means all the toy names that start with the letter 'S' and has 3rd letter as 't' will deleted.

10. In the following query how many rows will be deleted? **(NCERT)**
```
DELETE Student
WHERE Student_ID=109;
```
(Assuming a Student table with primary key Student_ID)

Ans.
```
DELETE FROM Student WHERE
Student_ID=109;
```
Here, the "FROM" clause is missing , so the command will produce an error.

11. If the value in the column is repeatable, how do you find out the unique values? **(NCERT)**

Ans. The DISTINCT clause in SQL is used to display only distinct values in a column of a table. Hence, if the column allows duplicate values the unique values can be extracted using the DISTINCT clause.

```
SELECT DISTINCT CLASS FROM Student ;
```
This displays only the unique classes.

12. What do you mean by an operator? Name any four operators used in queries.

Ans. An operator is a component of an expression that represents the action that should be taken over a set of values.

Four operators used in queries are

(i) Arithmetic operators

(ii) Comparison operators

(iii) Boolean/Logical operators

(iv) Between operator

13. How NOT operator is used with WHERE clause? Give an example.

Ans. The WHERE clause is used to retrieve some given data according to the condition and NOT operator reverses the result of it.
For example,
```
mysql>SELECT Name, Class, Games FROM
Student_table WHERE NOT Games = 'FootBALL';
```

14. What are the functions of ALTER TABLE command?

Ans. The main functions of ALTER TABLE command are
(i) Add or drop columns.
(ii) Change the column definition of a column.
(iii) Add or drop constraint.
(iv) Rename a column.

15. Write syntax of the conditions given below.
(i) Add a column in a table.
(ii) Delete a column from a table.

Ans.
```
(i) ALTER TABLE<table_name>ADD
    <column_name>datatype<value>;
(ii) ALTER TABLE<table_name>DROP
    COLUMN<column_name>;
```

16. Consider the following table PREPAID. Write MySQL commands for the statements given below.

S_No	C_Name	Model	Connection
1.	Sita	Nokia	Airtel
2.	Geeta	Samsung	Idea
3.	Ritesh	LG	BSNL
4.	Jayant	Micromax	Reliance

(i) DELETE a column name Model.

(ii) DELETE a customer record where connection type is BSNL.

Ans.
```
(i) mysql> ALTER TABLE PREPAID DROP Model;
(ii) mysql> DELETE FROM PREPAID WHERE
     Connection = 'BSNL';
```

17. What will be the output of the following queries on the basis of EMPLOYEE table?

Table : EMPLOYEE

Emp_Id	Name	Salary
E01	Siya	54000
E02	Joy	NULL
E03	Allen	32000
E04	Neev	42000

(i)
```
SELECT Salary + 100 FROM EMPLOYEE
   WHERE Emp_Id = 'E02';
```
(ii)
```
SELECT Name FROM EMPLOYEE
   WHERE Emp_Id = 'E04';
```
Ans. The output of the following queries

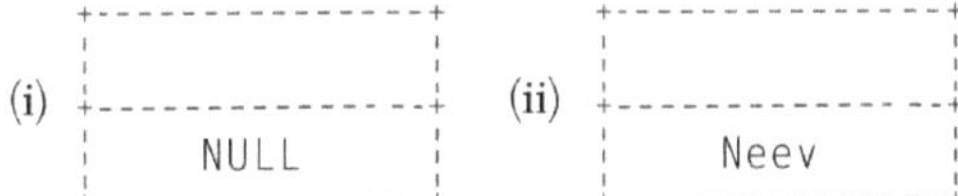

(i)

```
+----------------+
|                |
|      NULL      |
+----------------+
```

(ii)

```
+----------------+
|                |
|      Neev      |
+----------------+
```

18. What are the aggregate functions in SQL?

Ans. Aggregate function is a function where the values of multiple-rows are grouped together as input on certain criteria to form a single value of more significant meaning. Some aggregate functions used in SQL are SUM ( ), AVG( ), MIN(), etc.

19. What is the purpose of GROUP BY clause in MySQL? How is it different from ORDER BY clause? **[CBSE 2012]**

Ans. The GROUP BY clause can be used to combine all those records that have identical value in a particular field or a group of fields.

Whereas, ORDER BY clause is used to display the records either in ascending or descending order based on a particular field. For ascending order ASC is used and for descending order, DESC is used. The default order is ascending order.

20. Gopi Krishna is using a table Employee. It has the following columns :

```
Code, Name, Salary, Dept_code
```

He wants to display maximum salary department wise. He wrote the following command :

```
SELECT Deptcode, Max(Salary) FROM
Employee;
```

But he did not get the desired result.

Rewrite the above query with necessary changes to help him get the desired output. **[CBSE Delhi 2014]**

Ans.
```
SELECT Deptcode, Max(Salary)
```

```
FROM Employee
GROUP BY Deptcode;
```

21. Consider the following table Employee :

Table : Employee

100	Steven	King	Sking	1987-06-17	AD_PRES	24000.00	90
101	Neena	Kochhar	Nkochhar	1987-06-18	AD_VP	17000.00	90
102	Lex	De Haan	Ldehaan	1987-06-19	AD_VP	9000.00	60
103	Alexander	Hunold	Ahunold	1987-06-20	IT_PROG	6000.00	60
104	Bruce	Ernst	Bernst	1987-06-21	IT_PROG	4800.00	60
105	David	Austin	Daustin	1987-06-22	IT_PROG	4800.00	60
106	Valli	Pataballa	Vpataballa	1987-06-23	IT_PROG	4800.00	100

Write a query to get the total salary, maximum, minimum, average salary of employees (Job_ID wise), for Dept_ID 90 only.

Ans.
```
SELECT Job_ID, SUM(Salary), AVG(Salary),
MAX(Salary), MIN(Salary)
FROM Employee
WHERE Dept_ID = '90'
GROUP BY Job_ID;
```

• Long Answer Type Questions

22. What is the differences between HAVING clause and WHERE clause?

Ans. Differences between HAVING clause and WHERE clause are

WHERE clause	HAVING clause
WHERE clause is used to filter the records from the table based on the specified condition.	HAVING clause is used to filter record from the groups based on the specified condition.
WHERE clause implements in row operation.	HAVING clause implements in column operation.
WHERE clause cannot contain aggregate function.	HAVING clause can contain aggregate function.
WHERE clause can be used with SELECT, UPDATE, DELETE statement.	HAVING clause can only be used with SELECT statement.
WHERE clause is used with single row function like UPPER, LOWER etc.	HAVING clause is used with multiple row function like SUM, COUNT etc.

23. Answer the questions (i) to (v) on the basis of the following tables SHOPPE and ACCESSORIES.

Table : SHOPPE

Id	SName	Area
S001	ABC Computeronics	CP
S002	All Infotech Media	GK II
S003	Tech Shoppe	CP
S004	Geeks Tecno Soft	Nehru Place
S005	Hitech Tech Store	Nehru Place

Table : ACCESSORIES

No	Name	Price	Id
A01	Mother Board	12000	S01
A02	Hard Disk	5000	S01
A03	Keyboard	500	S02
A04	Mouse	300	S01
A05	Mother Board	13000	S02
A06	Keyboard	400	S03
A07	LCD	6000	S04
T08	LCD	5500	S05
T09	Mouse	350	S05
T10	Hard Disk	4500	S03

(i) To display Name and Price of all the Accessories in ascending order of their Price.

(ii) To display Id and SName of all Shoppe located in Nehru Place.

(iii) To display Minimum and Maximum Price of each Name of Accessories.

(iv) To display Name, Price of all Accessories and their respective SName, where they are available.

(v) To display name of accessories whose price is greater than 1000.

Ans.　(i)
```
SELECT Name, Price
FROM ACCESSORIES
ORDER BY Price;
```
(ii)
```
SELECT Id, SName
FROM SHOPPE
WHERE Area = 'Nehru Place';
```
(iii)
```
SELECT MIN(Price) "Minimum Price",
MAX(Price) "Maximum Price", Name
FROM ACCESSORIES
GROUP BY Name;
```
(iv)
```
SELECT Name, Price, SName
FROM ACCESSORIES A, SHOPPE S
WHERE A.Id = S.Id;
```
but this query enable to show the result because A.Id and S.Id are not identical.

(v)
```
SELECT Name From
ACCESSORIES
WHERE Price>1000;
```

24. Consider the following tables STORE and answer the questions:

Table: STORE

ItemNo	Item	Scode	Qty	Rate	LastBuy
2005	Sharpener Classic	23	60	8	31-JUN-09
2003	Balls	22	50	25	01-FEB-10
2002	Gel Pen Premium	21	150	12	24-FEB-10
2006	Gel Pen Classic	21	250	20	11-MAR-09
2001	Eraser Small	22	220	6	19-JAN-09
2004	Eraser Big	22	110	8	02-DEC-09
2009	Ball Pen 0.5	21	180	18	03-NOV-09

Write SQL commands for the following statements:

(i) To display details of all the items in the STORE table in ascending order of LastBuy.

(ii) To display ItemNo and Item name of those items from STORE table, whose Rate is more than ₹ 15.

(iii) To display the details of those items whose Supplier code (Scode) is 22 or Quantity in Store (Qty) is more than 110 from the table STORE.

(iv) To display minimum rate of items for each Supplier individually as per Scode from the table STORE.

(v) To display the item with its quantity which include pen in their name.

Ans.　(i)
```
SELECT * FROM STORE ORDER BY LastBuy;
```
(ii)
```
SELECT ItemNo, Item FROM STORE WHERE
Rate>15;
```
(iii)
```
SELECT * FROM STORE WHERE Scode = 22
OR Qty>110;
```
(iv)
```
SELECT MIN(Rate) FROM STORE GROUP BY
Scode;
```
(v)
```
SELECT Item, Qty FROM STORE WHERE Item
LIKE '%Pen%';
```

25. Consider the following tables STUDENT and STREAM. Write SQL commands for the statements (i) to (v).

Table : STUDENT

SCODE	NAME	AGE	STRCDE	POINTS	GRADE
101	Amit	16	1	6	NULL
102	Arjun	13	3	4	NULL
103	Zaheer	14	2	1	NULL
105	Gagan	15	5	2	NULL
108	Kumar	13	6	8	NULL
109	Rajesh	17	5	8	NULL
110	Naveen	13	3	9	NULL
113	Ajay	16	2	3	NULL
115	Kapil	14	3	2	NULL
120	Gurdeep	15	2	6	NULL

Table : STREAM

STRCDE	STRNAME
1	SCIENCE+COMP
2	SCIENCE+BIO
3	SCIENCE+ECO
4	COMMERCE+MATHS
5	COMMERCE+SOCIO
6	ARTS+MATHS
7	ARTS+SOCIO

(i) To display the name of streams in alphabetical order from table STREAM.

(ii) To display the number of students whose POINTS are more than 5.

(iii) To update GRADE to 'A' for all those students, who are getting more than 8 as POINTS.

(iv) ARTS+MATHS stream is no more available. Make necessary change in table STREAM.

(v) To display student's name whose stream name is science and computer.

Ans. (i)
```
SELECT STRNAME FROM STREAM ORDER BY
   STRNAME;
```
(ii)
```
SELECT COUNT(*) FROM STUDENT WHERE
   POINTS > 5;
```
(iii)
```
UPDATE STUDENT SET GRADE = 'A' WHERE
   POINTS > 8;
```
(iv)
```
DELETE FROM STREAM WHERE STRNAME
   = 'ARTS + MATHS';
```
(v)
```
SELECT NAME FROM STUDENT
   WHERE STUDENT.STRCDE = STREAM.STRCDE
   AND STRNAME = "SCIENCE + COMP";
```

26. Consider the following tables GARMENT and FABRIC. Write SQL commands for the statements (i) to (v).

Table : GARMENT

GCODE	DESCRIPTION	PRICE	FCODE	READYDATE
10023	PENCIL SKIRT	1150	F03	19-DEC-08
10001	FORMAL SHIRT	1250	F01	12-JAN-08
10012	INFORMAL SHIRT	1550	F02	06-JUN-08
10024	BABY TOP	750	F03	07-APR-07
10090	TULIP SKIRT	850	F02	31-MAR-07
10019	EVENING GOWN	850	F03	06-JUN-08
10009	INFORMAL PANT	1500	F02	20-OCT-08
10007	FORMAL PANT	1350	F01	09-MAR-08
10020	FROCK	850	F04	09-SEP-07
10089	SLACKS	750	F03	20-OCT-08

Table : FABRIC

FCODE	TYPE
F04	POLYSTER
F02	COTTON
F03	SILK
F01	TERELENE

(i) To display GCODE and DESCRIPTION of each GARMENT in descending order of GCODE.

(ii) To display the details of all the GARMENTs, which have READYDATE in between 08-DEC-07 and 16-JUN-08 (inclusive of both the dates).

(iii) To display the average PRICE of all the GARMENTs. Which are made up of FABRIC with FCODE as F03.

(iv) To display FABRIC wise highest and lowest price of GARMENTs from GARMENT table. (Display FCODE of each GARMENT alongwith highest and lowest price.)

(v) To display garment's description with their price whose fabric is silk.

Ans. (i)
```
SELECT GCODE, DESCRIPTION FROM GARMENT
   ORDER BY GCODE DESC;
```
(ii)
```
SELECT*FROM GARMENT
   WHERE READYDATE BETWEEN '08-DEC-07'
   AND '16-JUN-08';
```
(iii)
```
SELECT AVG(PRICE) FROM GARMENT WHERE
   FCODE = 'F03';
```

(iv) SELECT FCODE, MAX(PRICE), MIN(PRICE)
FROM GARMENT GROUP BY FCODE;

(v) SELECT DESCRIPTION, PRICE FROM GARMENT
WHERE GARMENT.FCODE = FABRIC.FCODE
AND TYPE = "SILK";

27. Consider the following tables. Write SQL commands for the statements (i) to (v).

Table : SENDER

SenderID	SenderName	SenderAddress	SenderCity
ND01	R Jain	2, ABC Appts	New Delhi
MU02	H Sinha	12, Newtown	Mumbai
MU15	S Jha	27/A, Park Street	Mumbai
ND50	T Prasad	122-K, SDA	New Delhi

Table : RECIPIENT

RecID	SenderID	RecName	RecAddress	RecCity
KO05	ND01	R Bajpayee	5, Central Avenue	Kolkata
ND08	MU02	S Mahajan	116, A Vihar	New Delhi
MU19	ND01	H Singh	2A, Andheri East	Mumbai
MU32	MU15	P K Swamy	B5, C S Terminus	Mumbai
ND48	ND50	S Tripathi	13, B1 D, Mayur Vihar	New Delhi

(i) To display the names of all Senders from Mumbai.

(ii) To display the RecID, SenderName, SenderAddress, RecName, RecAddress for every Recipient.

(iii) To display Recipient details in ascending order of RecName.

(iv) To display number of Recipients from each City.

(v) To display the detail of recipients who are in Mumbai.

Ans. (i) SELECT SenderName FROM SENDER WHERE
SenderCity = 'Mumbai';

(ii) SELECT RecID, SenderName,
SenderAddress, RecName, RecAddress
FROM RECIPIENT, SENDER WHERE
RECIPIENT.SenderID = SENDER.SenderID;

(iii) SELECT * FROM RECIPIENT ORDER BY
RecName;

(iv) SELECT COUNT(*) AS "No. of
Recipients", RecCity FROM RECIPIENT
GROUP BY RecCity;

(v) SELECT * FROM RECIPIENT
WHERE RecCity = "Mumbai";

28. Write the SQL commands for (i) to (v) on the basis of the table HOSPITAL.

Table : HOSPITAL

No.	Name	Age	Department	Dateofadm	Charges	Sex
1	Sandeep	65	Surgery	23/02/98	300	M
2	Ravina	24	Orthopaedic	20/01/98	200	F
3	Karan	45	Orthopaedic	19/02/98	200	M
4	Tarun	12	Surgery	01/01/98	300	M
5	Zubin	36	ENT	12/01/98	250	M
6	Ketaki	16	ENT	24/02/98	300	F
7	Ankita	29	Cardiology	20/02/98	800	F
8	Zareen	45	Gynaecology	22/02/98	300	F
9	Kush	19	Cardiology	13/01/98	800	M
10	Shailya	31	Nuclear Medicine	19/02/98	400	M

(i) To show all information about the patients of Cardiology Department.

(ii) To list the name of female patients, who are in Orthopaedic Department.

(iii) To list names of all patients with their date of admission in ascending order.

(iv) To display Patient's Name, Charges, Age for male patients only.

(v) To display name of doctor are older than 30 years and charges for consultation fee is more than 500.

Ans. (i) SELECT * FROM HOSPITAL WHERE Department
= 'Cardiology';

(ii) SELECT Name FROM HOSPITAL WHERE
Department = 'Orthopaedic' AND Sex
= 'F';

(iii) SELECT Name FROM HOSPITAL ORDER BY
Dateofadm;

(iv) SELECT Name, Charges, Age FROM
HOSPITAL WHERE Sex = 'M';

(v) SELECT NAME FROM HOSPITAL WHERE Age>30
AND Charges>500;

29. Write SQL commands for (i) to (v) on the basis of table INTERIORS.

Table : **INTERIORS**

No.	ITEMNAME	TYPE	DATEOF STOCK	PRICE	DISCO- UNT
1	Red rose	Double Bed	23/02/02	32000	15
2	Soft touch	Baby cot	20/01/02	9000	10
3	Jerry's home	Baby cot	19/02/02	8500	10
4	Rough wood	Office Table	01/01/02	20000	20
5	Comfort zone	Double Bed	12/01/02	15000	20
6	Jerry look	Baby cot	24/02/02	7000	19
7	Lion king	Office Table	20/02/02	16000	20
8	Royal tiger	Sofa	22/02/02	30000	25
9	Park sitting	Sofa	13/12/01	9000	15
10	Dine Paradise	Dining Table	19/02/02	11000	15
11	White Wood	Double Bed	23/03/03	20000	20
12	James 007	Sofa	20/02/03	15000	15
13	Tom look	Baby cot	21/02/03	7000	10

(i) To show all information about the Sofa from the INTERIORS table.

(ii) To list the ITEMNAME, which are priced at more than 10000 from the INTERIORS table.

(iii) To list ITEMNAME and TYPE of those items, in which DATEOFSTOCK is before 22/01/02 from the INTERIORS table in descending order of ITEMNAME.

(iv) To insert a new row in the INTERIORS table with the following data

```
{14, 'TrueIndian', 'Office Table',
'25/03/03', 15000, 20}
```

(v) To display the name of item with their price which have discount more than 20.

Ans. (i)
```
SELECT * FROM INTERIORS WHERE TYPE
= 'Sofa';
```

(ii)
```
SELECT ITEMNAME FROM INTERIORS WHERE
PRICE > 10000;
```

(iii)
```
SELECT ITEMNAME, TYPE FROM INTERIORS
WHERE DATEOFSTOCK < '22/01/02'
ORDER BY ITEMNAME DESC;
```

(iv)
```
INSERT INTO INTERIORS VALUES
(14,'TrueIndian', 'Office Table',
'25/03/03',15000,20);
```

(v)
```
SELECT ITEMNAM, PRICE FROM INTERIORS
WHRE DISCOUNT>20;
```

30. Given the following tables for a database LIBRARY.

Table : **BOOKS**

Book_Id	Book_ Name	Author_ Name	Publishers	Price	Type	Qty
F0001	The Tears	William Hopkins	First Publ	750	Fiction	10
F0002	Thunder bolts	Anna Roberts	First Publ	700	Fiction	5
T0001	My First C++	Brain & Brooke	EPB	250	Text	10
T0002	C++ Brainwo rks	A.W. Rossaine	TDH	325	Text	5
C0001	Fast Cook	Lata Kapoor	EPB	350	Cookery	8

Table : **ISSUED**

Book_Id	Quantity_Issued
F0001	3
T0001	1
C0001	5

Write SQL queries for (i) to (v).

(i) To show Book name, Author name and Price of books of EPB Publishers.

(ii) To list the names from books of Fiction type.

(iii) To display the names and price of the books in descending order of their price.

(iv) To increase the price of all books of First Publ Publishers by 50.

(v) To display the detail of book whose quantity less than 10.

Ans. (i)
```
SELECT Book_Name, Author_Name, Price
FROM BOOKS WHERE Publishers = 'EPB';
```

(ii)
```
SELECT Book_Name FROM BOOKS WHERE Type
= 'Fiction';
```

(iii)
```
SELECT Book_Name, Price FROM BOOKS
ORDER BY Price DESC;
```

(iv)
```
UPDATE BOOKS SET Price = Price + 50
WHERE Publishers = 'First Publ';
```

(v)
```
SELECT *FROM BOOKS
WHERE Qty<10;
```

31. Write SQL commands for (i) to (v) on the basis of table STUDENT

Table : STUDENT

SNO	NAME	STREAM	FEES	AGE	SEX
1	ARUN KUMAR	COMPUTER	750.00	17	M
2	DIVYA JENEJA	COMPUTER	750.00	18	F
3	KESHAR MEHRA	BIOLOGY	500.00	16	M
4	HARISH SINGH	ENG. DR	350.00	18	M
5	PRACHI	ECONOMICS	300.00	19	F
6	NISHA ARORA	COMPUTER	750.00	15	F
7	DEEPAK KUMAR	ECONOMICS	300.00	16	M
8	SARIKA VASWANI	BIOLOGY	500.00	15	F

(i) List the name of all the students, who have taken stream as COMPUTER.

(ii) To count the number of female students.

(iii) To display the number of students stream wise.

(iv) To display all the records in sorted order of name.

(v) To display the stream of student whose name is Harish.

Ans. (i) SELECT NAME FROM STUDENT WHERE STREAM ='COMPUTER';

(ii) SELECT COUNT(*) FROM STUDENT WHERE SEX = 'F';

(iii) SELECT STREAM, COUNT(*) FROM STUDENT GROUP BY STREAM;

(iv) SELECT * FROM STUDENT ORDER BY NAME;

(v) SELECT STREAM FROM STUDENT WHERE NAME LIKE "%HARISH%";

32. Given the following family relation. Write SQL commands for questions (i) to (v) based on the table FAMILY

Table : FAMILY

No.	Name	Female Members	Male Members	Income	Occupation
1	Mishra	3	2	7000	Service
2	Gupta	4	1	50000	Business
3	Khan	6	3	8000	Mixed
4	Chaddha	2	2	25000	Business
5	Yadav	7	2	20000	Mixed
6	Joshi	3	2	14000	Service
7	Maurya	6	3	5000	Farming
8	Rao	5	2	10000	Service

(i) To select all the information of family, whose Occupation is Service.

(ii) To list the name of family, where female members are more than 3.

(iii) To list all names of family with income in ascending order.

(iv) To count the number of family, whose income is less than 10000.

(v) To display the detail of family whose income is more than 10000 and occupation is mixed type.

Ans. (i) SELECT * FROM FAMILY WHERE Occupation = 'Service';

(ii) SELECT Name FROM FAMILY WHERE FemaleMembers > 3;

(iii) SELECT Name, Income FROM FAMILY ORDER BY Income;

(iv) SELECT COUNT(*) FROM FAMILY WHERE Income < 10000;

(v) SELECT *FROM FAMILY WHERE INCOME > 10000 AND Occupation = "Mixed";

33. Consider the following tables PRODUCT and CLIENT. Write SQL commands for the statement (i) to (v).

Table : PRODUCT

P_ID	ProductName	Manufacturer	Price
TP01	Talcom Powder	LAK	40
FW05	Face Wash	ABC	45
BS01	Bath Soap	ABC	55
SH06	Shampoo	XYZ	120
FW12	Face Wash	XYZ	95

Table : CLIENT

C_ID	ClientName	City	P_ID
01	Cosmetic Shop	Delhi	FW05
06	Total Health	Mumbai	BS01
12	Live Life	Delhi	SH06
15	Pretty Woman	Delhi	FW12
16	Dreams	Bengaluru	TP01

(i) To display the details of those Clients, whose City is Delhi.

(ii) To display the details of products, whose Price is in the range of 50 to 100 (both values included).

(iii) To display the ClientName, City from table CLIENT and ProductName and Price from table PRODUCT, with their corresponding matching P_ID.

(iv) To increase the Price of all products by 10.

(v) To display the product detail whose manufacturer is ABC and price less than 50.

Ans. (i) `SELECT * FROM CLIENT WHERE City='Delhi';`

(ii) `SELECT * FROM PRODUCT WHERE Price BETWEEN 50 AND 100;`

(iii) `SELECT ClientName, City, ProductName, Price FROM CLIENT, PRODUCT WHERE CLIENT.P_ID = PRODUCT.P_ID;`

(iv) `UPDATE PRODUCT SET Price = Price + 10;`

(v) `SELECT *FROM PRODUCT WEHRE Manufacturer = "ABC" AND Price < 50;`

34. Study the following tables DOCTOR and SALARY and write SQL commands for the questions (i) to (v).

Table : DOCTOR

ID	NAME	DEPT	SEX	EXPERI-ENCE
101	John	ENT	M	12
104	Smith	ORTHOPEDIC	M	5
107	George	CARDIOLOGY	M	10
114	Lara	SKIN	F	3
109	K George	MEDICINE	F	9
105	Johnson	ORTHOPEDIC	M	10
117	Lucy	ENT	F	3
111	Bill	MEDICINE	F	12
130	Morphy	ORTHOPEDIC	M	15

Table : SALARY

ID	BASIC	ALLOWANCE	CONSULTATION
101	12000	1000	300
104	23000	2300	500
107	32000	4000	500
114	12000	5200	100
109	42000	1700	200
105	18900	1690	300
130	21700	2600	300

(i) Display NAME of all doctors who are in MEDICINE department having more than 10yrs experience from the table DOCTOR.

(ii) Display the average salary of all doctors working in ENT department using the tables DOCTOR and SALARY. SALARY = BASIC + ALLOWANCE.

(iii) Display the minimum ALLOWANCE of female doctors.

(iv) Display the highest consultation fee among all male doctors.

(v) To display the detail of doctor who have experience more than 12 years.

Ans. (i) `SELECT NAME FROM DOCTOR WHERE DEPT = 'MEDICINE' AND EXPERIENCE > 10;`

(ii) `SELECT AVG(BASIC + ALLOWANCE) FROM SALARY WHERE SALARY.ID IN(SELECT ID FROM DOCTOR WHERE DEPT = 'ENT');`

(iii) `SELECT MIN(ALLOWANCE) FROM SALARY WHERE SALARY.ID IN(SELECT ID FROM DOCTOR WHERE SEX = 'F');`

(iv) `SELECT MAX(CONSULTATION) FROM SALARY WHERE SALARY.ID IN(SELECT ID FROM DOCTOR WHERE SEX = 'M');`

(v) `SELECT * FROM DOCTOR WHERE EXPERIENCE>12;`

35. Study the following tables FLIGHTS and FARES and write SQL commands for the questions (i) to (iv).

Table : FLIGHTS

FL_NO	STARTING	ENDING	NO_FLIGHT	NO_STOPS
IC301	MUMBAI	DELHI	8	0
IC799	BENGALURU	DELHI	2	1
MC101	INDORE	MUMBAI	3	0
IC302	DELHI	MUMBAI	8	0
AM812	KANPUR	BENGALURU	3	1
IC899	MUMBAI	KOCHI	1	4
AM501	DELHI	TRIVANDRUM	1	5
MU499	MUMBAI	MADRAS	3	3
IC701	DELHI	AHMEDABAD	4	0

Table : FARES

FL_NO	AIRLINES	FARE	TAX%
IC701	INDIAN AIRLINES	6500	10
MU499	SAHARA	9400	5
AM501	JET AIRWAYS	13450	8
IC899	INDIAN AIRLINES	8300	4
IC302	INDIAN AIRLINES	4300	10
IC799	INDIAN AIRLINES	10500	10
MC101	DECCAN AIRLINES	3500	4

(i) Display FL_NO and NO_FLIGHT from KANPUR to BENGALURU from the table FLIGHTS.

(ii) Arrange the contents of the table FLIGHTS in the ascending order of FL_NO.

(iii) Display the FL_NO and fare to be paid for the flights from DELHI to MUMBAI using the tables FLIGHTS and FARES, where the fare to be paid = FARE + FARE * TAX % 100.

(iv) Display the minimum fare INDIAN AIRLINES is offering from the table FARES.

(v) To display the detail fares of Indian airlines.

Ans. (i) `SELECT FL_NO, NO_FLIGHT FROM FLIGHTS WHERE STARTING = 'KANPUR' AND ENDING = 'BENGALURU';`

(ii) `SELECT * FROM FLIGHTS ORDER BY FL_NO;`

(iii) `SELECT FL_NO, FARE + FARE * TAX%100 FROM FARES WHERE FL_NO = (SELECT FL_No FROM FLIGHTS WHERE STARTING = 'DELHI' AND ENDING = 'MUMBAI');`

(iv) `SELECT MIN(FARE) FROM FARES GROUP BY AIRLINES HAVING AIRLINES = 'INDIAN AIRLINES';`

(v) `SELECT * FROM FARES WHERE AIRLINES = "Indian Airlines";`

36. Write SQL commands for (i) to (iv) on the basis of the table SPORTS

Table : SPORTS

STUD-ENTNO	CLASS	NAME	GAME1	GRADE	GAME2	GRADE1
10	7	Sameer	Cricket	B	Swimming	A
11	8	Sujit	Tennis	A	Skating	C
12	7	Kamal	Swimming	B	Football	B
13	7	Veena	Tennis	C	Tennis	A
14	9	Archana	Basketball	A	Cricket	A
15	10	Arpit	Cricket	A	Athletics	C

(i) Display the games taken up by the students, whose name starts with 'A'.

(ii) Write a query to add a new column named MARKS.

(iii) Write a query to assign a value 200 for Marks for all those, who are getting grade 'B' or grade 'A' in both GAME1 and GAME2.

(iv) Which command will be used to arrange the whole table in the alphabetical order of NAME?

(a) `SELECT FROM SPORTS ORDER BY NAME;`

(b) `SELECT*SPORTS ORDER  BY NAME;`

(c) `SELECT*FROM SPORTS ORDER NAME;`

(d) `SELECT*FROM SPORTS ORDER BY NAME;`

Ans. (i) `SELECT GAME1, GAME2 FROM SPORTS WHERE NAME LIKE 'A%';`

(ii) `ALTER TABLE SPORTS ADD(MARKS NUMBER(3));`

(iii) `UPDATE SPORTS SET MARKS = 200 WHERE GRADE = 'A' OR GRADE = 'B' OR GRADE1 = 'A' OR GRADE1 = 'B';`

(iv) (d) `SELECT * FROM SPORTS ORDER BY NAME;`

37. Write SQL commands for (i) to (iv) on the basis of table EMPLOYEE

Table : EMPLOYEE

S NO	NAME	BASIC	DEPARTMENT	DATO FAPP	AGE	SEX
1	KARAN	8000	PERSONNEL	27/03/97	35	M
2	DIVAKAR	9500	COMPUTER	20/01/98	34	M
3	DIVYA	7300	ACCOUNTS	19/02/97	34	F
4	ARUN	8350	PERSONNEL	01/01/95	33	M
5	SABINA	9500	ACCOUNTS	12/01/96	36	F
6	JOHN	7400	FINANCE	24/02/97	36	M
7	ROBERT	8250	PERSONNEL	20/02/97	39	M
8	RUBINA	9450	MAINTENANCE	22/02/98	37	F
9	VIKAS	7500	COMPUTER	13/01/94	41	M
10	MOHAN	9300	MAINTENANCE	19/02/98	37	M

(i) Which command will be used to list the names of the employees, who are more than 34 years old sorted by NAME.

(a) `SELECT NAME FROM EMPLOYEE WHERE AGE>34 ORDER BY NAME;`

(b) `SELECT * FROM EMPLOYEE WHERE AGE>34 ORDER BY NAME;`

(c) `SELECT NAME FROM EMPLOYEE WHERE AGE>34;`

(d) `SELECT NAME FROM EMPLOYEE AGE>34 ORDER BY NAME;`

(ii) Write a query to display a report, listing NAME, BASIC, DEPARTMENT and annual salary. Annual salary equals to BASIC * 12.

(iii) Insert the following data in the EMPLOYEE table

11, 'VIJAY', 9300, 'FINANCE', '13/7/98', 35, "M"

(iv) Write a query to count the number of employees, who are either working in PERSONNEL or COMPUTER department.

Ans. (i) (a) `SELECT NAME FROM EMPLOYEE WHERE AGE > 34 ORDER BY NAME;`

(ii) `SELECT NAME, BASIC, DEPARTMENT, BASIC*12 "Annual Salary" FROM EMPLOYEE;`

(iii) `INSERT INTO EMPLOYEE VALUES(11, 'VIJAY', 9300, 'FINANCE', '13/7/98', 35,'M');`

(iv) `SELECT COUNT(*) FROM EMPLOYEE WHERE DEPARTMENT = 'PERSONNEL' OR DEPARTMENT = 'COMPUTER';`

38. Write SQL commands for (i) to (iv) on the basis of table COLLEGE

Table : **COLLEGE**

No	Name	Age	Department	DateofJoin	Basic	Sex
1	Shalaz	45	Biology	13/02/88	10500	M
2	Sameera	54	Biology	10/01/90	9500	F
3	Yagyen	43	Physics	27/02/98	8500	M
4	Pratyush	34	Chemistry	11/01/93	7500	M
5	Aren	51	Mathematics	22/01/91	8500	M
6	Reeta	27	Chemistry	14/02/94	9000	F
7	Urvashi	29	Biology	10/02/93	8500	F
8	Teena	35	Mathematics	02/02/89	10500	F
9	Viren	49	Mathematics	03/01/88	9000	M
10	Prakash	22	Physics	17/02/92	8000	M

(i) Write a query to change the Basic salary to 10500 of all those teachers from COLLEGE, who joined the COLLEGE after 01/02/89 and are above the age of 50.

(ii) Write a query to display Name, Age and Basic of all those from COLLEGE, who belong to Physics and Chemistry department only.

(iii) Which command will be used to delete a row from table COLLEGE, in which NAME is VIREN?

(iv) Insert the following data in the given table COLLEGE

11, 'Saurav', 50, 'Chemistry', '18/05/93', 12000, 'M'

Ans. (i) `UPDATE COLLEGE SET Basic = 10500 WHERE DateofJoin>'01/02/89' AND Age>50;`

(ii) `SELECT Name, Age, Basic FROM COLLEGE WHERE Department='Physics' OR Department='Chemistry';`

(iii) `DELETE FROM COLLEGE WHERE Name = 'VIREN';`

(iv) `INSERT INTO COLLEGE VALUES (11, 'Saurav', 50, 'Chemistry', '18/05/93', 12000, 'M');`

Chapter Test

Multiple Choice Questions

1. Riya wants to remove a column "Name" from her table , which command she has to use?
    (a) ALTER TABLE   (b) CLEAR
    (c) UPDATE   (d) None of these

2. The clause with ALTER TABLE command that renames a column is
    (a) RENAME   (b) CHANGE
    (c) DROP   (d) CHANGENAME

3. We can use the aggregate functions in select list or the .... clause of a select statement. But they cannot be used in a .... clause.
    (a) WHERE, HAVING   (b) GROUP BY, HAVING
    (c) HAVING, WHERE   (d) GROUP BY, WHERE

4. Select correct SQL query from below to find the temperature in increasing order of all cites.
    (a) SELECT city FROM weather ORDER BY temperature;
    (b) SELECT city, temperature FROM weather;
    (c) SELECT city, temperature FROM weather ORDER BY temperature;
    (d) SELECT city, temperature FROM weather ORDER BY city;

5. The HAVING clause acts like a WHERE clause, but it identifies columns that meet a criterion, rather than rows.
    (a) True   (b) False
    (c) Depend on query   (d) Depend on column

Short Answer Type Questions

6. Explain usage of IS NULL and IS NOT NULL clauses.   **(NCERT)**

7. With respect to the following table structure write queries for the following

GameID	GName	Type	Players

    (i) To display the details of games of "OUTDOOR" type.
    (ii) To display GName and Players for games where players is more than 2.

8. Explain working of AND and OR operators in queries.

9. Write a query to display the Sum, Average, Highest and Lowest marks of the students grouped by subject and sub-grouped by class.

10. The following query is producing an error. Identify the error and also write the correct query.
    SELECT * FROM EMP ORDER BY NAME WHERE SALARY>=5000;

Long Answer Type Questions

11. With respect to the following table "BOOK" write SQL commands for the questions (i) to (iv).

Table : Book

BookID	Bname	Publisher	Price	DtofPub
B1	Science Fiction	TMH	1200	2020-09-08
B2	Stories	PHI	900	NULL
B3	Ramayana	PHI	1700	NULL
B4	Beginners Cooking	Oswal	1400	1990-12-03

    (i) Display details of books published before year 2000.
    (ii) Display names and publishers of books whose price is less than 1000.
    (iii) Display names of books who do not have a date of publication.
    (iv) Increase price of all books by 200.

12. Write SQL commands with respect to the Employee table given below.

Table : Employee

Eno	Ename	Dept	Desig	DtofJoin	Salary
1	Jack	Sales	MGR	2012-09-12	89000
2	Priya	Accts	MGR	2005-04-22	56000
3	Ria	Pers	Clerk	2000-01-09	25000
4	Anil	Pers	Officer	1994-04-03	67000
5	Sumit	Sales	Officer	NULL	19000
6	Akash	Sales	Officer	NULL	20000

(i) Display name and department of employees whose name begins with" S".

(ii) Display details of employees whose designation ends with "r".

(iii) Display details of employees whose name has 1st letter "P" 3rd letter "i".

(iv) Display name,deptartment and salary of employees whose department name ends with "s".

13. Consider the following table GARMENT, write SQL commands for the statements (i) to (v).   [CBSE Question Bank 2021]

Table : GARMENT

GCODE	DESCRIPTION	PRICE	FCODE	READYDATE
10023	PENCIL SKIRT	1150	F03	19-DEC-08
10001	FORMAL SHIRT	1250	F01	12-JAN-08
10012	INFORMAL SHIRT	1550	F02	06-JUN-08
10024	BABY TOP	750	F03	07-APR-07
10090	TULIP SKIRT	850	F02	31-MAR-07
10019	EVENING GOWN	850	F03	06-JUN-08
10009	INFORMAL PANT	1500	F02	20-OCT-08
10007	FORMAL PANT	1350	F01	09-MAR-08
10020	FROCK	850	F04	09-SEP-07
10089	SLACKS	750	F03	20-OCT-08

(i) To display GCODE and DESCRIPTION of each GARMENT in descending order of GCODE.

(ii) To display the details of all the GARMENT, which have READYDATE in between 08-DEC-07 and 16-JUN-08 (inclusive if both the dates).

(iii) To display the average PRICE of all the GARMENT, which are made up of fabric with FCODE as F03.

(iv) To display fabric wise highest and lowest price of GARMENT from GARMENT table. (Display FCODE of each GARMENT along with highest and lowest price).

(v) To display GCODE whose PRICE is more than 1000.

Answers

Multiple Choice Questions

1. (a)   2. (b)   3. (b)   4. (c)   5. (b)

For Detailed Solutions

Scan the code

Interface Python with SQL

In this Chapter...

- Connecting to MySQL form Python
- Creating Table
- Insert Operation
- Update Operation
- Delete Operation
- Read Operation

While developing real life applications, we need to connect it with database in order to encounter such situation where the data stored in database need to be manipulated/changed. Python allows us to connect our application to the databases like MySQL,MongoDB, SQLite and many others.

In this chapter, we will discuss Python - MySQL connectivity and learn to perform different database operations in python.

Connecting to MySQL from Python

User can write Python script using mysql. connector library after installing Python MySQL connector. It can connect to MySQL databases from Python.

Install mysql connector

To connect the Python application with MySQL database, we must import the mysql.connector module in the program.

The mysql.connector is not a build-in module, we need to install it. Execute the following command to install it using pip installer.

```
>python -m pip install mysql-connector
```

If you are using Anaconda Jupyter then type following command on terminal

```
conda install -c anaconda
mysql-connector-python
```

Steps for Creating Database Connectivity

There are various steps for creating database connectivity as follows

Step 1   Import mysql.connector module

To import mysql.connector module, write the following command :

```
import mysql.connector
```
Or

```
import mysql.connector as mydb
```

Here, mydb is an identifier which can be choose by user.

Step 2   Create the connection object

To create a connection between the MySQL database and Python application, use connect() method mysql.connector module is used. Pass the database details like HostName, UserName and database Password. This method returns the connection object.

Syntax

```
Connection_object
        = mysql.connector.connect(
host = HostName,
user = UserName,
passwd = password
)
```

e.g.

```
import mysql.connector
```

```
    con = mysql.connector.connect(
       host = "localhost",
       user = "root",
       passwd = "arihant"
    )
    print(con)
```

Output

<mysql.connector.connection.MYSQL Connection object at Ox7fb142edd780>

If you want to connect to specific database, you have to specify the database name in connect() method.

e.g.

```
    import mysql.connector
    con = mysql.connector.connect(
       host = "localhost",
       user = "root",
    passwd = "arihant",
    database = "mysql"
    )
    print(con)
```

Step 3 Creating the cursor object

The cursor object is used to define as an abstraction that specified in Python DB-API 2.0. It provides the facility to the user to work on multiple separate environment through the same connection to the database. Cursor object can be create using cursor () method of connection object. It is an important term to the database for executing queries.

Syntax

```
    cursor_object = connection_object.
                                 cursor()
```

e.g.

```
    import mysql.connector
    con = mysql.connector.connect(
       host = "locolhost",
       user = "root",
       password = "arihant",
       database = "mysql"
    )
    print (con)
    cursor = con.cursor()
```

print (cursor)

Output

<mysql.connector.connection.MySQL connection object at O × 7fb142edd780>
MySQLCursor : (Nothing executed yet)

Step 4 Execute the Query

After creating the cursor, SQL query can be execute using execute() function.

Syntax

```
    cursor_object.execute (query)
```

Step 5 Clean up the environment

This is the final step for creating database connectivity. There is necessary to close the connection which you created.

Syntax

```
    connection_object.close()
```

e.g. We created the connection con, so to close this connection use following command

```
    con.close()
```

To Show the List of Existing Database

If you want to display the name of all existing database, use following query

Syntax

```
    >show databases
```

e.g.
```
    import mysql.connector
    con = mysql.connector.connect(
       host = "localhost",
       user = "root",
       passwd = "arihant")
    cursor = con.cursor()
    try:
       db = cursor.execute("show databases")
    except:
       con.rollback()
    for i in cursor:
       print(i)
    con.close()
```

Output

('information_schema',)

('my',)

('mysql',)

('test',)

Creating the New Database

To create the new database, use following command

Syntax

```
    create database (database_name)
```

e.g.
```
    import mysql.connector
    con = mysql.connector.connect(
       host = "localhost",
       user = "root",
       passwd = "arihant"
    )
    cursor = con.cursor()
    try:
       cursor.execute("create database Python
       DB")
       db = cursor.execute("show databases")
    except:
       con.rollback()
    for i in cursor:
```

```
      print(i)
con.close()
```
Output

('PythonDB',)

('information_schema',)

('my',)

('mysql',)

('test',)

Creating Table

We can create a table using CREATE TABLE statement.

Syntax
```
CREATE TABLE Table_Name
(
    column1 datatype constraint,
    column2 datatype constraint,
    :
    columnN datatype
)
```

Here, we will create table Student in database PythonDB with five columns as Name, Class, RollNo, Address and Percentage.

e.g.
```
import mysql.connector
con = mysql.connector.connect
(host = "localhost",
user = "root",
passwd = "arihant",
database = "PythonDB")
cursor = con.cursor()
try:
    db = cursor.execute ("create table
    Student
    (Name Varchar(30)NOT NULL,
    RollNo Int(10) Primary key,
    Class Varchar(5),
    Address Varchar(50),
    Percentage Float (15)))
except:
    con.rollback()
con.close()
```
In Python shell,
```
>>> use PythonDB;
Database changed
>>> desc Student;
```

Field	Type	Null	Key	Default	Extra
Name	Varchar<30>	NO		NULL	
RollNo	Int<10>	NO	PRI	NULL	
Class	Varchar<5>	YES		NULL	
Address	Varchar<50>	YES		NULL	
Percentage	Float<15>	YES		NULL	

```
5 rows in set <0.06 sec>
```

Alter Table

If user wants to alter existing table, ALTER TABLE statement is used.

Syntax
```
ALTER TABLE Table_Name ADD ColumnName
Datatype
```

e.g. We will add new column Age in table Student.
```
import mysql.connector
con = mysql.connector.connect
    (host = "localhost",
    user = "root",
    passwd = "arihant",
    database = "PythonDB")
cursor = con.cursor()
try:
    cursor.execute("alter table Student
add
    Age int(5) not null")
except :
    con.rollback()
con.close()
```
In Python shell,
```
>>>desc Student;
```

Field	Type	Null	Key	Default	Extra
Name	varchar(30)	NO		NULL	
RollNo	int(10)	NO	PRI	NULL	
Class	varchar(5)	YES		NULL	
Address	varchar(50)	YES		NULL	
Percentage	float(15)	YES		NULL	
Age	int(5)	NO		NULL	

Insert Operation

Insert operation is required when you want to create your records into a database's table. INSERT INTO statement is used to add a record.

1. Add Single Record into a Table

In Python, to add single record into a table, we can mention the format specifier (%s) in place of value.

e.g. without format specifier
```
import mysql.connector
con = mysql.connector.connect
    (host = "localhost",
    user = "root",
    passwd = "arihant",
    database = "PythonDB")
cursor = con.cursor()
sql = "insert into Student (Name,
RollNo, Class, Address, Percentage,
Age) values ('Riya', 27, 12, 'Delhi',
```

```
73, 15)"
try :
   cursor.execute (sql)
   con.commit()
except :
   con.rollback()
con.close()
```

e.g. with format specifier

```
import mysql.connector
con = mysql.connector.connect
   (host = "localhost",
   user = "root",
   passwd = "arihant",
   database = "PythonDB")
cursor = con.cursor()
sql = "insert into Student (Name,
RollNo, Class, Address, Percentage,
Age )values (%s, %s, %s, %s, %s, %s)"
values = ("Riya", 27, 12, "Delhi", 73, 15)
try :
   cursor.execute(sql, values)
   con.commit()
except:
   con.rollback()
con.close()
```

In Python shell,

```
>>>select *from Student;
```

Name	RollNo	Class	Address	Percentage	Age
Riya	27	12	Delhi	73	15

2. Insert Multiple Rows or Records

You can also insert multiple records at a time. To insert multiple records, use format specifier (%s) makes it easy. For this executemany() is used because it executes more than one statements together.

e.g.

```
import mysql.connector
con = mysql.connector.connect
   (host = "localhost",
   user = "root",
   passwd = "arihant",
   database = "PythonDB")
cursor = con.cursor()
sql = "insert into Student (Name,
   RollNo, Class, Address,
   Percentage, Age) values (%s, %s,
   %s, %s, %s, %s)
values = [("Ayush", 33, 11,
      "Delhi", 97, 14),
      ("Kiran", 22, 11,
```

```
      "Pune", 88, 15),
      ("Nisha", 28, 12,
      "Meerut", 95, 16)]
try :
   cursor.executemany(sql,values)
   con.commit()
except:
   con.rollback()
con.close()
```

In Python Shell,

```
>>>select*From Student;
```

Name	RollNo	Class	Address	Percentage	Age
Riya	27	12	Delhi	73	15
Ayush	33	11	Delhi	97	14
Kiran	22	11	Pune	88	15
Nisha	28	12	Meerut	95	16

Update Operation

Update operation means to update one or more records on any database, which are already exist in that database. For this, UPDATE statement is used.

Syntax

```
UPDATE Table_Name SET column_Name = value
WHERE condition
```

e.g. In Student table, we will update the class of those student whose Roll No is 22.

```
import mysql.connector
con = mysql.connector.connect
(host = "localhost", user = "root",
   passwd = "arihant",
   database = "PythonDB")
cursor = con.cursor()
try :
   cursor.execute ("update Student set
         Class = 12 where RollNo =
22")
   con.commit()
except :
      con.rollback()
con.close()
```

In Python Shell,

```
>>>SELECT *FROM Student;
```

Name	RollNo	Class	Address	Percentage	Age
Riya	27	12	Delhi	73	15
Ayush	33	11	Delhi	97	14
Kiran	22	12	Pune	88	15
Nisha	28	12	Meerut	95	16

Delete Operation

This operation is required when you want to delete some records from the database. For this, DELETE FROM statement is used.

Syntax

```
DELETE FROM Table_Name WHERE condition
```

e.g.

In Student table, we will delete the record of that student whose Roll No is 33.

```
import mysql.connector
con = mysql.connector.connect
(host = "localhost", user = "root",
    passwd = "arihant",
    database = "PythonDB")
cursor = con.cursor()
try:
    cursor.execute ("delete from Student
    where RollNo = 33")
    con.commit()
except:
    con.rollback()
con.close()
```

In Python Shell,

```
>>>SELECT *FROM Student;
```

Name	RollNo	Class	Address	Percentage	Age
Riya	27	12	Delhi	73	15
Kiran	22	12	Pune	88	15
Nisha	28	12	Meerut	95	16

Read Operation

This operation is used to fetch some useful information from the database. By following methods, you can fetch the data from database

1. fetchone()

It returns the next row from the result set as tuple. If there are no more rows to retrieve, None is returned.

e.g. To fetch only one record

```
import mysql.connector
con = mysql.connector.connect
(host = "localhost",
    user = "root",
    passwd = "arihant",database =
"PythonDB")
cursor = con.cursor()
```

```
try:
    cursor.execute ("Select Name,
    RollNo, Address, Percentage from
        Student")
    display = cursor.fetchone()
    print(display)
except:
    con.rollback()
con.close()
```

Output

('Riya', 27, 'Delhi', 73)

2. fetchmany ([size])

It returns the number of rows specified by the size argument. When called repeatedly this method fetches the next set of rows of a query result and returns a list of tuples. If no more rows are available, it returns an empty list.

e.g. To fetch many records from database PythonDB

```
import mysql.connector
con = mysql.connector.connect
(host = "localhost", user = "root",
    passwd = "arihant",database =
"PythonDB")
cursor = con.cursor()
try:
    size = int(input("Enter the value of
    numbers of rows."))
    cursor.execute("Select*from Student")
    display = cursor.fetchmany(size)
    for i in display:
        print (i)
except:
    con.rollback()
con.close()
```

Output

Enter the value of no. of rows : 2

('Riya', 27, 12, 'Delhi', 73, 15)

('Kiran', 22, 12, 'Delhi', 88, 15)

3. fetchall()

It fetches all the rows of a query result. It returns all the rows as a list of tuples. An empty list is returned if there is no record to fetch.

e.g. To fetch all records from database PythonDB

```
import mysql.connector
con = mysql.connector.connect
(host = "localhost", user = "root",
    passwd = "arihant",
```

```
    database = "PythonDB")
cursor = con.cursor()
try :
    cursor.execute ("select *from
    Student")
    display = cursor.fetchall()
    for i in display :
            print(i)
except :
```

```
        con.rollback ()
        con.close()
```

Output

('Riya', 27, 12, 'Delhi', 73, 15)

('Kiran', 22, 12, 'Delhi', 88, 15)

('Nisha', 28, 12, 'Meerut', 95, 16)

Note *rowcount is read only attribute and returns the number of rows that were affected by an execute() method.*

Chapter Practice

Objective Questions

• Multiple Choice Questions

1. User can write Python script using
 (a) mysql.connector library
 (b) sql.connect library
 (c) mysql.connect library
 (d) None of the above

Ans. (*a*) User can write Python script using mysql.connector library after installing Python MySQL connector.

2. Which of the following method is used to create a connection between the MySQL database and Python?
 (a) connector ( )   (b) connect ( )
 (c) con ( )   (d) cont ( )

Ans. (*b*) connect ( ) is used to create a connection between the MySQL database and Python.

3. What is default value of host?
 (a) host   (b) localhost
 (c) global host   (d) None of these

Ans. (*b*) localhost is the default value of host.

4. Which command is used to display the name of existing databases?
 (a) display databases; (b) result databases;
 (c) show databases;   (d) output databases;

Ans. (*c*) show databases; command is used to display the name of existing databases.

5. .... operation is required when you want to create your records into a database's table.
 (a) Update (b) Delete (c) Read (d) Insert

Ans. (*d*) Insert operation is required when you want to create your records into a database's table.

6. Which method returns the next row from the result set as tuple?
 (a) fetchone ( )   (b) fetchmany ( )
 (c) fetchall ( )   (d) rowcount

Ans. (*a*) fetchone ( ) returns the next row from the result set as tuple. If there are no more rows to retrieve, None is returned.

• Case Based MCQs

Direction *Read the case and answer the following questions.*

7. Consider the table Faculty in which Riya wants to add two rows. For this, she wrote a program in which some code is missing. Help her to complete the following code.

```
import mysql.connector
mycon = mysql.____.connect         # Statement1
         (host = "localhost",
          user = "root", passwd = "system",
          database = "Test")
cursor = con.cursor ( )
sql = "INSERT___Faculty (F_ID,  # Statement2
Fname, Lname, Hire_date,Salary,Course_Name)
      VALUES
      (%s, %s, %s, %s, %s, %s)"
___ = [(101, 'Riya', 'Sharma',# Statement3
      '12-10-2004', 35000, 'Java
      Advance'), (102, 'Kiyaan',
      'Mishra', '3-12-2010', 28000,
      'Data Structure')]
try:
   cursor.executemany (sql, val)
   mycon.___ ( )                  # Statement 4

except:
   mycon.rollback ( )

   ___                            # Statement5
```

(i) Choose the correct option to fill the blank as marked Statement1.
 (a) connect   (b) connector
 (c) con   (d) mycon

(ii) Identify the correct option to fill the blank as marked statement?
 (a) INTO   (b) IN
 (c) TO   (d) DATA

(iii) Identify the correct option to fill the blank as marked Statement3.

(a) val   (b) value
(c) data   (d) d

(iv) Choose the correct option to fill the blank as marked Statement4.

(a) com   (b) committment
(c) commit   (d) None of these

(v) Choose the correct option to fill the blank as marked Statement5.

(a) con.close()   (b) my.close ()
(c) y.close ()   (d) mycon.close ()

Ans. (i) (*b*) connector is the correct option to fill the blank in line as marked Statement1.connector can connect to databases from Python.

(ii) (*a*) INTO is the correct option to fill the blank as marked Statement2.

(iii) (*a*) val is the correct option to fill the blank as marked Statement3.

(iv) (*c*) commit is the correct option to fill the blank as marked Statement4.

(v) (*d*) mycon. close() is the correct option to fill the blank in Statement5. It is used to close the connection.

• Short Answer Type Questions

1. Which data will get added in table Company by following code?

```
import mysql.connector
con = mysql.connector.connect (
    host = "localhost",
    user = "system",
    passwd = "hello",
    database = "connect")
cur = con.cursor ( )
sql = "insert into Company
        (Name, Dept, Salary)
values (%s, %s, %s)"
val = ("ABC", "DBA", 35000)
cur.execute (sql, val)
con.commit ( )
```

Ans. "ABC", "DBA", 35000

2. The table Company of database connect contains the following records

Name	Dept	Salary
ABC	DBA	35000
XYZ	Analyst	42000
ABC1	DBA	40000

What will be the output of following code?

```
import mysql.connector
con = mysql.connector.connect
```

```
        (host = "localhost",
        user = "system",
        passwd = "hello",
        database = "connect")
cur = con.cursor()
cur.execute ("select Name,
Salary from Company")
display = cur.fetchone()
print(display)
```

Ans. ('ABC', 35000)

3. Write the code to create the connection in which database's name is Python, name of host, user and password can taken by user. Also, print that connection.

Ans.
```
import mysql.connector
mycon = mysql.connector.connect(
        host = "localhost",
        user = "test",
        passwd = "testData",
        database = "Python")
print(mycon)
```

4. Write the code to create a table Product in database Inventory with following fields :

Fields	Datatype
PID	varchar(5)
PName	char(30)
Price	float
Rank	varchar(2)

Ans.
```
import mysql.connector
mycon = mysql.connector.connect
        (host = "localhost", user = "system",
        passwd = "hello",
        database = "Inventory")
cur = mycon.cursor ( )
db = cur.execute ("CREATE TABLE Production
        (PID varchar (5) Primary key,
        PName   char (30),
        Price   float,
        Rank    varchar(2)))"
mycon.close( )
```

5. Given below is a table Item in database Inventory.

ItemID	ItemName	Quantity	UnitPrice
101	ABC	5	120
102	XYZ	7	70
103	PQR	8	65
104	XYZ	12	55

Riya created this table but forget to add column ManufacturingDate. Can she add this column after creation of table? If yes, write the code where user's name and password are system and test respectively.

Ans. Yes, she can add new column after creation of table.

```
import mysql.connector
mycon = mysql.connector.connect(
        host = "localhost",
        user = "system",
        passwd = "test",
        database = "Inventory")
cursor = mycon.cursor ( )
cursor.execute ("ALTER TABLE Item ADD
            ManufacturingDate Date
            NOT NULL")
mycon.close ( )
```

6. Consider the following table structure

Faculty with fields as

```
        F_ID(P)
        Fname
        Lname
        Hire_date
        Salary
```

Write the Python code to create the above table.

Ans.
```
import mysql.connector
mycon = mysql. connector.connect (
        host = "localhost",
        user = "root",
        passwd = "system",
        database = "School")
cursor = mycon.cursor ( )
db = cursor.execute ("CREATE TABLE
    Faculty (
F_ID  varchar (3) Primary key,
Fname varchar (30) NOT NULL,
Lname varchar (40),
Hire_date Date,
Salary  Float))
mycon.close ( )
```

7. Consider the table Persons whose fields are P_ID, LastName, FirstName, Address, City. Write a Python code to add a new row but add data only in the P_Id, LastName and columns as 5, Peterson, Kari respectively.

Ans.
```
import mysql.connector
con = mysql.connector.connect
        (host = "localhost",
        user = "admin",
        passwd = "admin@123",
        database = "system")
cursor = con.cursor ( )
sql= "INSERT INTO Persons (P_ID, LastName,
    FirstName) VALUES
        (5, 'Peterson', 'Kari')"
```

```
try:
    cursor.execute (sql)
    con.commit ( )
except:
    con.rollback ( )
con.close ( )
```

8. Consider the table Student whose fields are

SCODE	Name	Age	strcde	Points	Grade
101	Amit	16	1	6	NULL
102	Arjun	13	3	4	NULL
103	Zaheer	14	2	1	NULL
104	Gagan	15	5	2	NULL
105	Kumar	13	6	8	NULL

Write the Python code to update grade to 'A' for all these students who are getting more than 8 as points.

Ans.
```
import mysql.connector as mydb
con = mydb.connect (host = "localhost",
        user = "Admin",
        passwd = "Admin@123",
        database = "system")
cursor = con.cursor ( )
sql = "UPDATE Student SET Grade = 'A'
        WHERE Points > 8"
try :
    cursor. execute (sql)
    con.commit ( )
except :
    con.rollback ( )
con.close ( )
```

9. Write the code to create the following table Student with the following fields

RollNo

FirstName

LastName

Address

ContactNo

Marks

Course

Rank

In the table, Rank should be Good, Best,   Bad, Worst, Average.

Ans.
```
import mysql.connector
mycon = mysql.connector.connect (
        host = "localhost",
        user = "root",
        passwd = "system",
        database = "School")
cursor = mycon.cursor ( )
```

```
db = cursor.execute
     (“CREATE TABLE Student(
RollNo      Int(5)         Primary key,
FirstName   varchar(30)   NOT NULL,
LastName    varchar(30),
Address     varchar(50),
ContactNo   varchar(20),
Marks       Float,
Course      char(20),
Rank char(10) check (Rank IN(‘Good’,
‘Best’, ‘Bad’, ‘Worst’, ‘Average’))))
mycon.close ( )
```

10. Consider the table Faculty whose columns' name are

```
     F_ID, Fname, Lname, Hire_date,
     Salary, Course_name
```

Write the code to insert the following record into the above table.

| 101 | Riya | Sharma | 12-10-2004 | 35000 | Java Advance |
| 102 | Kiyaan | Mishra | 3-12-2010 | 28000 | Data Structure |

Ans.
```
import mysql.connector
mycon = mysql.connector.connect
        (host = “localhost”,
         user = “root”, passwd = “system”,
         database = “Test”)
cursor = con.cursor ( )
sql = “INSERT INTO Faculty (F_ID, Fname,
       Lname, Hire_date, Salary,
       Course_Name) VALUES
       (%s, %s, %s, %s, %s, %s)”
val = [(101, ‘Riya’, ‘Sharma’,
       ‘12-10-2004’, 35000, ‘Java
       Advance’), (102, ‘Kiyaan’,
       ‘Mishra’, ‘3-12-2010’, 28000,
       ‘Data Structure’)]
try:
   cursor.executemany (sql, val)
   mycon.commit ( )
except :
   mycon.rollback ( )
mycon.close ( )
```

11. Consider the table MobileStock with following fields

```
    M_Id, M_Name, M_Qty, M_Supplier
```

Write the Python code to fetch all records with fields M_Id, M_Name and M_Supplier from database Mobile.

Ans.
```
import mysql.connector as mydb
mycon = mydb.connect (host = “localhost”,
        user = “root”, passwd = “system”,
        database = “Mobile”)
cursor = mycon.cursor ( )
```

```
sql = “SELECT M_Id, M_Name, M_Supplier
       FROM MobileStock”
try:
   cursor. execute (sql)
   display = cursor. fetchall ()
   for i in display:
      print (i)
except :
   mycon.rollback ( )
mycon.close ( )
```

12. Consider the following table Traders with following fields

TCode	TName	City
T01	Electronic Sales	Mumbai
T03	Busy Store Corp	Delhi
T02	Disp House Inc	Chennai

Write Python code to display the names of those traders who are either from Delhi or from Mumbai.

Ans.
```
import mysql. connector
mycon = mysql.connector.connect
        (host = “localhost”, user = “root”,
         passwd = “system”,
         database = “Admin”)
cursor = mycon. cursor ( )
sql = “SELECT * FROM Traders WHERE
       City = ‘Mumbai’ OR City = ‘Delhi’”
try:
   cursor.execute(sql)
   dis = cursor.fetchall ( )
   for i in disp:
          print (i)
except :
   mycon.rollback ( )
mycon.close ( )
```

• Long Answer Type Questions

13. Create following table using Python code where

Database	—	Test
Table	—	Watches
User name	—	Root
Password	—	System

WatchId	WatchName	Price	Type	Qty_store
W001	High Time	10000	Unisex	100
W002	Life Time	15000	Ladies	150
W003	Wave	20000	Gents	200
W004	High Fashion	7000	Unisex	250
W005	Golden Time	25000	Gents	100

Ans.
```
import mysql.connector
my = mysql.connector.connect
    (host = "localhost",
     user = "Root", passwd = "System",
     database = "Test")
cursor = my.cursor ( )
db = cursor.execute ("CREATE TABLE Watches
    (Watch_Id   varchar(5)   Primary Key,
    WatchName   char(20)      NOT NULL,
    Price       float,
    Type        varchar (20),
    Qty_store   Int(5)        NOT NULL))"
sql = "INSERT INTO Watches
    (WatchId, WatchName, Price, Type,
    Qty_store) VALUES (%s, %s, %s,
    %s, %s)"
val = [("W001", "High Time", 10000,
    "Unisex", 100),
    ("W002", "Life Time", 15000,
    "Ladies", 150),
    ("W003", "Wave", 20000,
    "Gents", 200),
    ("W004", "HighFashion", 7000,
    "Unisex", 250),
    ("W005", "Golden Time", 25000,
    "Gents", 100)]
try:
    cursor. executemany (sql, val)
    my.commit ( )
except :
    my.rollback ( )
my.close ( )
```

14. Here is a table Club

MemberId	MemberName	Address	Age	Fee
M001	Sumit	New Delhi	20	2000
M002	Nisha	Gurgaon	19	3500
M003	Niharika	New Delhi	21	2100
M004	Sachin	Faridabad	18	3500

Write the Python code for the following

(i) Update the Address of member whose MemberId is M003 with Noida.

(ii) Delete the record of those member whose name is Sachin.

Ans. (i)
```
import mysql.connector
mycon = mysql.connector.connect
(host = "localhost",
user = "Admin", passwd = "Admin@123",
database = "System")
cursor = mycon.cursor ( )
try:
    cursor.execute ("UPDATE Club SET
```

```
    Address = "Noida" WHERE MemberId
        = "M003")")
    mycon.commit ( )
except :
    mycon.rollback ( )
mycon.close ( )
```

(ii)
```
import mysql. connector
mycon = mysql. connector.connect
    (host = "localhost",
     user = "Admin",
     passwd = "Admin@123",
     database = "System")
cursor = mycon.cursor ( )
try:
    cursor.execute ("DELETE FROM Club
    WHERE MemberName = 'Sachin')"
    cursor.commit ( )
except:
    mycon.rollback ( )
mycon.close ( )
```

15. Consider the table MobileMaster

M_Id	M_Company	M_Name	M_Price	M_Mf_Date
MB001	Samsung	Galaxy	4500	2014-02-12
MB002	Nokia	N1100	2250	2011-04-15
MB003	Sony	Experia M	9500	2017-11-20
MB004	Oppo	SelfieEx	8500	2010-08-21

Write the Python code for the following

(i) To display details of those mobiles whose price is greater than 8000.

(ii) To increase the price of mobile Samsung by 2000.

Ans. (i)
```
import mysql.connector as mydb
mycon = mydb.connect
        (host = "localhost",
         user = "root",
         passwd = "system",
         database = "Admin")
cursor = mycon.cursor ( )
sql = "SELECT * FROM MobileMaster
WHERE M_Price > 8000"
try:
    cursor.execute (sql)
    display = cursor. fetchall ( )
    for i in display:
            print(i)
except:
    mycon.rollback ( )
mycon.close ( )
```

(ii)
```
import mysql.connector as mydb
mycon = mydb.connect
```

```
        (host = "localhost",
         user = "root",
         passwd = "system",
         database = "Admin")
  cursor = mycon.cursor ( )
  sql = "UPDATE MobileMaster SET M_Price
      = M_Price + 2000
      WHERE M_Company = 'Samsung'"
  try:
      cursor.execute (sql)
      mycon.commit ( )
  except :
      mycon.rollback ( )
  mycon.close( )
```

16. Write the Python code for (i) and (ii) on the basis of table College.

No	Name	Age	Department	DateofJoin	Basic	Sex
1	Aren	51	Mathematics	22/01/91	8500	M
2	Reeta	27	Chemistry	14/02/94	9000	F
3	Viren	49	Mathematics	03/01/88	9000	M
4	Prakash	22	Physics	17/02/92	8000	M
5	Shalaz	45	Biology	13/02/88	10500	M
6	Urvashi	29	Biology	10/02/93	8500	F

(i) To insert a new row in the table College with the following data

15, "Atin", 27, "Physics", "15/05/02", 8500, "M"

(ii) To delete a row from table in which name is Viren.

Ans. (i)
```
import mysql.connector as mydb
con = mydb.connect (
    host = "localhost",
    user = "root",
    passwd = "admin@123",
    database = "Management")
cursor = con.cursor ( )
sql = "INSERT INTO College (No, Name,
        Age, Department, DateofJoin,
        Basic, Sex) VALUES
        (15, 'Atin', 27, 'Physics',
        '15/05/02', 8500, 'M')"
cursor.execute (sql)
con.close ( )
```

(ii)
```
import mysql.connector as mydb
con = mydb.connect
        (host = "localhost",
        user = "root",
        passwd = "admin@123",
        database = "Management")
cursor = con.cursor ( )
try:
    cursor.execute (DELETE FROM College
            WHERE Name = "Viren" " )
    con.commit ( )
except :
    con.rollback ( )
con.close ( )
```

Multiple Choice Questions

1. What is an identifier in following command?

```
import mysql.connector as db
```

(a) import   (b) mysql

(c) connector   (d) db

2. To add a new column into a table, which command is used?

(a) ALTER TABLE   (b) UPDATE FROM

(c) INSERT INTO   (d) All of these

3. To insert multiple records into table, which method is used to execute statements?

(a) execute ( )   (b) executemany ( )

(c) executeall ( )   (d) None of these

4. Which of the following statement is correct?

(a) DELETE INTO

(b) DELETE TABLE

(c) DELETE ALL

(d) DELETE FROM

5. It fetches all the rows of a query result.

(a) fetchall ( )   (b) fetchmany ( )

(c) fetchwhole ( )   (d) allfetch ( )

Short Answer Type Questions

6. Create the connection of Python with MySQL, in which

```
database name = System
User = Admin
Password = Admin@123
```

7. Write the code to create a table stationery in database School with following fields.

Fields	Datatype
I_Code	Varchar(3) (P)
I_Name	Char(30)
Qty.	Int
Price	Float

8. Which data will get added in the table Mobile by following code?

```
import mysql.connector
mycon = mysql.connector.connect
        (host = "localhost",
        user = "Admin",
        passwd = "Admin@123",
        database = "connect")
cursor = mycon.cursor ( )
sql = "INSERT INTO Mobile (Name, Model,
      Price, Qty)
      VALUES (%s, %s, %s, %s)"
val = ("Samsung", "Galaxy Pro", 28000, 3)
cursor.execute (sql,val)
mycon.commit ( )
```

9. Consider the table Inventory with following fields ID, Name, Qty, Amount, Manufacturing Date. Write the Python code to fetch all records with fields ID, Name, Qty, Amount from database.

10. Consider the table Employee whose columns' name are

```
E_ID, EmpName, JoiningDate,
Salary, Department
```

Write the code to insert the following record into the above table:

E101	Atin	12-10-2009	35000	DBA
E102	Sandeep	7-8-1999	58000	Business Analyst

Long Answer Type Questions

11. Create following table using Python code

Table : College

No	Name	Age	Department	Date of Join	Basic	Sex
1	Shalaz	45	Biology	13/02/88	10500	M
2	Sameera	54	Biology	10/01/90	9500	F
3	Pratyush	34	Chemistry	11/01/93	7500	M
4	Reeta	27	Chemistry	14/02/94	9000	F
5	Urvashi	29	Biology	10/02/93	8500	F
6	Teena	35	Mathematics	02/02/89	10500	F

12. Consider the table FLIGHTS

FL_No	Starting	Ending	No_Flight	No_Stops
IC301	Mumbai	Delhi	8	0
IC799	Bengluru	Delhi	2	1
MC101	Indore	Mumbai	3	0
AM812	Kanpur	Bengluru	3	1

Write the Python code for the following

(i) To display details of those flights whose number of flights greater than 5.

(ii) To increase the number of flights of flight Indore to Mumbai by 3.

Answers

Multiple Choice Questions

1. (d)   *2. (a)*   *3. (b)*   *4. (d)*   *5. (a)*

For Detailed Solutions

Scan the code

Practice Paper 1*
(Solved)

General Instructions

- Time : 2 Hours
- Max. Marks : 35

1. There are 9 questions in the question paper. All questions are compulsory.
2. Question no. 1 is a Case Based Question, which has five MCQs. Each question carries one mark.
3. Question no. 2-6 are Short Answer Type Questions. Each question carries 3 marks.
4. Question no. 7-9 are Long Answer Type Questions. Each question carries 5 marks.
5. There is no overall choice. However, internal choices have been provided in some questions. Students have to attempt only one of the alternatives in such questions.

As exact Blue-print and Pattern for CBSE Term II exams is not released yet. So the pattern of this paper is designed by the author on the basis of trend of past CBSE Papers. Students are advised not to consider the pattern of this paper as official, it is just for practice purpose.

1. **Direction** *Read the following passage and answer the questions that follows*

   Mr. Rajeshwar has created a stack whose size is fixed for 10 elements and wants to perform some operations on it. He wants to push certain elements and pop some elements from it. He is confused about the operations and how the elements will behave on pushing and popping?

Chevrolet
Suzuki
Honda
Mercedes
RolsRoyce

   Help him to find the answers of the following questions.

   (i) How many elements can he push more to the stack?
   (a) 3   (b) 5
   (c) 4   (d) 1

   (ii) How many elements he needs to take out before "RolsRoyce" will come out?
   (a) 2   (b) 3
   (c) 4   (d) 1

   (iii) If 3 elements are popped out and 2 pushed in , what will be the strength of the stack?
   (a) 2   (b) 4
   (c) 0   (d) 1

(iv) If "Tata" and "Datsun" are pushed to the initial stack respectively , which element will be popped out as a result of a pop operation now?

   (a) Chevrolet   (b) Datsun

   (c) Tata   (d) RolsRoyce

(v) If 2 elements are popped out and 4 pushed into the initial stack, how many times a loop needs to iterate to traverse the stack?

   (a) 6   (b) 3

   (c) 7   (d) 4

2. Write the name of benefits of networking.

Or Write any two uses of Internet.

3. What do you understand by the term database?

Or What is a DBMS? Expand and explain in short.

4. Differentiate between ALTER and UPDATE commands in SQL.

Or How is char data type different from varchar data type?

5. Which data will get added in table Company by following code?

```
import mysql.connector
  con = mysql.connector.connect (
      host = "localhost",
      user = "system",
      passwd = "hello",
      database = "connect")
  cur = con.cursor ( )
  sql = "insert into Company
        (Name, Dept, Salary)
  values (%s, %s, %s)"
  val = ("ABC", "DBA", 35000)
  cur.execute (sql, val)
  con.commit ( )
```

6. What is the use of baud rate?

Or A company wants to form a network on their five computers to a server within the company premises. Represent star and ring topologies diagrammatically for this network.

7. Trine Tech Corporation (TTC) is a professional consultancy company. The company is planning to set up their new offices in India with its hub at Hyderabad. As a network adviser, you have to understand their requirement and suggest them the best available solutions. Their queries are mentioned as (i) to (v) below.

Physical locations of the blocks of TTC

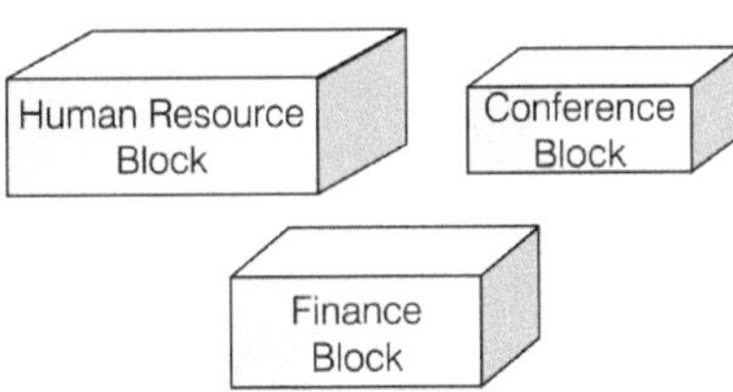

Block to block distance (in m)

Block (From)	Block (To)	Distance
Human Resource	Conference	110
Human Resource	Finance	40
Conference	Finance	80

Expected number of computers

Block	Computers
Human Resource	25
Finance	120
Conference	90

(i) Which will be the most appropriate block, where TTC should plan to install their server?

(ii) Draw a block to block cable layout to connect all the buildings in the most appropriate manner for efficient communication.

(iii) What will be the best possible connectivity out of the following, you will suggest to connect the new set up of offices in Bengalore with its London based office.

    (a) Satellite Link

    (b) Infrared

    (c) Ethernet

(iv) Which of the following device will be suggested by you to connect each computer in each of the buildings?

    (a) Switch

    (b) Modem

    (c) Gateway

(v) Company is planning to connect its offices in Hyderabad which is less than 1 km. Which type of network will be formed?

Or Granuda consultants are setting up a secured network for their office campus at Faridabad for their day-to-day office and web based activities. They are planning to have connectivity between 3 buildings and the head office situated in Kolkata.

Answer the questions (i) to (v) after going through the building positions in the campus and other details, which are given below.

Distance between various buildings

Building RAVI to Building JAMUNA	120 m
Building RAVI to Building GANGA	50 m
Building GANGA to Building JAMUNA	65 m
Faridabad Campus to Head Office	1460 km

Number of computers

Building RAVI	25
Building JAMUNA	150
Building GANGA	51
Head Office	10

(i) Suggest the most suitable place (i.e. block) to house the server of this organisation. Also, give a reason to justify your suggested location.

(ii) Suggest a cable layout of connections between the building inside the campus.

(iii) Suggest the placement of the following devices with justification:

    (a) Switch   (b) Repeater

(iv) The organisation is planning to provide a high speed link with its head office situated in the Kolkata using a wired connection. Which of the following cable will be most suitable for this job?

    (a) Optical fibre   (b) Co-axial cable

    (c) Ethernet cable

(v) Consultancy is planning to connect its office in Faridabad which is more than 10 km from Head office. Which type of network will be formed?

8. Explain the role of database management system in maintaining huge volumes of data of different domains. Explain your views using an example.

Or A table "Sports" exists with 3 columns and 5 rows. What is its degree and cardinality? 2 rows are added to the table and 1 column deleted. What will be the degree and cardinality now?

9. Answer the questions (i) to (v) on the basis of the following tables SHOPPE and ACCESSORIES.

Table : SHOPPE

Id	SName	Area
S001	ABC Computeronics	CP
S002	All Infotech Media	GK II
S003	Tech Shoppe	CP
S004	Geeks Tecno Soft	Nehru Place
S005	Hitech Tech Store	Nehru Place

Table : ACCESSORIES

No	Name	Price	Id
A01	Mother Board	12000	S01
A02	Hard Disk	5000	S01
A03	Keyboard	500	S02
A04	Mouse	300	S01
A05	Mother Board	13000	S02
A06	Keyboard	400	S03
A07	LCD	6000	S04
T08	LCD	5500	S05
T09	Mouse	350	S05
T10	Hard Disk	4500	S03

(i) To display Name and Price of all the Accessories in ascending order of their Price.

(ii) To display Id and SName of all Shoppe located in Nehru Place.

(iii) To display Minimum and Maximum Price of each Name of Accessories.

(iv) To display Name, Price of all Accessories and their respective SName, where they are available.

(v) To display name of accessories whose price is greater than 1000.

Or What is the differences between HAVING clause and WHERE clause?

Explanations

1. (i) (*b*) Though the capacity of the stack is 10 , so he can push a maximum of 5 elements.
    (ii) (*c*) Though there are 4 elements above "RolsRoyce", so 4 elements need to be taken out.
    (iii) (*b*) Popping 3 elements means 2 remain. Now, pushing 2 elements means strength becomes 4.
    (iv) (*b*) Since 'Datsun' is pushed at the end, it will be popped out first.
    (v) (*c*) Since, there are 5 elements in stack and we popped out 2 elements from it, then 3 elements remain. Now, we push 4 elements into stack, then total elements are 7. Hence, a loop needs to iterate to traverse the stack is 7 times.

2. Some of the benefits of networking are
    (i) File sharing
    (ii) Hardware sharing
    (iii) Application sharing
    (iv) User communication
    (v) Access to remote database

Or

Two uses of Internet are as follows
    (i) Internet is used for communication and information sharing.
    (ii) Business use the Internet to provide access to complex databases.

3. A database is a huge collection of data accumulating in a particular system. It comprises of historical data, operational and transactional data. The database grows everyday with the transactions dealing with it.

A database has the following properties
    (i) It is a collection of data elements representing real-world information.
    (ii) It is logical, coherent and internally consistent.

Or

A Database Management System is a software system that enables users to define, create and maintain the database and provides controlled access to this database.

The primary goal of a DBMS is to provide a way to store and retrieve database information that is both convenient and efficient. Data in a database can be added, deleted, changed, sorted or searched, all using a DBMS.

4. Differences between ALTER and UPDATE commands in SQL are

ALTER command	**UPDATE command**
It belongs to DDL category.	It belongs to DML category.
It changes the structure of the table.	It modifies data of the table.
Columns can be added, modified , deleted etc.	Data can be changed, updated with values and expressions.

Or

Differences between char data type and varchar data type are

Char	**Varchar**
It is fixed length.	It is variable length.
Wastage of memory.	Memory usage only as per data size.
Less useful.	Better data type.

5. "ABC", "DBA", 35000

6. Baud rate is a measure of the number of symbols (signals) transferred or line changes every second. It may represent more than one binary bit.

Every symbol can represent or convey one or several bits of data. For a binary signal of 20 Hz, this is equivalent to 20 baud.

Or

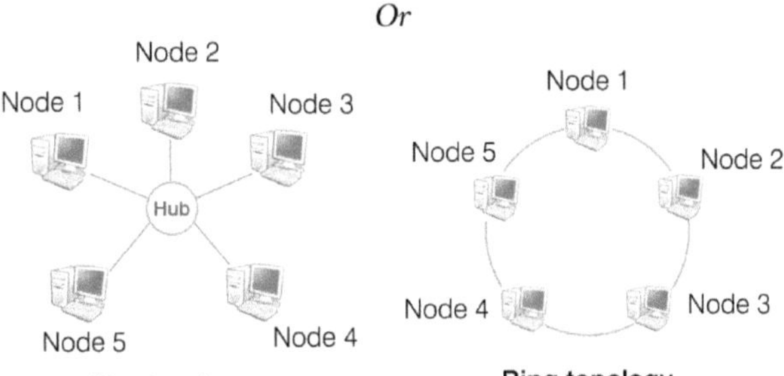

7. (i) TTC should install its server in finance block as it is having maximum number of computers.

(ii)

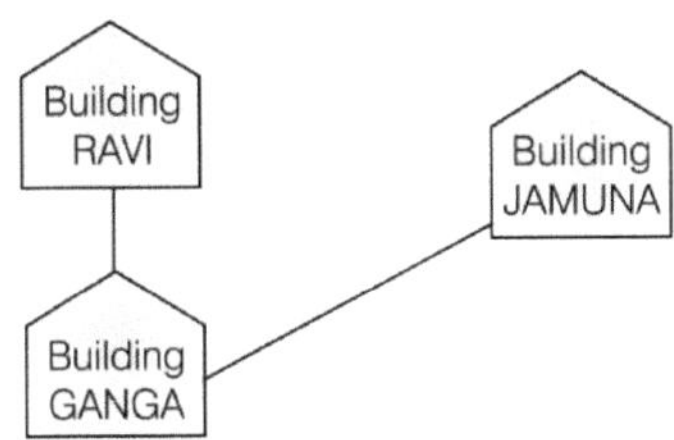

The above layout is based on minimum cable length required, which is 120 metres in the above case.

(iii) (a) Satellite Link   (iv) (a) Switch

(v) LAN

Or

(i) The most suitable place to house the server is JAMUNA because it has maximum number of computers.

(ii)

(iii) (a) Switches are needed in every building to share bandwidth in every building.

(b) Repeaters may be skipped as per above layout, (because distance is less than 100 m) however, if building RAVI and building JAMUNA are directly connected, we can place a repeater there as the distance between these two buildings is more than 100 m.

(iv) (a) Optical fibre

(v) MAN

8. A database management system is a specialised software that helps maintain large volumes of data pertaining to a real life system . Examples of such systems include business houses , transport systems, libraries , schools etc.

It not only stores bulk data in structured way but also helps to add , modify ,search , update and delete data from such databases. Examples of DBMS softwares are MySQL , Microsoft SQL Server , Oracle etc.

Application program accesses the data stored in the database by sending request to the DBMS.

For example, MySQL, INGRES, MS-ACCESS etc.

The purpose of a Database Management System is to bridge the gap between information and data. The data stored in memory or on disk must be converted to usable information

Or

The term degree refers to the total number of columns in a table. The term cardinality refers to the total number of rows in a table.

Initially, Sports table has 3 columns and 5 rows, so

Degree : 3

Cardinality : 5

After operations, 2 rows are added to the table and 1 column deleted.

Now, degree : 2 cardinality : 7.

9. (i)
```
SELECT Name, Price
FROM ACCESSORIES
ORDER BY Price;
```
(ii)
```
SELECT Id, SName
FROM SHOPPE
WHERE Area = 'Nehru Place';
```
(iii)
```
SELECT MIN(Price) "Minimum Price",
MAX(Price) "Maximum Price", Name
FROM ACCESSORIES
GROUP BY Name;
```
(iv)
```
SELECT Name, Price, SName
FROM ACCESSORIES A, SHOPPE S
WHERE A.Id = S.Id;
but this query enable to show the result because
A.Id and S.Id are not identical.
```
(v)
```
SELECT Name From
ACCESSORIES
WHERE Price>1000;
```

Or

Differences between HAVING clause and WHERE clause are

WHERE clause	HAVING clause
WHERE clause is used to filter the records from the table based on the specified condition.	HAVING clause is used to filter record from the groups based on the specified condition.
WHERE clause implements in row operation.	HAVING clause implements in column operation.
WHERE clause cannot contain aggregate function.	HAVING clause can contain aggregate function.
WHERE clause can be used with SELECT, UPDATE, DELETE statement.	HAVING clause can only be used with SELECT statement.
WHERE clause is used with single row function like UPPER, LOWER etc.	HAVING clause is used with multiple row function like SUM, COUNT etc.

Practice Paper 2*
(Unsolved)

General Instructions

■ **Time :** 2 Hours
■ **Max. Marks :** 35

1. There are 9 questions in the question paper. All questions are compulsory.
2. Question no. 1 is a Case Based Question, which has five MCQs. Each question carries one mark.
3. Question no. 2-6 are Short Answer Type Questions. Each question carries 3 marks.
4. Question no. 7-9 are Long Answer Type Questions. Each question carries 5 marks.
5. There is no overall choice. However, internal choices have been provided in some questions. Students have to attempt only one of the alternatives in such questions.

As exact Blue-print and Pattern for CBSE Term II exams is not released yet. So the pattern of this paper is designed by the author on the basis of trend of past CBSE Papers. Students are advised not to consider the pattern of this paper as official, it is just for practice purpose.

1. Direction *Read the following passage and answer the questions that follows*

Table: Book_Information   **Table: Sales**

Column Name
Book_ID
Book_Title
Price

Column Name
Store_ID
Sales_Date
Sales_Amount

Basis on above table information, answer the following questions.

(i) Which SQL statement allows you to find the highest price from the table Book_Information?
   (a) SELECT Book_ID,Book_Title,MAX(Price) FROM Book_Information;
   (b) SELECT MAX(Price) FROM Book_Information;
   (c) SELECT MAXIMUM(Price) FROM Book_Information;
   (d) SELECT Price FROM Book_Information ORDER BY Price DESC;

(ii) Which SQL statement allows you to find sales amount for each store?
   (a) SELECT Store_ID, SUM(Sales_Amount) FROM Sales;
   (b) SELECT Store_ID, SUM(Sales_Amount) FROM Sales ORDER BY Store_ID;
   (c) SELECT Store_ID, SUM(Sales_Amount) FROM Sales GROUP BY Store_ID;
   (d) SELECT Store_ID, SUM(Sales_Amount) FROM Sales HAVING UNIQUE Store_ID;

(iii) Which SQL statement lets you to list all store name whose total sales amount is over 5000 ?
   (a) SELECT Store_ID, SUM(Sales_Amount) FROM Sales GROUP BY Store_ID HAVING SUM(Sales_Amount) > 5000;
   (b) SELECT Store_ID, SUM(Sales_Amount) FROM Sales GROUP BY Store_ID HAVING Sales_Amount > 5000;
   (c) SELECT Store_ID, SUM(Sales_Amount) FROM Sales WHERE SUM(Sales_Amount) > 5000 GROUP BY Store_ID;
   (d) SELECT Store_ID, SUM(Sales_Amount) FROM Sales WHERE Sales_Amount > 5000 GROUP BY Store_ID;

(iv) Which SQL statement lets you find the total number of stores in the SALES table?
   (a) SELECT COUNT(Store_ID) FROM Sales;
   (b) SELECT COUNT(DISTINCT Store_ID) FROM Sales;
   (c) SELECT DISTINCT Store_ID FROM Sales;
   (d) SELECT COUNT(Store_ID) FROM Sales GROUP BY Store_ID;

(v) Which SQL statement allows you to find the total sales amount for Store_ID 25 and the total sales amount for Store_ID 45?
   (a) SELECT Store_ID, SUM(Sales_Amount) FROM Sales WHERE Store_ID IN (25, 45) GROUP BY Store_ID;
   (b) SELECT Store_ID, SUM(Sales_Amount) FROM Sales GROUP BY Store_ID HAVING Store_ID IN (25, 45);
   (c) SELECT Store_ID, SUM(Sales_Amount) FROM Sales WHERE Store_ID IN (25,45);
   (d) SELECT Store_ID, SUM(Sales_Amount) FROM Sales WHERE Store_ID = 25 AND Store_ID =45 GROUP BY Store_ID;

2. What are the aggregate functions in SQL?

Or What is the purpose of GROUP BY clause in MySQL? How is it different from ORDER BY clause?

3. Explain working of AND and OR operators in queries.

Or Write a query to display the Sum, Average, Highest and Lowest marks of the students grouped by subject and sub-grouped by class.

4. What is the use of foreign key field?

Or What are the components of a database system?

5. What do you understand by the term cardinality of a table? How can it be modified?

Or What is a primary key? How many primary keys can be there in a table?

6. What is the purpose of switch in a network?

Or Illustrate the layout for connecting five computers in a bus and a star topology of networks.

7. In twisted pair cable, two insulated wires are twisted around each other which provides protection against noise. Explain.

Or Explain the three main parts of an optical fibre cable.

8. Consider the table MobileStock with following fields

```
M_Id, M_Name, M_Qty, M_Supplier
```

Write the Python code to fetch all records with fields **M_Id, M_Name** and **M_Supplier** from database Mobile.

Or Consider the table Faculty whose columns' name are

```
F_ID, Fname, Lname, Hire_date, Salary, Course_name
```

Write the code to insert the following record into the above table.

| 101 | Riya | Sharma | 12-10-2004 | 35000 | Java Advance |
| 102 | Kiyaan | Mishra | 3-12-2010 | 28000 | Data Structure |

9. With respect to the following table "BOOK" write SQL commands for the questions (i) to (iv).

Table : Book

Book ID	Bname	Publisher	Price	DtofPub
B1	Science Fiction	TMH	1200	2020-09-08
B2	Stories	PHI	900	NULL
B3	Ramayana	PHI	1700	NULL
B4	Beginners Cooking	Oswal	1400	1990-12-03

(i) Display details of books published before year 2000.

(ii) Display names and publishers of books whose price is less than 1000.

(iii) Display names of books who do not have a date of publication.

(iv) Increase price of all books by 200.

Or Write SQL commands with respect to the Employee table given below.

Table : Employee

Eno	Ename	Dept	Desig	DtofJoin	Salary
1	Jack	Sales	MGR	2012-09-12	89000
2	Priya	Accts	MGR	2005-04-22	56000
3	Ria	Pers	Clerk	2000-01-09	25000
4	Anil	Pers	Officer	1994-04-03	67000
5	Sumit	Sales	Officer	NULL	19000
6	Akash	Sales	Officer	NULL	20000

(i) Display name and department of employees whose name begins with" S".

(ii) Display details of employees whose designation ends with "r".

(iii) Display details of employees whose name has 1st letter "P" 3rd letter "i".

(iv) Display name,deptartment and salary of employees whose department name ends with "s".

Practice Paper 3*
(Unsolved)

1. **Direction** *Read the following passage and answer the questions that follows*

   Web server is a special computer system running on HTTP through web pages. The web page is a medium to carry data from one computer system to another. The working of the web server starts from the client or user. The client sends their request through the web browser to the web server. Web server takes this request, processes it and then sends back processed data to the client. The server gathers all of our web page information and sends it to the user, which we see on our computer system in the form of a web page. When the client sends a request for processing to the web server, a domain name and IP address are important to the web server. The domain name and IP address are used to identify the user on a large network.

   (i) Web servers are
      (a) IP addresses
      (b) computer systems
      (c) web pages of a site
      (d) a medium to carry data from one computer to another

   (ii) What does the web server need to send back information to the user?
      (a) Home address   (b) Domain name
      (c) IP address   (d) Both (b) and (c)

   (iii) What is the full form of HTTP?
      (a) HyperText Transfer Protocol
      (b) HyperText Transfer Procedure
      (c) Hyperlink Transfer Protocol
      (d) Hyperlink Transfer Procedure

(iv) The .... translates Internet domain and host names to IP address.
- (a) domain name system
- (b) routing information protocol
- (c) Internet relay chart
- (d) network time protocol

(v) Computer that requests the resources or data from another computer is called as ....
- (a) server
- (b) client
- (c) Both (a) and (b)
- (d) None of these

2. What do you mean by an operator? Name any four operators used in queries

Or How NOT operator is used with WHERE clause? Give an example.

3. What are the functions of ALTER TABLE command?

Or Write syntax of the conditions given below.
(i) Add a column in a table.
(ii) Delete a column from a table.

4. Explain two problems that can occur during transmission of data.

Or Write down any two points of differences between LAN, MAN and WAN.

5. Define tree topology. Also, write down its two limitations.

Or What is the significance of HTTP?

6. Write the code to create a table Product in database Inventory with following fields :

Fields	Datatype
PID	varchar(5)
PName	char(30)
Price	float
Rank	varchar(2)

Or Write the code to create the connection in which database's name is Python, name of host, user and password can taken by user. Also, print that connection.

7. Write the rules that are used while converting an infix expression to postfix using stack.

Or Write the algorithm for push in a static stack.

8. List some of the advantages of data structure.

Or Write a function popdata() with a list of student names as parameter and display only those names that are of length more than 10.

9. Consider the following tables. Write SQL commands for the statements (i) to (v).

Table : SENDER

SenderID	SenderName	SenderAddress	SenderCity
ND01	R Jain	2, ABC Appts	New Delhi
MU02	H Sinha	12, Newtown	Mumbai
MU15	S Jha	27/A, Park Street	Mumbai
ND50	T Prasad	122-K, SDA	New Delhi

Table : RECIPIENT

RecID	SenderID	RecName	RecAddress	RecCity
KO05	ND01	R Bajpayee	5, Central Avenue	Kolkata
ND08	MU02	S Mahajan	116, A Vihar	New Delhi
MU19	ND01	H Singh	2A, Andheri East	Mumbai
MU32	MU15	P K Swamy	B5, C S Terminus	Mumbai
ND48	ND50	S Tripathi	13, B1 D, Mayur Vihar	New Delhi

(i) To display the names of all Senders from Mumbai.

(ii) To display the RecID, SenderName, SenderAddress, RecName, RecAddress for every Recipient.

(iii) To display Recipient details in ascending order of RecName.

(iv) To display number of Recipients from each City.

(v) To display the detail of recipients who are in Mumbai.

Or Write the SQL commands for (i) to (v) on the basis of the table HOSPITAL.

Table : **HOSPITAL**

No.	Name	Age	Department	Dateofadm	Charges	Sex
1	Sandeep	65	Surgery	23/02/98	300	M
2	Ravina	24	Orthopaedic	20/01/98	200	F
3	Karan	45	Orthopaedic	19/02/98	200	M
4	Tarun	12	Surgery	01/01/98	300	M
5	Zubin	36	ENT	12/01/98	250	M
6	Ketaki	16	ENT	24/02/98	300	F
7	Ankita	29	Cardiology	20/02/98	800	F
8	Zareen	45	Gynaecology	22/02/98	300	F
9	Kush	19	Cardiology	13/01/98	800	M
10	Shailya	31	Nuclear Medicine	19/02/98	400	M

(i) To show all information about the patients of Cardiology Department.

(ii) To list the name of female patients, who are in Orthopaedic Department.

(iii) To list names of all patients with their date of admission in ascending order.

(iv) To display Patient's Name, Charges, Age for male patients only.

(v) To display name of doctor are older than 30 years and charges for consultation fee is more than 500.